WITHDRAWN

FOR A
"CHRISTIAN AMERICA"

RUTH MURRAY BROWN

A HISTORY OF THE RELIGIOUS RIGHT

FOR A

"CHRISTIAN AMERICA"

Prometheus Books
59 John Glenn Drive
Amherst, New York 14228-2197

Published 2002 by Prometheus Books

Inquiries should be addressed to
Prometheus Books
59 John Glenn Drive
Amherst, New York 14228–2197
VOICE: 716–691–0133, ext. 207
FAX: 716–564–2711
WWW.PROMETHEUSBOOKS.COM

06 05 04 03 02   5 4 3 2 1

Library of Congress Cataloging-in-Publication Data

Brown, Ruth Murray, 1927–2002
    For a "Christian America" : a history of the religious right / Ruth Murray Brown.
        p. cm.
    Includes bibliographical references and index.
    ISBN 1–57392–973–5 (alk. paper)
    1. Conservatism—Religious aspects—Christianity—History—20th century. 2
Christianity and politics—United States—History—20th century. I. Title.

BR526 .B77 2002
320.52'0973—dc21

                                                                        2002021305

Printed in Canada on acid-free paper

CONTENTS

PART I. "PRO-FAMILY": PROTECTING OUR FAMILIES AND SAVING OUR COUNTRY

PART II. "CHRISTIAN NATION": RESTORING THE VISION OF THE FOUNDERS

PART III. THE ISSUES AND HOW THEY EVOLVED

LIST OF GRAPHS AND TABLES

ACKNOWLEDGMENTS

My biggest debt of gratitude, of course, is to those whom I interviewed and observed from 1976 to 1983, and from 1995 to 1998. In each time period I conducted lengthy interviews with about sixty persons randomly chosen from a list of activists, and with others who were in leadership positions or had particularly interesting stories to tell. Most were eager to participate, in part because they felt they were being misrepresented in the popular media. They let me come into their homes and take an hour or more of their time; they offered me refreshments, and in some cases, meals; they offered their blessings on my work, and they encouraged me to contact them again if I needed anything else.

I called many of them back later for further information, some of them many times. When I called some of the 1980 interviewees for updates in 1997, they were still glad to help. Traveling hundreds of miles for interviews could have been a tiresome and unpleasant chore, but because of the unfailing kindness of those I met, it was not.

I am especially grateful to the leadership of the Oklahoma White House Conference on Families in 1979, and to Ken Wood, executive director of the Oklahoma Christian Coalition in 1997. Without them, I would not have had access to lists from which I could draw random samples. In both time periods, I also requested responses to mail surveys and acted as participant and observer at meetings, lobbying events, and rallies. Many others cooperated in providing these kinds of information.

For financial support while working on the anti-ERA movement, I was fortunate to have grants from the National Endowment for the Humanities—a Summer Stipend in 1978 and a Fellowship for College Teachers in 1982. Their vote of confidence and their financial support was crucial at that early stage. By 1995, when I began work on the contemporary movement, I was retired from teaching. Since 1992, the Social Security Administration and the Oklahoma Teachers' Retirement System have provided me with income for living expenses as well as for travel and supplies. I am grateful to them as well.

Special thanks are also due to the good friends, family members, and colleagues who read parts of the manuscript and offered helpful suggestions.

FOREWORD

In the late 1970s I heard a television interview with Lindsay Wagner, a TV actress and minor celebrity known for her role as The Bionic Woman. It sticks in my sociological mind for what it revealed about the changing American culture. She was asked about her "domestic life" at the time and answered that she was living with a man whom she named. In an apparent effort to introduce some excitement into a faltering interview, the interviewer challenged Miss Wagner, asking her if this arrangement was "right." The actress replied that anything that makes one happy is "right."

I thought at the time, and still do, that even less than two decades before that interview, a public admission of a man and woman living together and not married to each other would not have been so easily made public. Not that many Americans ever had such arrangements or a similar sense of morality. What had changed was the public acceptability of it. What was unthinkable had become thinkable. What had been expressed in public as deviant and immoral had become normalized. The social and cultural changes that have swept American life in the past forty years have been profound and have touched our lives at levels of daily activity and in the most intimate areas. For some these changes have been embraced with satisfaction. For others they have been viewed with apprehension and sorrow. For many they have been matters of indifference or resignation. In *For a "Christian America"* Ruth Murray Brown has described the rise of a major and politically significant opposition to many of the changes in American life. The Christian Right represents both an effort to resist such changes and to enhance the role of religion through political action. In an unfolding history, from the countermovement against the Equal Rights Amendment in the seventies to the present constellation of issues, she describes the organizations, issues, and leading figures that have composed the movement. Presenting factual material and analyzing the issues, her work provides an indispensable guide to a movement of great importance to American politics and culture.

While the movement owes much to the cultural upheavals of the sixties, it is hardly the first time that American politics has been filled with lifestyle and religious issues or witnessed the creation and mobilization of religious organizations in a concern for moral behavior. To mention just a few: The controversies surrounding laws banning various activities on Sundays, the attempts to pass a constitutional amendment banning polygamy, the Prohibition movements (which I have studied extensively), and the issues of gambling and pornography as well as abortion (which involves Catholic organizations as well.)

During the sixties and early seventies and since, America has become both a more diverse and a more homogeneous society. It became more diverse in two senses. In one sense immigration brought in more new groups of different cultures and skin colors—Latin American, Polynesian, East Asian, South Asian, and Eastern European. It produced a broader collection of religions—Muslim, Buddhist, and Hindu to add to the list of Protestant, Catholic, Christian sects, and Judaic.

It became more diverse in another sense. Groups already present in the United States became more organized, more affluent, and more visible. This is evident especially in the American "family." The oft-perceived typical American family has been a mother, a father, and their biological offspring. This is no longer the typical case. Single parents are far more common than in the past. Divorce is more commonly accepted as is cohabitation, childbirth out-of-wedlock, and in vitro fertilization. The homosexual has come out of the closet, is organized into communities, and is politically visible. Minorities are no longer excluded from the world of political life. The dominance of a single form of family is no longer the rule.

We have become more homogeneous also in two senses. In one sense we are now similarly exposed to a common mass culture, especially through the media of popular culture—television, radio, movies, and public education. Media make people aware of the diversity that exists in American society. Such media have broken down isolations and cultural enclaves that kept us unaware of the oppositions that exist to our own often exclusive styles of life. A pro-life woman, interviewed by Kristin Luker for the study "The Politics of Abortion," remarked that she had never met anyone who supported abortion on demand. Such is hardly atypical of all sides of the issues of America's "culture wars." Gloria Steinem and Jerry Falwell are both part of America's celebrity culture.

A second sense in which America is more homogeneous is in a greater equality of political power. Civil Rights, the sexual revolution, and feminism have all brought into the public arena a much wider spectrum of groups. Higher education has contributed to a declining devotion to fundamentalist religion and the rise of what the Christian Right calls "secular humanism."

These aspects of social and cultural change are understandably threats to the dominance of religion in American life, both as an aspect of our culture and as a powerful institution. Adherents of religious beliefs and institutions are aware of the vacuum of public morality and the conflict engendered by it. For Bible-centered people the conflicts are sharpened. The conflict between scientists and fundamentalists is real, as the arguments and agitations over creationism suggest.

The Christian Right described in this significant volume is, however, only one segment of the spectrum of those who feel ill at ease in the changing American culture. (Jerry Falwell tried to capitalize on this in his organization of the Moral Majority.) It is the organized political action of the Christian Right that makes it significant in American politics; it has the capacity to affect elections through its mobilization of partisans and the institutional support of many churches, chiefly Protestant. Dr. Brown recounts its victories, such as the prevention of the ratification of the Equal Rights Amendment, and its failures, such as most of the Supreme Courts decisions on church-state relationships.

The Christian Right that Ruth Murray Brown describes is deeply Protestant and especially prevalent among Southern Baptists, Church of Christ members, and less-established but similarly Bible-centered groups.

It has not found a way of getting out of an exclusivity which minimizes its possible recruitment among Latinos and African Americans, where religiosity finds strongly committed people, nor among many secular humanists who might agree with them on some specific issues although are repelled by others and by the Bible-centered character of their doctrine.

In my city of San Diego a legal and political conflict has existed for most of the past two decades over a very large cross erected on the top of a hill, which prominently overlooks the city. Built in 1950, it has been the center of several appellate court decisions concerning the constitutional amendment about church and state relationships. At present the cross still stands. Whether or not it remains, the struggles it engenders are not likely to disappear.

> Joseph R. Gusfield, Ph.D.
> Professor Emeritus in Sociology
> University of California, San Diego

PREFACE

F or much of my life, I have chafed under the constraints of the oft-
repeated advice "don't talk about politics or religion," for those are
the two topics that interest me most.

Therefore it is not surprising that I chose to study a movement based
on the belief that religion had been wrongly purged from its proper place
in American life. Although the Christian Right seemed in its first stages
to be a conflict between traditional women and the feminist movement,
even then a concern about the effect of government policy on religious
practice was an underlying theme. During the twenty-five year history of
the movement, the issue broadened and evolved to focus on the relationship between church and state.

Having grown up in a parsonage, my childhood was spent in the church
milieu, and I met my husband at a church college. After marrying, I continued the life of a traditional woman, spending seventeen years as a stay-
at-home mom, but remaining active in politics as a volunteer. When my
youngest child entered first grade, I returned to graduate school and then
embarked on an absorbing career, teaching political science and sociology
at a local college. Thus I was in a position to understand the viewpoints of
the traditional women who started the pro-family movement by opposing
the Equal Rights Amendment, and also of the feminists they opposed.

In 1975 my students showed me copies of an anonymous flyer about
a child care bill pending in Congress and told me that the flyers had come

through church channels. I soon learned that some of the same individuals and churches responsible for the dissemination of that flyer were also opposing the Equal Rights Amendment. With a newly minted Ph.D. and an interest in social policy, it seemed almost providential that a religiously motivated social movement was developing around me. I determined to meet the movement participants and to learn what I could about them and their movement.

It was only fair that while I was asking questions of the Christian conservatives, they wanted to know about me as well. Their first question was: "Are you one of us or one of them?" They were suspicious of me because they believed—and in many cases they were right—that national news coverage of their movement usually depended on interviews with national leaders and often contained inaccurate stereotypes of the grassroots participants. As late as 1993, a newspaper article described Christian conservatives as "largely poor, uneducated, and easy to command."

While academic writers about pro-family movement participants presented a more balanced view, their work had not been circulated widely among the general public, and even academics, as some recent research shows, are sometimes prejudiced against the Christian conservatives. As a result, my respondents had formed their own stereotypes of academics as irreligious liberals. So I had to persuade them that I was sincerely interested in their ideas and intended to represent them fairly in what I wrote.

In writing this book, I hope that I can dispel some of the stereotype-based suspicion each side has of the other—admittedly a difficult task. In common with others who have done such work, I have had to contend not only with conservative suspicion of academics and the media, but also with the general public's suspicion of Christian conservatives. I can't count the number of times that someone who had just learned of my work—sometimes a friend of mine—would say, "How can you talk to THOSE people?" those "hypocrites," those "closed-minded people," or those "extremists"?

Actually, it was very easy, for with a few exceptions, they were none of those things. Many Americans put them in somewhat the same position as racial or ethnic minorities—people whom we scarcely know, but we are sure are not like us. In some ways they are not, of course, but in other ways they are. No good purpose is served when such a large proportion of the American people has so little respect for the beliefs of from one-quarter to one-third of our citizens. They are not all extremists, and they are not all alike. Christian Right adherents are in general agreement with the movement's agenda, but they disagree among themselves on the details.

I have tried to be fair and accurate in what I say about the movement, utilizing the best available sources to put what I learned in Oklahoma in context. I do so in the hope that more Americans will have a more balanced view of the Christian conservatives. Therefore I have tried to make it accessible and interesting to those who have not immersed themselves in the latest academic takes on it.

My answer to my respondents' question "Are you one of us, or one of them?" is this: "I agree with many of your concerns about the trends in American society—excessive violence on TV and in movies, lack of civility in daily interactions, and more acceptance of behavior that used to be unacceptable. But I am not sure about some of your proposed solutions, or even that government action is what is needed." As I send this book out into the world, I suspect that parts of it will be denounced by some on both sides. That may be the best outcome I can hope for, indicating that I have succeeded in presenting an evenhanded account.

INTRODUCTION

As conservative Oklahoma women gathered at their state capital in 1972 to urge legislators *not* to ratify the Equal Rights Amendment, I asked them why they opposed it. I knew that the ERA was a feminist project, one of the many causes espoused by the turbulent movements of the sixties. The anti-ERA women had watched in horror as they had seen antiwar activists, student protesters, civil rights marchers, and "uppity" women rebelling against the norms of personal behavior by flaunting long hair, tacky clothing, and coarse language. They were especially disturbed by the loose sexual norms and acceptance of drugs that seemed to go along with it. They told me that they feared passage of the ERA would only accelerate these other symptoms of moral decline.

On a very personal level, they feared that entrenching feminist values in the Constitution would mean the end of their Bible-based way of life. Most were active members of fundamentalist and evangelical churches. Their fundamentalist understanding of the Bible was that women were to be responsible for home and family and to be submissive to their husbands. As one of them said:

> It would affect my life more than anything else—it would affect my religion—it would affect my own financial situation in that it would change the Social Security laws. It would affect my home life in that my daughter would have to go to war. It would affect everything in my life—if this Equal Rights Amendment were passed! (Myrtle Kelly, October 13, 1981).

15

To her and to others like her, the real threat of the ERA was not just the specifics of unisex restrooms or of drafting women, or even of legalizing abortion—things emphasized by the popular media—but the broader threat of government interference with the right of families to raise their children in the ways prescribed by their religion. They saw defeating the ERA as a way of restoring those rights and halting moral decline. What they didn't know was that they were also laying the foundation for what came to be called the Christian Right.

There were other women in the capitol hallways, too—women who favored the ERA. The two groups began calling themselves "Pros" and "Antis." Before long I was hooked on the ERA controversy. I talked to those in both groups, attended meetings of both groups, and was fascinated by the stereotypes each formed of the other. Some of the Pros were church members too, but their churches were not fundamentalist. I was not a fundamentalist either, but my upbringing had brought me into contact with that movement, and I understood what it meant to the conservative women.

Thus began a project of interviewing, participating, observing, and attending rallies and conventions that continued for more than twenty-five years. In addition to exploring the religious basis of their crusade and learning about the churches from which they came, I also inquired about the background of the leaders, how the organizations developed their strategy, how new leaders were recruited and trained, how the organizations changed over time, and how they worked together.

As the ERA ratification battle dragged on longer than anyone had expected, I continued to interview and observe the Christian conservatives who had moved on to oppose other perceived threats to the Bible-based family—public school curricula and textbooks which seemed to denigrate traditional morality. By 1977 they were calling themselves the "pro-family movement."

The crusade against the ERA was won by 1982. But the STOP-ERA organization continued as Eagle Forum. By then it had been joined by other organizations—the Moral Majority, Focus on the Family, Traditional Values Coalition, Concerned Women for America—committed to stopping "moral decline" and restoring what they saw as America's Christian heritage. I sought out members of these groups, too, and talked to them when I could. I came to see that the early fight against the ERA was just one facet of the struggle to regain what they believed was a lost Christian heritage.

From urging public recognition of their own religious claims, Christian conservatives began arguing that their right to free exercise of their religion was being abridged. This was a subtle shift, one that some observers suggest was simply a strategic move to attract a more sympathetic response.[1] Be that as it may, my interviews showed that the grassroots participants were in complete agreement with the new approach.

Jerry Falwell's Moral Majority was organized in 1979 after Falwell had led a series of rallies all around the United States, preaching that America could be saved from God's judgment only by a return to Judeo-Christian morality. The belief that America was founded on biblical law and should continue to abide by it had a long history among evangelicals in the United States. The Puritans of the Massachusetts Bay Colony believed that they had a covenant with God to establish his law in the new land, and that his blessings would flow only so long as they kept the covenant.[2]

By 1990 the Moral Majority had collapsed and the Christian Coalition had taken its place. The "Christian America" theme still dominated the rhetoric of what was by then called the "Christian Right." In the early years, the fear that the government was interfering in family life was implicit in the crusade to defeat the ERA. It evolved into an effort to keep unchristian influences out of the schools, and finally, into an explicit crusade for public recognition of Christianity in schools, courtrooms, and public buildings. This brought the Christian Right into conflict with Supreme Court interpretations of the separation of church and state.

To place the conflict over church-state relationships in context, a quick review of its historical background is in order. Those who settled in the new land before the Revolution were a mixed lot. Some dissenters had come to escape religious persecution in Europe, but they did not hesitate to set up their own established churches and in some cases to persecute their own dissenters. Others were accustomed to paying taxes for the support of established churches and thought it an essential component of good government. Even those like James Madison, Thomas Jefferson, Benjamin Franklin, and George Washington, who were "discontented with orthodox religion," did not want to harm the church. For whatever reasons, nine of the thirteen colonies had established churches at the time of the Revolution, but few colonists were active members—no more than about 7 percent of the population, according to Martin Marty, the premier historian of American religion.[3]

Although the framers of the Constitution were defying the traditions of Western civilization when they decided *not* to establish a national religion, there was surprisingly little conflict about the decision. Some of the framers, aware of the chaos and conflict over religion that had plagued the countries of Europe for centuries, thought it best for governments to be neutral about religion. Some represented the four colonies which had never had an established church, or the five others which had already removed civil support for the church or had multiple establishments.[4] Only in Virginia had there been a controversy over the idea of state establishment. Jefferson and Madison had favored the 1786 Bill for Establishing Religious Freedom and withdrawing support from its state church, but Patrick Henry had opposed it.

The Bill of Rights, added in 1791, went beyond the 1789 Constitution, which had merely declined to establish a national religion. The First Amendment's provision that "Congress shall make no law respecting an establishment of religion, or prohibiting the free exercise thereof," ensured there would never be a national establishment. After Massachusetts, the last state to do so, disestablished its state religion in 1833, legal disestablishment was in place everywhere in the United States. Churches were on their own. Government would not support them financially, and no citizen would be coerced to join a church or prevented from holding public office because of his religion.

Despite the lack of a legal, or *de jure* establishment, there was a de facto establishment, an establishment in practice if not in law, of the moderate Protestants, primarily Congregationalists, Episcopalians, and Presbyterians.[5] Those evangelical (which in those days meant non-Catholic) sects dominated elected and appointed offices. The phrases in the Declaration of Independence—"Nature's God," the "Creator," and "Divine Providence"—reflected their view of religion's importance, and that of many citizens, while avoiding specific theological doctrines. That view was reflected in our national seal and in the traditions of opening congressional sessions and Supreme Court sessions with religious expressions. Although moderate Protestantism faced no serious challenge at the time, those phrases and practices did not give preference to any sect over another, to Protestantism over Catholicism, or even to Christianity over other religions, with the possible exception of polytheistic ones.

By the middle of the nineteenth century, even the de facto establishment of the older European-based churches and their domination of the culture was in jeopardy. Enthusiastic Methodist and Baptist preachers, although they had little education and were poorly paid if at all, converted thousands along the expanding frontier of the new nation.[6] The new sects were especially active in the South and the middle states, but they made inroads in the original colonies as well. The persecution of Baptists in New England made members of that sect the staunchest defenders of religious freedom and disestablishment.

The badly outnumbered evangelical denominations of the North were challenged further by the newer evangelicals after the northern seminaries began to teach a new kind of "modernist" theology. "Modernist" theology seemed to the vigorous new sects to denigrate biblical truth by shifting the emphasis from the meaning of the words themselves to the context of the times in which they were written. Modernists argued, for instance, that if St. Paul's letters to the early churches were written in expectation of Jesus' immediate return, they were less relevant to a time two centuries later. If the Old Testament came out of a patriarchal, slave-owning society, then its words about the roles of women and servants could not be taken at face value. If modern science had discovered new truths which the biblical writers could not possibly have known, modern readers should accept that scientific evidence over the literal words of the biblical creation account. If there was a conflict between reason and biblical authority, modernism chose reason.

Those who objected to modernism, insisting that the Bible's words are literally true for all times, became known as "fundamentalists." The name derived from a series of little booklets titled *The Fundamentals,* published in 1910 by Milton and Lyman Stewart. The booklets defended the truth of the biblical accounts of the Creation, Jesus' virgin birth, his miracles, and his death and resurrection. By the time of the First World War, American evangelicalism had split into two camps, the conservative fundamentalists and the liberal or moderate modernists.

The split between modernists and fundamentalists added a new dimension to the earlier North-South split over the question of slavery in each of the two new sects, Methodists and Baptists. The northern branches of those church bodies were more inclined to adopt "modernism" while the southern branches remained "fundamentalist." Northerners perceived the South as less modern in other ways—less industrialized, more rural, its people poorer and with less education. Ironically, the modernist denominations came to be called "mainline," although the fundamentalists continued to surpass them in membership.[7]

Southern fundamentalists lost still more respect when their challenge to the teaching of evolution resulted in a national spectacle in 1925. Fundamentalism was pitted against modern science in the Scopes trial, in which an obscure Tennessee teacher was charged with teaching evolution. John T. Scopes, the teacher, was indeed convicted, but the conviction was reversed on appeal. The trial's more lasting effect was created by H. L. Mencken's reports about the trial, with his scathing description of the South and of its fundamentalists as ignorant country bumpkins: "In ten thousand country towns, the evangelical pastors are propagating their gospel, and everywhere the yokels are ready for it" was only one of his gibes.[8] The incident so humiliated fundamentalists that they withdrew from public roles, retreating to their homes and their southern churches. Fundamentalism came to be associated with theological intransigence and with radical separation from the world as well as separation from other religious groups.

By this time, there were two de facto "establishments": the fundamentalists in the South, and the modernists in the North. Fundamentalism's de facto establishment was able to dominate public life in the South. Their influence in state legislatures was magnified by the overrepresentation of rural residents in those bodies, but they were also influential in city councils and school boards. School classes were opened with prayer, school assemblies were often devoted to religious programs, and public monuments and official seals were religious in nature.

After World War II, even the de facto fundamentalism in the South faced a challenge. Southern segregation policies were challenged by the Civil Rights movement as it won Supreme Court cases. Christian prayer in schools was challenged by atheists and Jews as they won other Supreme Court cases. In the 1950s and 1960s, disestablishment finally came to southern fundamentalism.[9] Nor were the challenges limited to the South, or to religious practices. The power of rural fundamentalists was further reduced by the Supreme Court decision[10] requiring apportionment of state legislative seats to reflect the growing numbers of citizens in urban areas. Young people were in revolt on campuses across the nation. While protesting the Vietnam War, southern segregation, and women's traditional roles, they also sparked the "sexual revolution," challenging the moral codes of traditional Christianity.

This is why Christian conservatives say that "it began with the six-ties." It was inevitable that there would be a backlash against the fast pace of social change engendered by the liberal sixties movements. This brief historical summary explains why it was southerners, fundamentalists, and particularly women who, tending to be the guardians of morality, were the instigators of the backlash. It was particularly ironic that the Equal Rights Amendment, the supporters of which naïvely supposed would be supported by all women, became the opening wedge for a conservative countermovement to feminism in particular and liberalism in general.

Sex education in schools and the Supreme Court decisions removing organized prayer from the schools were bad enough. But the Equal Rights Amendment would, from the Christian conservative point of view, allow the government to interfere in God's plan for the family. Not only was the government attacking fundamentalist religion, it was trying to establish in its place the "religion" of secular humanism. Christian conservatives defined secular humanism as giving higher priority to human wants and needs than to God's word as revealed in the Bible. Feminists were accused of seeking their own selfish ends rather than accepting their role in "God's plan."

After Oklahoma women showed the way, women all over the country, most of them with no previous experience in politics, did what no one thought possible—stopped the Equal Rights Amendment cold. For them, it was a moral issue. Because of their opposition to the feminist movement, they were sometimes called antifeminists. But even before the proposed amendment was defeated, the women had taken on other moral issues and had become the nucleus of the "pro-family movement," the first phase of the Christian (or Religious) Right. It was a women's movement at first, but also a religious movement, with its greatest strength in the South.

Because fundamentalists had separated themselves from politics since the Scopes trial in 1925, their participation in a political movement was something most Americans in the 1970s had not seen before. But in the years before the 1970s, fundamentalist pastors (largely male) had been preaching against moral decline, seeing the comfortable world they had built for themselves as surrounded by Babylon, the evil empire of biblical times. Finally, they, too, organized against it, using their own church networks in the 1980s to create the Moral Majority, Christian Voice, and other political groups.

The churches of these women and men were typically based in the

South or in southern California, and the political organizations they created reflected the conservative culture of their southern establishment—a literal interpretation of the Bible, traditional "Bible-based" morality, and historically, single-party politics. But growing urban areas and rising levels of education and income were already changing southern culture. Southerners were moving out of the South and northerners were moving in, accelerating what John Egerton had described in his 1974 book as "the Americanization of Dixie, and the Southernization of America." Although far from being homogenized, the regions were becoming more similar.[11] One of the consequences was the spread of conservative churches in both the South and the North. (Southern Baptist churches can now be found in every state.) Others were the Republicanization of the South, and as a result of that, the further conservatization of the Republican Party.

Democratic politics and conservative religion had coexisted comfortably in the South ever since Reconstruction. The new political movements of the 1970s and 1980s forced a reassessment of Democratic dominance. Experiences like this one, described by a young woman in rural Oklahoma, occurred all over the South:

> I was a Democrat because my mother was a Democrat, and she was a Democrat because her parents were Democrats, and none of us knew why. My mother . . . got copies of the Republican and Democrat platforms, and she read 'em both. I wasn't politically active at all. . . . I just voted straight Democratic and didn't even know who they were. I was talking to my mother one day and she said she was changing to Republican, and I said "I'm going to stay Democrat," and she said, "Have you read the Democrat platform?" and I told her no, and so she brought out the piece of paper, and I read it, and I said, "I do not believe in this!" So . . . I went down and changed. (Sandra Grogan Jeter, September 12, 1980)

Not only did southerners change their registration from Democrat to Republican, but the Republican Party, under the influence of the Christian Right, became more friendly to traditional southern moral concerns. The congressional ratings prepared by the Christian Coalition, which saw itself as the arbiter of morality in politics, were a good indicator of the extent to which southern values had spread outside the South. The ratings, based on about ten selected issues, revealed the percentage of each congressperson's votes that were in agreement with the Coalition's position.[12] In the 105th Congress (1997–1998), the average Christian Coalition score for the Republicans was 86.94 percent, while the Democrats, who had controlled the "solid South" just after World War II, had an average score of only 22.17 percent.[13]

Christian Right activists are a powerful force in many southern states, but the South is not the only region where they are to be found. Nine of the eleven former Confederate states, along with six other states, refused to ratify the Equal Rights Amendment. An index of Christian Right influence in the Republican Party, tabulated by the periodical *Campaigns and Elections* in 1994, showed that it had "great" influence in seven of the eleven Confederate states plus Oklahoma, with "strong influence" in two other southern states and three nonsouthern states.[14] Six state congressional delegations with an average Christian Coalition score of 70 percent or higher were from the South or border states, along with eight nonsouthern states.

This book reports what I have learned from the Christian Right activists and from the literature the movement has produced. My research was driven by three questions: What were the underlying themes that drove the movement's activism? How has the movement changed over time? How has their agenda and the rationale for it changed over time?

The most persistent complaint of Christian conservatives over the twenty-five-year period was that the separation of church and state threatened to remove religion from public and even private life. That theme was implicit throughout the early interviews as respondents deplored the rising tide of secularism in the culture, but it did not reveal itself clearly until sometime later. At the beginning, even as they worried about cultural trends, the activists were preoccupied with strategic decisions about ERA, the next vote, or the next hearing. The series of specific cultural trends that they opposed—radical feminism, acceptance of abortion and homosexuality, teaching sex education and creationism in schools, sex- and violence-filled television and movies, and the overarching theme of protest against secularism—are reported in parts one and two of this book, along with the history of the movement itself.

The interviews and the long time frame of my research also allowed me to answer the second question of how the movement changed over time. The early chapters focus on the way the movement of fundamentalist women spread out of the South to other regions and enlisted both sexes.

The development of the pro-family movement from the anti-ERA protest during the years 1972–1979 is described in the rest of part one. The process of change, facilitated by the White House Conference on Families in 1979, was gradual and hardly noticed at the time, but by the dawning of the new century, the movement was clearly different than it had been in the 1970s. During the transitional period, other organizations, appealing to other constituencies, with different issue-emphases, and often led by men, joined the movement. By the end of the 1980s, there was less railing against the evil empire of Babylon and more longing for the promised land of Zion.[15] From opposing what they saw as attempts to establish a religion of secular humanism, they had moved to fighting against a reinterpretation of the religion clauses of the First Amendment and to demanding a return to what the activists believed was the Founding Fathers' original purpose: a "Christian America." There was even an attempt to amend the Constitution to "clarify" the First Amendment's religion clause by adding a specific right "to pray, acknowledge religious belief, heritage, or tradition on public property, including public schools."[16]

Part two describes the transition and the second phase, lasting into the 1990s. Not only did the message subtly evolve, but the organizations themselves became more bureaucratized, professionalized, and centralized. The Christian Right seemed less like a social movement and more like other interest groups employing lobbyists and using letter-writing and telephone campaigns to influence legislators. There was increasing use of television and radio programs as well as glossy publications to disseminate the message that America should return to its Christian heritage. There were more organizations, working on more issues, and appealing to a greater variety of religious groups.

The sources and content of fundamentalist beliefs are not common knowledge among Americans, of whom only one-third at most are fundamentalists. Many of those who are not fundamentalist know its beliefs only in caricature if at all. To put the Christian Right agenda in context, I have explained fundamentalist beliefs and described four different church groups leading the Christian Right, the Churches of Christ and the Mormons in chapter 4, the Baptists in chapter 8, and the charismatic churches in chapter 10. The way these groups are organized and the kind of members they attract are significant for their participation in the Christian Right.

The chapters in part three, using interviews with activists in the late

1970s and again in the late 1990s, answer the third question. They analyze how opinions have changed in each of four issue-areas, and how those opinions have been shaped by the writers and leaders of the Christian Right. Each of the four issues embodies a protest against government intrusion into family lives and against government interference with the prerogatives of parents to raise their children according to their own moral standards. Family and an emphasis on reproductive and sexuality issues were important for the original anti-ERA movement. Educational issues were a natural outgrowth of concern for families and children. Humanism was soon identified as the real culprit in "removing God" from school curricula and textbooks. Finally, Christian conservatives sought a return to America's Christian heritage, by reinterpreting the religion clause in the First Amendment.

The conclusion summarizes the changes in the Christian Right throughout its first quarter-century and provides a glimpse of the possibilities for its future. During the time that I have been interviewing participants, reading organizational literature, and observing local, state, and national meetings, the secular media have written the obituary of the Christian Right at least three times. Subsequent events proved those reports to have been exaggerated. Even if the heyday of the highly visible organizations is past, as some observers believe it is, those who support Christian conservative values have developed a parallel culture to perpetuate those values for years in the future. They are better educated and more sophisticated than they were twenty-five years ago. When their children begin taking their places as educators, journalists, lawyers, and public officials, they may well be in a position to change the culture. I hope this book will help other Americans to understand this movement as its adherents become increasingly more visible in American life.

NOTES

1. Matthew Moen, "From Moralism to Liberalism," chap. 6 in *The Transformation of the Christian Right* (Tuscaloosa: University of Alabama Press, 1992).

2. George M. Marsden, *Religion and American Culture* (New York: Harcourt-Brace Jovanovich, 1990).

3. Martin Marty, *Righteous Empire: The Protestant Experience in America* (New York: Dial, 1970), p. 38.

4. Rhode Island, Delaware, Pennsylvania, and New Jersey had no established church. Those not supporting the church financially or having multiple establishments were Maryland, North Carolina, Vermont, South Carolina, and New York.

5. Marty, *Righteous Empire*, pp. 19, 69–70.

6. Roger Finke and Rodney Stark, *The Churching of America, 1776–1990: Winners and Losers in our Religious Economy* (New Brunswick, N.J.: Rutgers University Press, 1992), chap. 3.

7. Ibid.

8. H. L. Mencken, *American Mercury*, Editorial (October 1925), quoted in Mayo DuBasky, *The Gist of Mencken: Quotations from America's Critic* (Metuchen, N.J.: Scarecrow, 1990), p. 43.

9. I credit Philip E. Hammond, *Religion and Personal Autonomy: The Third Disestablishment in America* (Columbia: University of South Carolina Press, 1992), with suggesting that the period since World War II was one of "disestablishment," although I have interpreted it somewhat differently than he did.

10. *Baker v. Carr,* 369 U.S. 186 (1962).

11. John Egerton, *The Americanization of Dixie, the Southernization of America* (New York: Harper's, 1974).

12. Examples were abortion, fetal tissue research, education savings accounts, pornography and obscenity, balanced budget amendment, and occasionally, confirmation of presidential appointees.

13. Calculated from the Christian Coalition Scorecard.

14. John C. Green, et al., "Less Than Conquerors: The Christian Right in State Republican Parties," chap. 7 in *Social Movements and American Political Institutions*, Anne N. Costain and Andrew S. McFarland (Lanham, Md.: Rowman and Littlefield, 1998).

15. Margaret Lamberts Bendroth, in *Fundamentalism and Gender: 1875 to the Present* (New Haven: Yale University Press, 1993), first described it in this way.

16. Excerpted from the Religious Freedom Amendment, proposed by Rep. Ernest Istook (R-Okla.). Sen. Henry Hyde (R-Ill.) has introduced a similar proposal for a Religious Equality Amendment.

PART I

"PRO-FAMILY"

PROTECTING OUR FAMILIES
AND SAVING OUR COUNTRY

1

HOW IT ALL BEGAN

WOMEN FOR RESPONSIBLE LEGISLATION

Congress voted to submit the Equal Rights Amendment to the states on Wednesday, March 22, 1972. Only thirty-two minutes later, Hawaii became the first state to ratify.[1] When six more states ratified in the next seven days, the proposed amendment's supporters were jubilant, predicting that the required thirty-eight states would ratify by the end of the year. Passage seemed assured in Oklahoma as well when the state senate approved it by a voice vote on Thursday, March 23.[2]

But there was opposition from an unexpected quarter. The *Phyllis Schlafly Report* for February 1972, titled "What's Wrong with the Equal Rights Amendment?" had already arrived in the homes of several women on Schlafly's mailing list in Oklahoma, including Ann Patterson, who was to become the leader of the anti-ERA forces in the state. When Patterson and the others learned that the amendment would probably be ratified on Monday without a hearing, they talked to a friendly legislator in the House, a fellow Republican, and secured a promise that the ERA would be held up in the Rules Committee there. Patterson said: "We didn't know anything about the amendment at all. In fact, I thought it was a good thing until I read Phyllis' *Report*. But we thought they ought to take time to consider it more carefully."[3]

On Wednesday, March 29, the ERA failed by a vote of fifty-two to thirty-six in the Oklahoma House of Representatives, the first setback in the ERA ratification process, but the vote attracted little attention. There were feminist organizations in the state, but they had not prepared for the vote. Those opposing the amendment were no better prepared than those favoring it, for they had no organization at all. The women who received Phyllis Schlafly's newsletter had heard nothing from her about feminism or the ERA before the historic February issue. That issue had been written only because a friend in Connecticut had insisted that Schlafly appear in a debate on the ERA when she would have preferred not to. But she quickly took charge when it became clear that a grassroots crusade was underway.

The anti-ERA organization which became the nucleus of the pro-family movement was born the weekend after the ERA's defeat in Oklahoma. Ann Patterson in Oklahoma City contacted Phyllis Schlafly in St. Louis and volunteered to use her mailing list to call conservative women in other states. In her calls, she told them what the Oklahoma women had done and encouraged them to do the same. She was pleased with the results. She said that she had called twenty-seven or twenty-eight states, and that all of them "stopped or slowed down at that time, although some ratified later."

Patterson then led the small band of conservative women in forming an ad hoc committee which they called Women for Responsible Legislation. Some of those in the new organization were her friends in Oklahoma on Schlafly's list; some were workers and donors from her husband's 1966 campaign for the U.S. Senate. She remained the de facto head of the Antis in Oklahoma throughout the ten-year period of the ratification contest.

Despite that first-in-the-nation defeat, the proponents of a national ERA still had no reason to suppose that it would not be quickly ratified. Twenty-two states ratified in 1972; the pace slowed in 1973, but by year's end there were thirty. Then it nearly stopped; from 1974 through 1982, the Pros succeeded in getting only five more ratifications, bringing the total to thirty-five. Meanwhile, legislatures in five of the ratified states had voted to rescind their ratification, although it is not clear whether such a move was legally valid. It was a moot point, however, for after ten years of struggle, the ERA was still three states short of the necessary three-fourths of the states, or thirty-eight.

ANN PATTERSON

Ann Patterson, the leader of the anti-ERA forces in Oklahoma, was in her late forties at the time of the first ERA vote. She had grown up as a Republican in Nebraska. She met her husband-to-be when he was stationed there during World War II. "Pat" Patterson was an Oklahoman and a Democrat, as were virtually all Oklahomans at that time. After the war, they married and settled in Oklahoma, where he soon joined her party. The Pattersons were in the forefront of the trend that eventually turned the solid Democratic South to almost solid Republican. Both were active in Republican politics even before Pat ran for the Senate in 1966. Ann "went around with him to all the little towns and we really had

Ann Patterson, the founder of the anti-ERA campaign in Oklahoma, also initiated the formation of similar organizations in other states. She is shown here with her grandchild, symbolizing her belief that a woman's primary role is with her family. (*James Patterson*)

a good time—it was a fun campaign." Although Pat Patterson was defeated in that election, the contacts the Pattersons made in the campaign were valuable in his wife's later campaign against the ERA.

The Pattersons were also Episcopalians. Pat was a vestryman and warden in the church and the author of a lay readers' training course and some Sunday school lessons. Ann taught Sunday school. Most of those who joined the anti-ERA effort in Oklahoma, however, were fundamentalists of the Churches of Christ, drawn in by Beverly Findley, a member of that church body. (More about that church body later, in chapter 4.) The campaign brought together people whose religious backgrounds were very different and who might not otherwise have met.

Patterson had long been active in civic and cultural affairs in Oklahoma City. She had been a member of Junior League and of Planned Parenthood, although she came to oppose Planned Parenthood later because of its association with abortion rights. She had attended at least one of the public meetings of the John Birch Society, and she knew the leaders well enough that they worked together in planning public hearings on the ERA. In answer to a question about it, she said only:

> I had a very dear friend whose father was a prof at the University. She was a home member of the John Birch Society. Several times at her house, Fieldmen of the society showed films and talked about them. We read the Blue Book of the John Birch Society and my husband had some questions about it. But I do use some of their research. They do excellent research and have good publications. (Ann Patterson, November 18, 1978)

She said, however, that she never identified the John Birch Society as the source of an anti-ERA argument, even if it was.

My longest interview with Ann Patterson took place at her home, when we talked for several hours. After that, we spoke to each other at meetings and conferences, and had many telephone conversations, some long, some short. I have quoted her frequently from this series of interviews in this book, especially in this chapter. By the end of the ERA campaign, the interviews were a series of friendly conversations, not a structured series with limited topics. She was quite cordial, although I always felt that she was a little wary of me. Often she would refuse to answer a question, or would parry it, but because we talked so often, I nearly always found the answer in some later conversation.

Patterson's conservative views were in line with those of her parents. Her mother had told her that "Women had so many responsibilities, and ... every woman had a man who would vote with her in mind," even though her own mother (Patterson's grandmother) had written to her (Patterson's mother) saying she should work for woman's suffrage. Patterson herself then commented, "I wonder how many men voted differently after they no longer had the responsibility for their wives. I have a lot of influence with my husband, which I think is more important than the fact that I vote" (November 18, 1978).

Patterson's arguments against the ERA were mostly legal. She did not emphasize the religious reasons for opposing the ERA, as did most of those activists who worked with her. Her view of what it means to be a woman was relevant to her opposition to the ERA and her disagreement with feminism. The following excerpt from Patterson's interview was similar to those made by the antisuffrage movement in the early part of the twentieth century.[4] It was echoed by other respondents, and in Phyllis Schlafly's writings:

> I have a good feeling about being a woman. There are some things that I do better. We are different. Women have so many responsibilities in church anyway that men won't take, why should women take on these others? When the women take hold, the men drop out, and I don't like to see that happen. (Patterson, at her home, November 18, 1978)

THE HEARINGS

In planning strategy, the Anti women, organized as Women for Responsible Legislation, did not have the luxury of deciding what would be easiest or best for them to do. Their strategy was determined for them by the rules of legislative procedure, as was most of the strategy of the anti-ERA movement. The first vote had gone their way, but there would be another, and the outcome of that might depend on how they presented their case in the hearings. So the first task was to plan for the hearings. Patterson explained that she was able to work well with the John Birch Society, but also hinted that she did not entirely agree with them.

For instance, when she found that the John Birch Society had signed up for all the time allotted to the Antis in the hearings, she persuaded them to let her have some of the time for other statements:

> [When I found that] the John Birch Society people had already signed up all the time . . . I talked with [their regional coordinator]. Of course they were most interested in the conspiracy thing . . . so I told him that we had . . . a woman who had escaped from Latvia. . . . She had pledged to spend her time fighting Communism when she got to America. . . . So he withdrew all his people when he saw that we had it all taken care of. So we work together well like that. (Ann Patterson, March 11, 1982)

The hearings were an educational experience for Oklahoma women, for there had not been much discussion of the ERA before then. The galleries were full for most of the sessions. Both Pros and Antis brought out their best speakers, and the issue was aired thoroughly. But the legislature did not take it up again that year, and the following year it was voted down for the second time.

RECRUITMENT

After the hearings, Ann Patterson and Beverly Findley, the head of an organization of women from the Churches of Christ, began to recruit activists and members for what they hoped would be a short campaign. Because of the newspaper publicity about the vote, they had plenty of invitations to speak. The issue was still new enough that people wanted to hear more about it. The groups to which they spoke were already sympathetic to anti-ETA rhetoric. Patterson started with the Republican Party because the woman who was president of the National Federation of Republican Women was coming for a state federation meeting in May. They had already told her that they would like to take a position opposing the amendment, and after her presentation, they did so.

After the Pros began to publicize the Methodist church's support for the ERA, some Methodist groups began to schedule debates about the issue, often inviting Patterson to take part. In spring 1972, she debated before the League of Women Voters (which subsequently took a position favoring the amendment) and Parents without Partners. She had expected the Republican Party and the League of Women Voters to take official positions on the issue, but she had mixed feelings about church groups.

> I am not one who believes in going to organizations and asking for a position. I don't think a consensus is fair, even if you take a vote. I don't think it's as valid for a church group to take a position as one like the League. I'm sure that 100 percent of the Mormons don't oppose the ERA, for instance. (Ann Patterson, November 18, 1978)

But when pressed about when churches should take a position, she hedged several times, then said that maybe this is something the church should take a look at, and finally decided that it was a valid political issue for the churches. She was already struggling with the American tradition of church-state separation, which was the source of so much controversy in the later stages of the movement. The membership of conservative churches offered a rich prize in dedicated activists, but she was vaguely uncomfortable about it, especially when liberal churches took the opposite position.

Research on social movements has consistently shown that the easiest way to recruit constituents and activists is to align the movement's ideology with that of existing networks, and to appeal to them through those networks.[5] Anti-ERA activists in Oklahoma were recruited from the John Birch Society, the Republican Party, the Oklahoma Farm Bureau, and the Oklahomans on Phyllis Schlafly's mailing list. The John Birch Society magazine, *American Opinion*, published an article opposing the ERA in November 1972.[6] The magazine also carried articles opposing gay rights, child care programs, public education, and feminism during the 1970s. Its members were therefore a likely source of recruits to oppose the ERA and related liberal or feminist causes.

Although the Republican Party did not oppose the ERA officially until much later, Phyllis Schlafly was more conservative than mainstream Republicans. (Oklahoma Republicans, in turn, were more conservative than Republicans in many other states.) The *Phyllis Schlafly Report* went to those who agreed with her more conservative views. So those who came from either of these groups (some individuals belonged to both) were already convinced of most of the legal and political arguments that Ann Patterson was making about the ERA.

The other groups, more likely to be recruited by one of their own members, were the fundamentalists of the Baptist church or the Churches of Christ and the Mormons, who had always had a conservative family policy. Except for the Mormons, whose church had taken an official position against the ERA, the religious groups had not been exposed to the legal and political rationale for opposing ERA. But the appeal used so successfully by Phyllis Schlafly—that it would harm the traditional family—was one that resonated with their existing beliefs. To be sure, the two appeals sometimes merged, as in the argument that existing laws protecting women would be invalidated by the ERA.

When I asked Patterson if she ever talked about religion with the Church of Christ women, she said, "Oh, not really. These women are so convicted that they are right, and they like me, which I appreciate." They worry because "they know that I drive around the state and all, late at night, and they know that I've been sprinkled, not immersed."

The mode of baptism, the ceremony marking the conversion of an adult or the dedication of a child by its parents, is one of the points of difference between fundamentalist and nonfundamentalist churches. Fundamentalists believe the only valid baptism is by total immersion in water, the way that Jesus was baptized by John the Baptist. Nonfundamentalist churches settle for a symbolic sprinkling of water upon the new convert's head. Another point of difference is that fundamentalist churches do not use a liturgy, responses and prayers from a printed prayer book, as the Episcopalian and other nonfundamentalist churches do.

Patterson was "not at home in the fundamentalist churches because 'I'm used to the liturgy,'" but she became disaffected with her own church because of its liberal stances on abortion and the role of women. She thought the local church should "speak out more and not let the national church direct them." She finally asked to have her name taken off the roll at her local church. When her priest asked, "What will you do for Christian fellowship?" she responded "I've had more Christian fellowship, working with this project for the last seven years, than I have ever known [before] on a day-to-day basis" (November 18, 1978).

BEVERLY FINDLEY

The way in which two conservative women from different religious traditions, Patterson an Episcopalian and Findley a member of the Church of Christ, met and worked together is an example of how the movement grew and developed. It is also the Oklahoma counterpart of the national cooperation between Lottie Beth Hobbs, the leader of the Church of Christ women, and Phyllis Schlafly. Their relationship, in turn, was mirrored in the later cooperation between leaders with differing emphases on religion and on politics in the Republican Party.

Patterson and Findley first met face-to-face at a 1974 John Birch Society seminar at Oklahoma Christian College, a college supported by individual Churches of Christ. Ann Patterson had met Becky Tilotta, a former Oklahoman, in 1973 at Schlafly's annual leadership meeting in St. Louis. At that meeting, she took names of some of Tilotta's friends in the

Churches of Christ in Oklahoma. So when she met Beverly Findley, she already knew about her. They immediately began planning another meeting to be devoted exclusively to the ERA, with Becky Tilotta as the speaker. Findley was herself a former member of the John Birch Society.

> I took a chapter and tried to do right by it, but I had to get out of it because it took so much time, and besides, I heard so much about Communism that it scared me to death. I just couldn't sleep at night. I couldn't take the literature. It was just too depressing. (June 1979)[7]

When I asked if she thought it was exaggerated, she replied:

> No, I think it was accurate. Oh, it may have been a little overdramatized, but there were just too many things to think about, and it scared me so bad that I just couldn't take it. So I just dropped out, but when the ERA came along, the children were older, and I thought I could handle it better. (June 1979)

Findley, the wife of an Oklahoma City firefighter, was a slim blonde, the mother of three children, and in her thirties at the time of her anti-ERA activism. Although she supported the ideal of subordinate roles for women in accordance with the teachings of her church, she did not hesitate to assume a leadership role when she saw something that needed to be done.

Findley removed her children from the public schools when busing was first ordered in Oklahoma City, then was instrumental in starting a private school in her church. One of her children, who was retarded, continued in the public schools' special education program until she was sixteen. Then Findley undertook the management of a biweekly country music program, the proceeds of which went to support a sheltered workshop for retarded young people and adults. Vivacious and talented, she was herself an artist and a country music singer.

RECRUITMENT

Describing the formation of Women Who Want to be Women in Oklahoma, Findley said:

People wonder how I got all this organized. It's really very simple. I just
notified the people I worshipped with. They are the people that think the
way I do, and I knew that they would be likely to feel the same [about
ERA] as I did. (March 9, 1982)

Oklahoma Christian College, where the seminar on the ERA was held,
was supported by members of the Churches of Christ, but not officially affiliated with the Churches of Christ—an important distinction to members of
those churches. The Churches of Christ, as individual churches, do not support colleges or other extrachurch ministries because the churches St. Paul
founded and described in the New Testament did not. For the same reason,
there are no hierarchical or coordinating organizations. Individual members,
however, can and do exchange newsletters with other members and cooperate on projects of mutual interest.

Those newsletters kept Church of Christ members better informed
than members of the denominations with more formal coordination structures. Beverly Findley used the church network because she knew that it
would be an effective means of communication. The seminar attracted
about five hundred people, although there had been no notices in general-
circulation newspapers. The next morning, when a small group met to
organize what they called Women Who Want to be Women in Oklahoma,
Findley found that the others were expecting her to take on the task.

During the five years that Beverly Findley was the Oklahoma Coordinator of the Four Ws, she and Ann Patterson were on the road, sometimes
together, sometimes not, speaking about the ERA, collecting names, and
setting up new chapters. Someone in a local community, usually a member
of the local Church of Christ, would contact Findley and ask her to come
and speak, which she did two or three times a week. Sometimes the meetings were held in churches, more often in a public library or other public
place. Occasionally, the meetings were publicized in the newspaper, but
the churches were the primary channels of communication.

Most of the churches wouldn't even announce a meeting at the services,
because there was a little stigma attached to it because it was political.
Not every church was that way, but most of them were. So it was usually just passed around among the members. (March 9, 1982)

At that time, these churches did not need the principle of separation of church and state to inhibit their political activities. Not being political was part of fundamentalist culture, partly because of the historic withdrawal of fundamentalists from political life after the Scopes trial. They called it "overstepping the bounds."

The conflict between religious-based opposition to the ERA and religious-based reluctance to take a political role was a common one for fundamentalist women. The opponents of woman suffrage faced a similar contradiction between their view of political action as unfeminine and the necessity to act politically in order to preserve their femininity by rejecting woman suffrage.[8]

While Beverly Findley was recruiting members from the Church of Christ and Ann Patterson was speaking to groups from other churches or to secular organizations, other organizations joined the anti-ERA coalition. The Oklahoma Farm Bureau cooperated, largely because some members of the John Birch Society and of Phyllis Schlafly's Eagle Forum were also members of the Farm Bureau.[9] In some towns, the Women's Christian Temperance Union (WCTU) was the focus of anti-ERA activity. This was ironic because the WCTU had had close ties with the earlier generation of feminists and had been part of the woman suffrage movement in the latter part of the nineteenth century.

APPEALING TO THE APPALLED

One of the most valuable recruiting tools "passed around among the members" was the "pink sheet," so called because it was printed on pink paper. It had been written by Lottie Beth Hobbs. It was clearly designed to appall its readers, just as Hobbs herself had been appalled when she first read about the ERA.

> In 1974 or 1975, I wrote the text and took it to my printer and told him to print up ten thousand copies in various colors. I asked him if he could think of some way to dress it up a little. So he looked at it, found pictures of two ladies in his clip-art collection, and drew the phone line around the page connecting them. . . . My sister-in-law came up with the title. She said when ladies were in the beauty shop or somewhere, the way to

Ladies)!
Have you Heard?

DO YOU KNOW WHO IS PLANNING YOUR FUTURE FOR YOU? ARE YOU
SURE THEY ARE PLANNING WHAT YOU REALLY WANT? IF NOT, IT'S
TIME TO WAKE UP AND SPEAK UP! THE HOUR IS LATE!

ARE YOU SURE YOU WANT TO BE "LIBERATED"?
God created you and gave you a beautiful and exalted place to fill. No women in
history have ever enjoyed such privileges, luxuries, and freedom as American women.
Yet, a tiny minority of dissatisfied, highly vocal, militant women insist that you
are being exploited as a "domestic drudge" and "a pretty toy". And they are determined to liberate you whether you want it or not!
What is "liberation"? Ask women in Cuba. Castro "liberated" Cuba! Remember?

WHAT IS THE EQUAL RIGHTS AMENDMENT?
On March 22, 1972, the U.S. Congress passed the Equal Rights Amendment (ERA)
and sent it to the states for ratification. If it is ratified by 38 states, it
will become law, enforced by the federal government, superseding all state laws
on related subjects.
The Amendment reads: "Equality of rights under the law shall not be denied or
abridged by the United States or by any states on account of sex." Simple, isn't it?
BUT HAVE YOU LOOKED AT THE HOOK INSIDE THE BAIT?

THE MOST DRASTIC MEASURE
Senator Sam Ervin called the ERA "the most drastic measure in Senate history."
Why? because it strikes at the very foundation of family life, and the home is the
foundation of our nation. Can you possibly avoid being drastically affected by the
ERA? NOT A CHANCE!
Actually, it is a Loss of Rights Amendment. How will it affect YOU?

DO YOU WANT TO LOSE YOUR RIGHT NOT TO WORK?
If you are married, you may choose to work outside your home. But you may
choose to stay at home, to rear your children, to be supported by your husband. The
ERA will abolish this right. It will invalidate all laws which require the husband
to support his family and will make the wife equally responsible for support. You
can be forced to supply half the family support, or all of it, if you are a better
wage earner (pp. 944, Yale Law Journal, which was inserted in the Congressional Record by Senator Birch Bayh, leading proponent of ERA).
What about your children? You can be forced to put them in a federal day care
center, if one is available. And to see that one is available is a major goal of the
National Organization for Women(NOW) - leaders in the movement to ratify the Equal
Rights Amendment.
Under the ERA, if a wife fails to support her husband, he can use it as grounds
for divorce (Yale Law Journal, P. 951).
This can work a special hardship on senior women who have spent their lives
rearing their families and are not prepared to enter the job market.

WILL THE ERA HELP DIVORCED WOMEN?
Divorced women will lose the customary right of child custody, child support, and
or alimony, and can be forced to pay child support and alimony, if her husband wins
custody of the children (Yale Law Journal, P. 952)

WHAT ABOUT OTHER EFFECTS ON FAMILY LIFE?
Wife and children will not be required to wear the name of husband and father.

The "pink sheet" prepared by Lottie Beth Hobbs of Fort Worth was a hugely successful recruiting tool for Women Who Want to be Women, Lottie Beth Hobbs's anti-
ERA organization. *(Women Who Want to be Women)*

get their attention was to say "Have you heard?" So we gave it the title, "Ladies Have You Heard?"[10] (Lottie Beth Hobbs, April 26, 1998)

Later they decided to use the "feminine" color, pink, for all of them. And so it came to be called "the pink sheet." Ann Patterson said:

> The pink sheet is something that I never would have been able to write. It's accurate, but it's a little too . . . well, it's an emotional way to promote the issue. I wouldn't have done it, and Phyllis would not have done it. But it fascinates me that this did happen, because in order to get lots of people involved, you have to use emotional appeals. (November 18, 1978)

The pink sheet was distributed in church literature tables, put on door-knobs in neighborhoods, printed in small-town newspapers, and copied and recopied by individuals and organizations all over the state and in other states as well. Hobbs reported that a woman in Georgia had told her that it kept that state from ratifying the ERA. Originally on letter-size paper, printed on both sides, its first page has a drawing of two women talking over the telephone with its cord looping all around the margin. It begins:

> God created you and gave you a beautiful and exalted place to fill. No women in history have ever enjoyed such privileges, luxuries, and freedom as American women. Yet a tiny minority of dissatisfied, highly vocal, militant women insist that you are being exploited as a "domestic drudge" and "a pretty toy." And they are determined to "liberate" you—whether you want it or not! What is "liberation"? Ask women in Cuba. Castro "liberated" Cuba! Remember? ("Pink Sheet")

Some of the paragraphs in the pink sheet appear to be almost verbatim quotations from Phyllis Schlafly's first three *Reports* on the ERA, although they were not attributed to her. Schlafly's *Reports*, in turn, had quoted and cited articles about the ERA in the *Yale Law Journal* and the *Harvard Civil Rights-Civil Liberties Law Review*.[11] The first law journal article was actually favorable to the ERA, but by quoting selectively, Schlafly was able to make the article's predictions of the ERA's consequences sound threatening to traditional women. The second article, unfavorable to the ERA, did indeed argue that the ERA might invalidate separate rest rooms or separate physical education classes for males and females.

When the pink sheet used quotations from the law journals, they were headlined so as to attract more attention and be even more appalling to traditional women. For example:

DO YOU WANT YOUR HUSBAND TO SLEEP
IN THE BARRACKS WITH WOMEN?

If your husband is in the armed forces, or a fireman, what can you expect under ERA? It will be illegal to have separate facilities—so your husband will be sharing sleeping quarters, restrooms, showers, and/or foxholes with women. ("Pink Sheet")

The only item in the pink sheet that had not appeared in some form in one of the three Schlafly *Reports* was this one, clearly intended to appall the members of conservative churches:

HOW WILL THE ERA AFFECT CHURCHES?

The National Organization for Women is demanding that "women be ordained in religious bodies where that right is still denied." To refuse to do this will be illegal under ERA. One goal of N.O.W. is to abolish the tax-exempt status of all churches.

The pink sheet aroused women from conservative churches who feared that these things might actually happen. Seeing the specter of government intrusion into their homes and even their churches, they flocked to join Women Who Want to be Women. Bunny Chambers, who later became the state coordinator for Women Who Want to be Women in Oklahoma was first recruited when she picked up a pink sheet while visiting a church in another part of the state. A woman I met at the state capitol told me that she had had the pink sheet reprinted in the local newspaper at her own expense in order to warn the members of her own community about the dangers of the ERA. Others had copied them and hung them on doorknobs in their neighborhoods. All agreed that it had been a superb recruiting tool. Hobbs described the media response:

Texas Monthly had an article likening it to too much cotton candy. On television news, a guy put it right up on the screen, and he said "these pink sheets are just showing up everywhere, and I don't know who's responsible for it, but it's got to be some group that's well organized and well financed." Well, I sat there and I just hooted, because I thought, "we are as well-organized as three drunks in a phone booth, and we don't have any money." I took the money right out of my pocket for the first 10,000. . . . I really think the Lord led us to do this, because at the time I really didn't know what I was doing at all! (April 24, 1998)

This technique of "appealing to the appalled" is not unusual for social movements. Social movements are organized around the belief that something needs to be changed. Their members may think something is wrong, they may think something is unfair, or they may actually be afraid of something. The probable consequences of the Equal Rights Amendment, as interpreted by Phyllis Schlafly and Lottie Beth Hobbs, were calculated to arouse fear in their constituents. Schlafly argued that the legal consequences would force women to go to work outside the home and to contribute to Social Security, and their sons to sleep in mixed-sex barracks. This was bad enough, but for the fundamentalist women, the belief that the ERA would violate what God had ordained made it even more frightening. It was "against God's plan."

FINANCES

Both the Antis and the Pros regularly complained to the press (and to me) about how much money the "other side" had to spend, while "poor-mouthing" their own finances. Ann Patterson said the fight against the ERA had been a "David and Goliath fight—there was no well-financed angel." The Pros, too, complained that they would have done more and had more paid field workers, a WATS line, and media promotion if they had had enough money. The Pros suspected that insurance companies were supporting the Antis, while the Antis suspected that Norman Lear and other Hollywood types were supporting the Pros. Neither side could offer hard evidence of such help.

Ann Patterson always avoided a direct answer to questions about finances, but some of the information dribbled out in the course of years of talking with her and others in her organization. Both the Pros and the Antis received in-kind contributions of office space, use of computers, and printing of materials. Gerry Lowe's chapter in a small city north of Oklahoma City received help from a wealthy member of the local Mormon church, and Ann Patterson admitted to receiving money from various wealthy supporters, although she would never say who they were.

The reality is that the big money on both sides came from outside the state. A comparison of the facilities and workers available to both sides suggests that the Pros probably had more of it, or spent it in more visible ways. The National Coalition for ERA, ERAmerica, NOW, the National Women's Political Caucus, and the League of Women Voters all provided funds to their state chapters, but the Oklahoma Pros complained that most of the money was wasted by the national offices and they never got what they needed. However, the Pros had twelve paid staff workers in Oklahoma, several rented offices (not luxurious, but usable), and money to pay national celebrities to come to the state.

The Antis had no state offices, only telephone lines in the leaders' homes, and no paid field-workers or coordinators. They brought in their own celebrity, Phyllis Schlafly, who provided her own funds. The John Birch Society arranged for U.S. Army General Andrew Gatsis to speak against putting women in the armed forces, and an unnamed "angel from the East" had provided funds for a training seminar at which Paul Weyrich, a leading Washington conservative, and Connie Marshner, a member of his staff, appeared. The Antis' other training seminars featured local people or Rosemary Thomson, Phyllis Schlafly's right-hand woman from Illinois. I heard no complaints from the local Antis that Schlafly wasted money or spent it unwisely.

When the state coordinators for the Antis traveled to other communities, the local women provided lodging and paid for gas. Their husbands usually covered the telephone bills. Recipients of the various newsletters, of which there were at least six during the ERA campaign, were asked to send a small fee, and if that was not enough, the newsletter writer paid the balance herself, or used the revolving fund of Women for Responsible Legislation.

The three most important networks for recruitment to the anti-ERA movement were the John Birch Society, the Republican Party, and the fundamentalist churches. In Oklahoma, the Farm Bureau contributed many members. Not surprisingly, the first to join the movement were individuals who belonged to more than one of these networks. For them, the appalling things that they heard about the ERA resonated with their preexisting beliefs. Recruitment, while important, is not enough without issue agreement.

Another factor in the success of the Anti movement was the skill and determination of the local and national leaders. They planned strategy, recruited members, and framed the issues in ways that continue to resonate with the members' beliefs. Ann Patterson and Beverly Findley fulfilled these functions for the Oklahoma members, and they succeeded in preventing ratification in Oklahoma. But ERA supporters could afford to lose some states, as long as they won at least thirty-eight. National leaders for the Antis needed to forestall the ratification in only thirteen states. The next chapter describes the efforts of Phyllis Schlafly.

NOTES

1. Eileen Shanahan, "Equal Rights Amendment Is Approved by Congress," *New York Times*, 23 March 1972, A1.

2. Associated Press, "Equal Rights for Women Amendment Clears Senate," *Daily Oklahoman*, 23 March 1972, A1.

3. This quotation is from a four-hour interview with Patterson in November 1978. Other quotations in this chapter are from this interview or from dozens of shorter interviews continuing until after the ERA was finally defeated.

4. Susan Marshall, *Splintered Sisterhood, Gender and Class in the Campaign against Woman Suffrage* (Madison: University of Wisconsin Press, 1997), notes several similarities between the antisuffrage movement and the anti-ERA movement on pages 231–33.

5. David A. Snow, Louis A. Zurcher, and Sheldon Ekland-Olson, "Social Networks and Social Movements: A Microstructural Approach to Differential Recruitment," *American Sociological Review* 45 (October 1980): 787–801.

6. John G. Schmitz, "Lookout! They're Planning to Draft Your Daughter," *American Opinion* 15, no. 10 (November 1972): 1–16.

7. This and other quotations from Beverly Findley are from a series of interviews with her from 1978 to 1982.

8. Susan E. Marshall, "Ladies against Women: Mobilization Dilemmas of Antifeminist Movements," *Social Problems* 32, no. 4 (April 1985): 348–61.

9. Samuel Berger, in Chapter 10 of *Dollar Harvest: The Story of the Farm Bureau* (Lexington, Mass.: D. C. Heath, 1971), describes the long-standing affinity of the Farm Bureau with the John Birch Society.

10. This and subsequent quotations from Lottie Beth Hobbs are from a lengthy interview with her at her office in Fort Worth, 24 April 1998.

11. Barbara Brown et al., "The Equal Rights Amendment: A Constitutional Basis for Equal Rights for Women," *Yale Law Journal* 80, no. 5 (April 1971): 871–985; Paul Freund, "The Equal Rights Amendment Is Not the Way," *Harvard Civil Rights-Civil Liberties Law Review* 6, no. 2 (March 1971): 215–87.

2

PHYLLIS SCHLAFLY AND EAGLE FORUM

One of the ladies that has inspired me and made me feel like I can do anything I want to, if I want to do it bad enough, is Phyllis Schlafly. I've met her, and to me, meeting Phyllis Schlafly is like . . . [she sighed, unable to think of an adequate comparison]. . . . She had her family, she raised her kids, she got her degree, she did the bar exams, and she's a lawyer. I really like stories like that, where poor people make good. (Sandra Grogan Jeter, September 12, 1980)

This comment, by Betty Grogan's daughter, is an example of the enthusiasm, almost adoration, Phyllis Schlafly inspired among the women who were involved with her in fighting the ERA. Schlafly's accomplishments are indeed impressive. Her family, like many others, endured hard times during the Great Depression. After her engineer-father lost his job, Phyllis Stewart's mother, a librarian, struggled to supplement the family income and to provide a genteel education for her daughters. Phyllis put herself through college by working the night shift in a World War II munitions plant and attending school in the daytime. In 1944, after only three years of this grueling schedule, she graduated Phi Beta Kappa from Washington University in St. Louis.

After graduation, she earned a master's degree in political science from Radcliffe and worked briefly as a congressional aide in Washington.

She then returned to St. Louis, where the conservative newsletter she was writing for a St. Louis bank caught the attention of local attorney Fred Schlafly. They married in 1949, and by 1964 had six children.

Schlafly made unsuccessful runs for Congress in 1952 and 1970. Her 1952 campaign used the slogan later adopted by the feminists, following the example of Bella Abzug in *her* campaign for Congress: "A woman's place is in the House." It didn't work for Schlafly, but she never claimed that her defeat was due to her being a woman. Nor does she have much sympathy for those in poverty today, despite the hardships of her childhood and youth. As she repeatedly emphasized during the ERA campaign, she still believes that the best way to help women is to make sure they are supported by men.

Schlafly has been active in Republican politics all her life. She was president of her state chapter of the Federation of Republican Women, traveled all over the country speaking to local and state chapters, and was the elected first vice president, usually a stepping-stone to the presidency of the National Federation. But at the 1967 national meeting, where she expected to be elected president, her candidacy was sabotaged by Ray Bliss, the chairman of the Republican National Committee, because of her authorship of a book entitled *A Choice, Not an Echo*,[1] detailing her view that a small group of "Eastern king-makers" had conspired to deny the Republican nomination to true conservatives ever since World War II.

The book was credited with helping Barry Goldwater become the 1964 Republican presidential nominee. After Goldwater was trounced in the November election by Lyndon Johnson, traditional Republicans did not feel kindly toward those like Schlafly who had supported the Goldwater candidacy. After her defeat at the Federation of Republican Women, Schlafly's supporters met with her in the hotel basement. Some of them, angry and bitter, urged the formation of their own conservative women's group. Cooler heads, particularly Maureen Reagan's, prevailed. They decided instead to "keep in touch" with one another.[2]

What better way to keep in touch than for Schlafly to write a newsletter? After all, she had been doing it for years, first for the St. Louis bank and then for her husband's family foundation, the anticommunist Cardinal Mindszenty Foundation. So she established the Eagle Trust Fund and began writing the *Phyllis Schlafly Reports*. Every month since 1967, a four-page folder has gone to those who had supported her at that convention and to others of like mind who subscribed later. In 1972 about 3,500 names were on the list; it grew to 50,000 by the end of the ERA campaign.

RELATIONSHIP TO THE OLD RIGHT

Phyllis's husband, Fred Schlafly, had always been both a devout Catholic and an active anticommunist. For a time, he was the president of the World Anti-Communist League.[3] His wife worked with him on his anti-communist projects until the fight against the ERA began to consume her time. In 1958, the Schlafly family established the Cardinal Mindszenty Foundation in honor of the Hungarian cardinal who spent twenty-three years in prison for resisting the Communist regime.[4] Fred Schwarz of the Christian Anti-Communism Crusade claimed to have suggested the formation of the Mindszenty Foundation to the Schlafly family.[5]

Both of the Schlaflys spoke at Fred Schwarz's Anti-Communism crusades, and at John Birch Society God and Country Rallies. Because of an obscure comment by Robert Welch,[6] the founder of the John Birch Society, that Schlafly was a loyal member of his society, she was often so identified (especially in liberal publications). She always denied that she was a member, elaborating on one occasion that the John Birch Society did not agree with her position supporting a strong national defense. The society downplayed the importance of a strong national defense because its members believed the real threat to America was internal subversion by Communists.

On the other hand, there had always been some support in the Republican Party for some of the John Birch Society positions. Phyllis Schlafly, as part of the most conservative wing of the party, supported some of them as well. A notice opposing the ERA appeared in the *John Birch Society Bulletin* for February 1973. The Birch Society had also consistently opposed the United Nations and attacked the public school system, positions supported by the pro-family movement, and later by the Christian Right. Further, as chapter 4 will show, John Birch Society members helped to recruit members for the STOP-ERA organization.

Because of such similarities, Jerome Himmelstein,[7] and others, have argued that the Christian Right was simply a continuation of the old anticommunist Right, including the John Birch Society, Fred Schwarz's, Christian Anti-Communism Crusade, and Billy James Hargis's Christian Crusade in Tulso. But the John Birch Society was never accepted by the Republican establishment, something the Christian Right was able to achieve in later years with a different approach and a different grassroots constituency.

The Old Right was already on life support by the time the pro-family movement was created. Joseph McCarthy's condemnation in 1954 was the first blow to the old anticommunist Right. Then the John Birch Society lost credibility in 1960 when it was revealed that Robert Welch, its founder, had accused the popular Dwight Eisenhower of being a "conscious agent of the Communist conspiracy."[8]

One of McCarthy's staunchest allies was Billy James Hargis, the fundamentalist preacher and head of Christian Crusade in Tulsa. Hargis's organization was similar in some ways to that of Jerry Falwell twenty years later, with a church, a mailing list, a radio program, and a college. He was also one of the early opponents of the Equal Rights Amendment.[9] Hargis lost his Tulsa empire in 1974 after he was accused of sexual misconduct with students in his college. Fred Schwarz continued to hold meetings of his Christian Anti-Communism Crusade until the mid-1970s, but it became increasingly difficult for him to attract a crowd.[10]

Another important difference between the two movements was that the Christian Right, as its popular name implies, recruited most of its adherents from conservative, especially fundamentalist, churches.[11] Despite its name, the Christian Anti-Communism Crusade was led by Fred Schwarz, a physician, and appealed to businessmen more than to church members. Allen Broyles, who studied the John Birch Society in 1964, reported that he met few active church members, although Robert Welch had once claimed that 40 percent of the membership was Catholic.[12] Even STOP-ERA's early organizers from the John Birch Society were soon greatly outnumbered by the massive recruitment of fundamentalist Christians to the anti-ERA movement.

EAGLE FORUM

In early 1972, alerted by the Oklahoma example and by Patterson's phone calls, those on Schlafly's mailing list in other states began organizing to oppose the ERA. In September 1972, Schlafly convened an anti-ERA workshop in St. Louis, inviting some of her friends from the National

Federation of Republican Women. At that meeting, Dorothy "Dot" Malone Slade of North Carolina and others agreed to head the anti-ERA effort in their states. Slade called upon her friends in the John Birch Society to help,[13] just as Ann Patterson had in Oklahoma. Some, but not all, of those who had been supporters of Schlafly since 1967 were fundamentalist church members; the Fundamentalists were more likely to be recruited later by one of their own, Lottie Beth Hobbs.

Beginning in November 1972 and continuing until the final defeat of the ERA, most of the monthly *Phyllis Schlafly Reports* included an additional section on issues related to the ERA. The new sections provided information for the anti-ERA effort in the states where her supporters were active. The other sections, like those she had written ever since 1967, kept the readers abreast of the other issues Schlafly cared about. National defense and foreign policy had always been her specialty, but she covered domestic issues as well. During the anti-ERA effort, she began to report on child care and education. Realizing that the ERA would not be an issue forever, she was preparing her readers to move on to other "pro-family" issues when they no longer were preoccupied with the ERA.

The monthly *Reports* were not only packed with information, but calculated to arouse strong emotions. They were never boring. Schlafly's writing, peppered with strong adjectives, was mostly pejorative when applied to liberal officeholders or their ideas. Although one might quibble about some of her adjectives or her interpretations of events, her research was thorough and the bare facts (although never presented "bare") were generally accurate. As an example of her style, the *Phyllis Schlafly Report* for May 1973, discussing the work of the various Governor's Councils on the Status of Women, concluded:

> It is time to put a stop to the shocking way that our State Legislators are being lobbied and our citizens are being politically propagandized at the taxpayers' expense. This is a complete subversion of the democratic process and a harbinger of what is in store for us in the future by way of Federal enforcement of the Equal Rights Amendment through the enabling clause called Section 2.

The *Report* mailings also included newsletters topped by the traditional octagonal red stop-sign, the STOP-ERA logo. They contained news

about the campaign, suggestions for action, and exhortations to keep up
the fight. It is impossible to exaggerate the importance of those newsletters and the accompanying suggestions on strategy. In her March 1976
Eagle Forum letter accompanying the report, she opposed government
support for child care programs:

> State nurseries for all children, regardless of family income, is a major
> objective of the anti-family women's lib movement. This is a natural
> corollary of their rationale that it is so unfair for society to expect mothers
> to care for their babies, and mothers must be relieved of this unequal
> burden in order to achieve their full equality (by working in more ful-
> filling paid employment, such as coal mines, construction work, etc.).

The letter went on to suggest a film called *Rockabye Baby* which would
lend credence to the fundamentalists' conviction that a mother's care is the
best for babies. The same letter praised the Georgia Eagle Forum for getting good publicity for their cause and explained how they did it. In the
early years of the anti-ERA movement, it was a seemingly hopeless protest
movement, ignored or derided by mainstream media and politicians. Therefore it had to use creative and innovative techniques to get press coverage.
If any of her state organizations had a good idea, as in the Georgia example,
Schlafly was quick to tell the others about it in her STOP-ERA letters.

At the beginning, STOP-ERA was not a formal organization, but a
collection of ad hoc local and state groups. This changed in August 1975
when Schlafly invited her subscribers to join a new organization: Eagle
Forum, the "alternative to women's lib." In November 1975, Eagle
Forum held its first national meeting. STOP-ERA was its Siamese twin.
Those who did not have a formal relationship with Eagle Forum were still
part of STOP-ERA. Phyllis Schlafly was acclaimed president of both
each year[14] and was still president of Eagle Forum in 2000.

Early in 1973, Schlafly told the *New York Times*[15] that anti-ERA organizations were active in twenty-six states, but particularly strong in Arizona, Florida, Illinois, Louisiana, Missouri, Ohio, Oklahoma, and Virginia.
All of those states except Ohio indeed refused to ratify, as did two others
listed in the same article as doubtful by pro-ERA organizations. Others
which failed to ratify were Utah and Nevada, both Mormon states, and the
southern states of Georgia, Mississippi, and North and South Carolina.

Eagle Forum's membership grew to about 50,000 by the end of the rat-ification period for the ERA.[16] Although the leading feminist organization, the National Organization for Women, claimed 220,000 members at the same time, the real test of an organization's strength is what it can do, not the number of names on its list. Schlafly's members could be counted on to do the things she suggested, whether to come to the capital to lobby, to send contributions for a lawsuit, to demand that the public library stock her books, or to write a letter to a radio station protesting its coverage of a news event. Not all the suggested projects were directly related to the ERA.

In August 1977, the Eagle Forum letter introduced a "library project." "Do your local libraries engage in book burning? Do they blacklist books they disagree with? Have your local libraries allowed the women's lib-bers to deny equal rights to pro-family books and ideas?" Readers were urged to check the card catalogues of their local libraries for "women's lib books" and "anti-lib, pro-family books." For guidance, the letter sup-plied lists of both types of books. Finally, readers were told to take the results of the survey to the librarian, mention how many of each type of book were in the library, and request that Schlafly's book, *The Power of the Positive Woman*, and other similar books be purchased. When I checked with libraries in my area a few weeks later, they reported that they had indeed received such calls.

Phyllis Schlafly took scattered ad hoc organizations, folded them into a national one, coordinated their activities, facilitated communication among them, made sure that the members were provided with new sugges-tions, trained them in lobbying and speaking, and encouraged them to per-severe in their quest to defeat the ERA. Even the Pros I talked to admitted to grudging admiration of her skill, although they disagreed with her.

Phyllis Schlafly was the "lady" admired by traditional women—always neat, well-groomed, and with a perfect figure. Her clothes were pastels, and she never wore pants. She sat perfectly straight in her chair, never crossing her legs. She boasted that she breast-fed all six of her chil-dren, taught them all to read at home, and that she could still wear her wedding dress. But her skill and tenacity won her a place in the world of male-dominated politics.

The same perfection her followers admired so much enraged her opponents. Unfortunately, they often showed it in appearances before col-lege audiences, press conferences, or televised debates, and invariably they came off looking second-best. She always knew what she was talking about, and she never appeared ruffled, no matter how rude her opponents were. Henry Schipper, who interviewed her in 1981, asked her about the event he had witnessed the night before, when Schlafly appeared before a "disruptive jeering college audience." Schlafly explained that she often had such experiences, but that "Nothing gets me upset. That's what infuriates them."[17]

SCHLAFLY'S LEADERSHIP STYLE

The worshipful attitude of Sandra Grogan Jeter and the other Antis toward Phyllis Schlafly suggests that her leadership style was what Max Weber called "charismatic" rather than bureaucratic. Weber was a German sociologist of the late nineteenth and early twentieth centuries who studied the nature of leadership and authority. He noted that bureaucracy was so superior "in precision, in stability, in the stringency of its discipline, and its reliability" that it would eventually become the dominant organizational form[18] because it sets up formal rules for procedure.

Just as Weber expected, bureaucracy is so pervasive today that almost any group organized for any purpose, even if only for recreation or fellowship, tends to draw up bylaws and conduct formal elections. The pro-ERA and feminist organizations such as the National Organization for Women, the National Women's Political Caucus, and ERAmerica were all replete with bureaucratic structures and procedures.

Eagle Forum, which thwarted all of those organizations in their attempts to secure ratification of ERA, had only enough bureaucracy to qualify as a nonprofit organization and fulfill tax-reporting requirements. Schlafly was elected by acclamation year after year, and the other officers were chosen by her. Although the grassroots activists of the Antis were less experienced than the Pro activists, the atmosphere in their offices was more harmonious and the work more effectively organized. Schlafly was able to maintain stability, reliability, and discipline with her leadership style.

Weber thought that charismatic authority was inherently unstable, and that its weakness would be apparent when the charismatic leader was no longer on the scene. That prediction has not yet been tested in Schlafly's case, but she has moved to put the organization on a firm footing. After her husband died in 1995, she moved out of the Schlafly home where Eagle Forum had been headquartered for twenty years. Although she was then seventy-one years old, she continued to speak around the country, to be active in the Republican Party, and to write the *Reports*.

DEVELOPMENT AND TRAINING LEADERS

> There were workshops from Friday afternoon to Sunday afternoon, and we had speakers.... Phyllis really makes you work.... Even at the meals there were speeches and workshops.... She had pastors come and hold services in the hotel on Sunday morning, so you couldn't get away from her. (Anna Mayer, rural woman, June 2, 1997)

This is how one of the participants described the weekend training conferences Phyllis Schlafly held each year in a St. Louis hotel. Her purpose was to sharpen the political skills of her associates in the states. Conferees gave short presentations in front of TV cameras, then other participants analyzed them. Not only did this training reduce the likelihood that the organization would be embarrassed by the behavior of its adherents, but it increased the self-confidence of the women themselves. If they learned how to do something, then did it, and found that it worked, they would be even more firmly committed to the organization that had thus enhanced their sense of self-worth.

Participants also had the opportunity to win awards and recognition, after having been nominated by others from their home state. Each invitation to the conference included a form on which to list three nominations. Only those who had done important work for the movement were invited to the annual St. Louis conference, and only those who had done outstanding work were honored with the Eagle Award each year. In order to spread the honors around the rule was that no one could win the award more than once.

COORDINATION

Ann Patterson respected Phyllis Schlafly for her knowledge, her research, her determination, and her organizational skill. They spoke frequently on the telephone, and Schlafly came to the state many times during the ten years of the ERA campaign. She came for special events, such as a speech at a university campus or a radio debate with a feminist speaker. She came to speak at a conference in Tulsa organized by Cleon Skousen, an Old Right author and organizer from Utah, and while there, attended some teas and receptions for Eagle Forum members.

Communities all over the nation had Eagle Forum chapters, each with leaders who had been personally approved by Phyllis Schlafly. The cooperating state organizations had various names. In Oklahoma, it was Ann Patterson's Women for Responsible Legislation. In North Carolina, it was NCAERA (North Carolina Against the ERA). Mississippi's Antis called themselves the Committee for Retention and Protection of Women's Rights. In other states it was called simply STOP-ERA. Each leader in a community or in a state, and for that matter, individual members, could call Schlafly to ask for advice or information. She was "the clearinghouse for information" as Ann Patterson put it. She always knew what was going on everywhere.

In November 1975, before local Eagle Forum chapters had been organized, Schlafly published a simple application form in the Eagle Forum newsletter accompanying the *Phyllis Schlafly Report*. The brief form invited applicants for chapter presidencies; it asked for the person's name, address, experience in politics, area to which she wished to be appointed (city or state), and, most important, the names of two persons known either to a state or national officer who could serve as a reference. Schlafly depended on people she already knew in each state and trusted them to evaluate these prospective leaders.

If the application was approved, the individual would be "appointed" president in the area, although there was a disclaimer warning that the appointment did not necessarily insure exclusive jurisdiction. Despite the invitation to her subscribers to apply for appointment as state presidents, I was told by Eagle Forum members from both Utah and Washington State in 1979 that Schlafly was then discouraging the formation of statewide organizations. Some states had them, to be sure, but Schlafly did not recommend it. The women from Utah said that they understood that she was afraid of the development of "prima donnas."[19] From these comments, and from other incidents involving Schlafly's interaction with the "girls" in the states, it is apparent that she preferred her associates not to be too independent. Schlafly was in the classic dilemma of the perfectionist—no one else could possibly do the job as well as she could, and she knew it. On the other hand, even she, disciplined and hard-working though she was, could not possibly do everything that needed to be done everywhere.

The pattern that has been described in the formation and early development of the movement in Oklahoma was repeated in other states as well. Initially recruited by experienced political women, and in many cases, by members of the John Birch Society, the rank and file of the anti-ERA movement was drawn from fundamentalist church members who saw the ERA as a threat to their deeply held convictions about Bible-based family life.

Schlafly could not have manufactured the tenacity and enthusiasm of those church members, and she had significant help from Lottie Beth Hobbs, herself a fundamentalist leader. But Schlafly welcomed, encouraged, and mentored the fundamentalists, hoping to channel their energy into other conservative causes when the ERA campaign was finally over. Although the anti-ERA movement was a countermovement, having come into being specifically to oppose the ERA, it became a movement in its own right by adopting other issues even before the ERA was defeated.

The Eagle Forum Trust Fund, controlled by Schlafly, was available when money was needed for lawsuits, for postage and printing costs, and for radio advertising during the last months of the ERA ratification struggle. Schlafly was also able to attract contributions from wealthy individuals whom she did not identify publicly, and the various state organizations had their "angels," but the true riches of Eagle Forum were in the voluntary efforts of its members, as well as of Schlafly herself. She coordinated their activities and developed the ideology sustaining their commitment.

AMENDMENT STRATEGY

The anti-ERA movement which later evolved into the pro-family movement came into being to counter the ERA, a centerpiece of the feminist agenda. As a countermovement, STOP-ERA's strategies were determined to some extent by those of the feminists.[20] At the same time, both the feminists and the antifeminists were subject to the Constitutionally prescribed procedures for amending it.

Adding an amendment to the U.S. Constitution is never easy, nor was it meant to be. The first step is for a proposed amendment to be passed by two-thirds of both the Senate and the House of Representatives or to be the subject of petitions in two-thirds of the states. Of over three thousand amendments introduced in Congress since the Constitution went into effect, only thirty-three have passed this first hurdle; none has been proposed by petitions.

The next step is approval by legislatures or conventions in three-fourths of the states. Six amendments, including the Equal Rights Amendment, have failed to achieve ratification after having been submitted by Congress. If the provisions of an amendment had already been approved in some other form by a good number of states, or if there was general approval of the amendment, ratification could be achieved quickly. If not, historical experience suggests it was likely to fail. All but three of the existing amendments were ratified within three years, and most were ratified in less than two years.[21]

Their failure to campaign first for state legislation or amendments similar to the national amendment turned out to be a fatal mistake on the part of the Pros. By contrast, the woman suffrage advocates of sixty years earlier had already won woman suffrage in several states before the national amendment was proposed, and they were ultimately successful, despite an active opposition movement.

The arithmetic of the three-fourths rule for ratifications gives a built-in advantage to the opponents of any amendment. They need to win in only one-fourth of the states. With fifty states in the Union, they need only to prevent ratification in thirteen states. In addition, opponents of almost any political proposal generally find it easier to raise doubts about the disadvantages of the proposal than for the proponents to explain its advantages. Phyllis Schlafly's strategy was to lay down a barrage of predictions of dreadful things that might come to pass if the ERA were adopted. Although the Pros scoffed at most of these predictions as highly unlikely, the doubt they created eroded support for the amendment.

The history of constitutional amendments shows that an amendment not passed quickly is not likely to pass at all. In spring 1972, an early ratification seemed likely, as the fast pace of ratifications reflected ERA's noncontroversial character at the beginning. But STOP-ERA's counterattack began only a few days after submission of the amendment. Within a year, the amendment had become controversial, and ratifications had begun to slow. Within two years, the ratifications had almost stopped, and several states tried to rescind.

A vote of the people could not determine ratification directly, but the legislature might be influenced by the outcome of a vote on the question. Legislatures also had discretion to require hearings first and to require a majority, a two-thirds, or a three-fourths vote of the legislature to ratify.

Most states required a simple majority, but Illinois's new constitution called for a three-fourths majority. Despite protests of the Pros, this provision kept Illinois from ratifying. Illinois was also a state that Phyllis Schlafly wanted to win, because her home in Alton, a suburb of St. Louis, was in Illinois. (Neither Illinois nor Missouri ratified the ERA.) Carol Felsenthal, in her biography of Schlafly, describes several Pro events in Illinois that were effectively overshadowed by Schlafly's clever tactics.

On one occasion, she arranged for a man in a gorilla suit to interrupt a speech by the national president of the League of Women Voters announcing a modest grant of funds to the Illinois anti-ERA campaign. After the gorilla suit had attracted the television cameras, Schlafly embarrassed the Pros by revealing that they had received even more from *Playboy* magazine, information that would not play well in Peoria, or most other Illinois towns.[22]

Although the Antis had some tactical and psychological advantage in the structure of the ratification process, they shared its downside with the Pros: they had to be ready to act and/or react to the opposition in any state at any time. Some states that had ratified early also began considering state ERAs, and the STOP-ERA movement wanted to prevent that as well. Even that was easier for the Antis, because of their dedicated grassroots supporters on call, than for the Pros, who thought it necessary to deploy workers to the states from the national organizations.

The final score at the end of the ratification period was thirty-five states for ratification, fifteen states against, and five states which had attempted to rescind. Even if the rescission resolutions were illegal, as some legal experts argued, there were still too few ratifications for final approval. Eagle Forum was not always able, however, to prevent states from adding provisions similar to the Equal Rights Amendment in their own state constitutions. Nine state ERAs were passed during the time of the conflict over a national ERA. It is particularly ironic that three of the states with state ERAs—Schlafly's home state of Illinois, as well as Virginia and Utah—did not ratify the national ERA. Schlafly's *Reports* did not dwell on those state ERAs, but instead on the six states that had turned down state ERAs in a referendum vote.

Both Pros and Antis gave Phyllis Schlafly most of the credit—or

Phyllis Schlafly leads the fight against ERA at the state capitol in her home state of Illinois. (*Bettman/Corbis*)

blame, depending on their point of view—for defeating the ERA. The women who had received her *Reports* after the 1967 National Republican Women's convention, most of whom were experienced political activists, took the leadership in the states in the beginning. They in turn, were able to recruit from other networks within each state.

But even the superbly organized campaign, with its skillful use of legal and social arguments, might not have succeeded without the large numbers of dedicated women from the conservative churches. As a Catholic, in a time when there was still a lot of mutual suspicion between Catholics and fundamentalists, Schlafly would not have been able to recruit them. It was Lottie Beth Hobbs of Fort Worth and her supporters in other states who brought them into the anti-ERA movement.

NOTES

1. Phyllis Schlafly, *A Choice Not an Echo* (Alton, Ill.: Pere Marquette, 1964).

2. This story was first told to me by Ann Patterson, who was at the meeting. It is also described in the *New York Times* (7 May 1967), 33.

3. Judy Klemesrud, "Opponent of ERA Confident of Its Defeat," *New York Times*, 15 December1975, A44.

4. "Mrs. Schlafly Fights against Communism," *St. Louis Globe Democrat*, 28 December 1963.

5. *Group Research Report,* Washington D.C. (13 April 1964); Sanford Ungar, "Reports and Comment: The Christian Anti-Communism Crusade," *Atlantic* 233, no. 6 (June 1974): 4–11.

6. Robert Welch, *John Birch Society Bulletin,* February 1960.

7. Jerome L. Himmelstein, *To the Right: The Transformation of American Conservatism* (Berkeley: University of California Press, 1990), chap. 2.

8. J. Allen Broyles, *The John Birch Society: The Anatomy of a Protest* (Boston: Beacon, 1964).

9. A fund-raising letter from Hargis reported by *Group Research* 11, no. 9, 31 May 1972.

10 Erling Jorstad, *The Politics of Doomsday: Fundamentalists of the Far Right* (Nashville: Abingdon, 1970); Ungar, *Report and Comment.*

11. Clyde Wilcox, "America's Radical Right Revisited: A Comparison of the Activists in Christian Right Organizations from the 1960s and the 1980s," *Sociological Analysis* 48, no. 1 (1987): 46–57; Broyles, *John Birch Society.*

12. Broyles, *John Birch Society*, chap. 7.

13. Donald G. Mathews and Jane Sherron DeHart, *Sex, Gender, and the Politics of ERA* (New York: Oxford University Press, 1990), pp. 59–60.

14. Eagle Forum newsletter, included with *Phyllis Schlafly Report*, January 1976.

15. Eileen Shanahan, "Equal Rights Amendment Is Approved by Congress," *New York Times*, 23 March 1972, A1.

16. Eagle Forum newsletter, mailed with *Phyllis Schlafly Report*, December 1980.

17. Henry Schipper, "An Interview with Phyllis Schlafly," *MS* (January 1982): 89; Carol Felsenthal, in her book *Sweetheart of the Silent Majority* (New York: Doubleday, 1981), refers to a number of other incidents, on pages 301–303. I heard Schlafly speak in public several times, but always before supportive audiences. The caustic comments about Schlafly that I heard were in my interviews with feminists.

18. Max Weber, *The Theory of Social and Economic Organization*, trans. A. M. Henderson and Talcott Parsons (New York: Oxford University Press, 1947), p. 337.

19. These interviews were at the Western States Rally in Boise, Idaho, March 23–24, 1979.

20. For a discussion of countermovements, see Clarence Lo, "Countermovements and Conservative Movements in the Contemporary U.S," *Annual Reviews of Sociology* 8 (1982): 107–34.

21. The outstanding contrary example was the latest amendment ratified, in 1992, dealing with congressional pay limits, but first submitted in 1789.

22. Carol Felsenthal, *The Sweetheart of the Silent Majority* (Garden City, N.Y.: Doubleday, 1981), p. 243.

3

WOMEN WHO WANT TO BE WOMEN

Women Who Want to be Women
Have made this bread for you
Because they love being homemakers
All the year through.
It's an honor to be a homemaker,
And this right we want to remain,
But the ERA would take away our choice
And have laws read: Men, Women, Same.
We cannot be the same as men,
We're just not created that way.
We have a place in life to fullfil [*sic*]
And are content to leave it that way.
So enjoy your bread,
Appreciate it too,
Cause unless the ERA is stopped,
The Homemaker May Be YOU!

Beverly Findley, the Oklahoma head of Women Who Want to be Women, wrote this little rhyme to be enclosed on cards with the homemade bread the women brought to legislators each year at the beginning of the legislative session. Bread Day, begun in 1975, became a feature of the opening week of every legislative session throughout the campaign. Bread Day was just one of the many unusual tactics used by the

Members of anti-ERA organizations brought homemade bread for the legislators every year near the beginning of the legislative session, as a symbol of their preferred role for women as homemakers. (*Daily Oklahoman*)

Antis in the ERA campaign. Homemade bread was an especially appropriate symbol for a group supporting the traditional role of women.

It is not clear which state's women first thought of this tactic, but it spread through Phyllis Schlafly's communication channels to all the states with active chapters. On Bread Day, each legislator was visited by a delegation of STOP-ERA members bearing a small loaf of homemade bread. Not all of the women baked bread, but those who did brought extra loaves so that there was always enough to go around.

Women Who Want to be Women was the sister organization to Phyllis Schlafly's Eagle Forum and the vehicle for Church of Christ women who opposed the ERA. The greatest strength of the Churches of Christ is in the middle South states of Oklahoma, Arkansas, and Tennessee, but Women Who Want to be Women also had strong leaders in Florida and Texas. Its women were the most enthusiastic members of the Oklahoma STOP-ERA movement. The founders of WWWW, or the Four Ws as it was soon abbreviated, were Lottie Beth Hobbs and Becky Tilotta of Fort Worth, Texas.

LOTTIE BETH HOBBS

Lottie Beth Hobbs was born in Abilene, Texas, in 1921, one of ten children. Her father worked a ranch and three farms, and her mother came from a family of teachers. Both parents were determined to send their children to college. Despite financial hardships, most of the children did graduate. Lottie Beth graduated from Abilene Christian College in 1943. She worked in defense plants during World War II, as did Phyllis Schlafly. After the war, she taught ladies' Bible classes, and then began writing books to use in the classes. A single woman, she supported herself by writing and distributing books. She was in demand as a speaker for ladies' Bible classes and conferences all over the South.

Hobbs told me that she first heard about the ERA in 1973, or possibly 1974, when she saw a leaflet about it while speaking at one of those meetings of women. As soon as she read it, she knew that something had to be done and mentioned it to the others. After the meeting, they came up to her and said, "Well, what are you going to do about it?" so she went to the library and got some feminist books. She was appalled.

> They were all so awful that I put them under the bed so my nieces and nephews wouldn't see them! But as I was digging more and more into it and found out the basis of it, I knew it was much bigger than just ERA. ERA was just one of the arms of the whole thing.
>
> Becky Tilotta helped me at first, but she married in 1975 and moved away, and left it in my lap. . . . I didn't want my name on the organization, and neither did she, so we came up with the name Women Who Want to be Women. . . . From what we could understand, the feminists weren't proud to be women. They put down women and wanted to be equal with men. We wanted to emphasize that we had a different philosophy, that we were proud of being women. (April 24, 1998)

In 1975 the Four Ws began cooperating with Schlafly's Eagle Forum. From 1975 to 1988, Hobbs put her career as a Bible study leader and author on hold and devoted most of her time to the Four Ws (renamed Pro-Family Forum after 1977) and to the anti-ERA campaign. As a Texas organization, one of its projects was the attempt in 1975 and again in 1977 to persuade the Texas legislature to rescind its ratification of the ERA. At their rally at the capitol in Austin to lobby for rescission, they wore pink, which led to the Antis being called "the ladies in pink."[1] But the Texas legislators, having ratified hastily in 1972 on the day after Oklahoma's failure to do so, were unwilling to reopen an issue that had become so contentious in the years since.

Hobbs also organized the large Pro-Family Rally in 1977 at the Houston Astrodome to show the strength of the antifeminists in the same city where the feminists had organized a national women's conference. (More about the counterrally in chapter 5.) After the rally, she continued to speak in other states about the ERA. Phyllis Schlafly asked her to be on the board of Eagle Forum, and she was also invited to join the Council for National Policy (CNP), a national coordinating committee organized by Paul Weyrich and his colleagues in what they were calling the New Right.

> We had a meeting in Washington to try to determine how we could all coalesce and how we could work together, and I found out later . . . that inevitably it falls apart, because the areas of disagreement seep in and I have found out you do a whole lot better just to let each organization do it how they want to do, using the methods you see best to do. To [try to] agree on everything, we're wasting our time and energy. (Lottie Beth Hobbs, April 24, 1998)[2]

She resigned from the CNP because she felt it was not a good use of her time. Time was especially important for her, for she had to support herself. She had given up writing books, her source of income, although she continued to sell copies of the books she had already written. The original ERA submission to the states provided for a seven-year ratification period, ending in 1979. When the ratification was extended to July 1982, Hobbs and the other Antis felt obligated to continue.

For Schlafly, fighting the ERA was an opportunity to recruit a new group of activists into conservative politics. When the ERA was defeated, she continued her commitment to conservative politics by joining other crusades on other issues. For Hobbs, on the other hand, fighting the ERA was another way of following her calling to teach women how to live in accordance with biblical principles. The two women's interests intersected at the point of antifeminism, although each had come to it by a different route. The emphasis on government as a danger to the moral order melded Schafly's conservative view of government's role with Hobbs's religious understanding of family life.

After the ERA was defeated, Hobbs disbanded Pro-Family Forum. Many of those who had joined it also returned to their own families and churches, although some remained active and took leadership positions in other local groups in later years. (At that time, almost half were over fifty years of age; one-third were over sixty-five.) Hobbs continued her issue-advocacy on a smaller scale by publishing a monthly newsletter titled the *Family Educator*, to reflect the new emphasis on educational issues. She finally stopped publishing it in 1994, when she returned to her career of writing books and speaking to church women's groups. By that time, other organizations had sprung up to continue the fight against moral decline.

CHILD CARE FLYER

While the pink sheet was being distributed, another flyer—this one of unknown origin—began to appear in churches and at workplaces. It also was distributed through informal networks. The purpose of the flyer was to mobilize opposition to a comprehensive child care bill being discussed in Congress. It purported to quote from the *Congressional Record*, but gave no citations. A search of the *Record* turned up some passages from which the quotations might have been derived, but the quotations were wildly inaccurate. One of the most appalling passages, another misquotation, implied that the child care bill would deny parents the right to require their children to take out the garbage.

A retired director of the Kansas Bible Camp in Hutchinson, Kansas, Richard Burson was apparently the source of most of the flyers in Oklahoma, although some were said to have come from Michigan. Burson said that "he had put out a thousand of the flyers" based on a three-page pamphlet he received from his brother-in-law's sister, who had picked it up at a revival in Missouri. He stopped distributing it about a week later, after he found that the material was misleading.[3] The reporter who discovered Burson's role tried to find the original source but never could. I was no more successful, despite contacting several persons active on the national level at that time.[4]

There were two reactions among those who saw the flyer. Some saw it as improbable and so outrageous that they quickly dismissed it. But others, for whom it seemed to confirm their own suspicions about the federal government's tendency to interfere in citizens' lives, had no doubt about it and were determined to fight the bill as vigorously as possible. The material resonated with Christian conservative beliefs about mothers' duty to take care of their own children, and with political conservatives' distrust in government. A union official from a nearby air force base saw no reason to doubt it.

> I don't trust the government at all. Democracy is eatin' us alive. I don't know whether we can save it. It's kind of scary when I think of governmental controls. This bill would just bring more state control. (John Clabes, AFCME—American Federation of State, County, and Municipal Employees—union official)

The newly organized Women Who Want to be Women in Oklahoma took on opposition to the child care bill as their first big project. It was literally true that in October and November 1975, everyone in the Oklahoma City area was talking about the bill. Members of STOP-ERA and Women Who Want to be Women urged the Oklahoma City PTA Council to oppose the bill. To their credit, the PTA Council members did not content themselves with reading the flyer. They secured copies of the original bill and discussed and debated its provisions thoroughly before finally deciding to oppose it.

Although the flyer itself was discredited, whoever wrote it had succeeded in catching the attention of a great many people who didn't ordinarily follow bills in Congress carefully, if at all. And that scrutiny led to its defeat in committee. Members of Congress from every state in the Union were inundated with mail about the bill, most of it negative.[5] The torrent of mail reaching Washington, D.C., about the child care bill gave the members of Congress a sample of the kind of grassroots passion that Oklahoma legislators already knew about from the struggle over ratification of the ERA. It also alerted Washington conservatives Paul Weyrich and Connie Marshner of the Committee for the Survival of a Free Congress to the political potential of the Christian conservatives.[6]

WHO WERE THE ANTIS?

Only a few state-level studies of the Antis are available. They show that the Churches of Christ and the Mormons, both with relatively small numbers in the southern states, contributed a disproportionate share of the anti-ERA campaigners in Oklahoma, Texas, and North Carolina, although Baptists were the majority in North Carolina. In all of those states, there were some Methodists among the Antis, but they were underrepresented in terms of their membership in the state population, except in Texas.[7]

TABLE 3.1
Percent of Members in States' Populations and among Anti-ERA Activists

	Texas		North Carolina		Oklahoma	
	State	Anti[8]	State	Anti[9]	State	Anti
Church of Christ	2.5	59.7	.2	45.1	5.2	43.0
Baptist	20.0	9.2	23.2	36.4	27.2	17.0
Mormon	.5	1.3	.4	n.a.	.5	9.0
Methodist	6.6	9.2	10.1	9.1	10.4	5.0

The situation was different outside the South, where there was more support for the ERA and the Antis were less likely to prevent ratification. In general, the Churches of Christ and the Baptists furnished the most anti-ERA activists in the southern states, Mormons in the West, and Catholics in the Northeast, along with a small number of Orthodox Jews.

Almost all of the Antis I interviewed attended church functions—usually women's Bible study classes—during the week, and most of them attended worship services twice on Sunday. Interviews could not be scheduled on the days when Bible study class was meeting. Further, prayer and "a personal relationship with the Lord" was a natural and necessary part of their lives. "I never miss Bible study if I can possibly help it. I just have to have that refreshment, and nothing else provides it like the word of the Lord," said one woman.

The opposition of Church of Christ women to the ERA was a product of their fundamentalist belief that the Bible is the Word of God, and that the ERA is "against God's plan." It was not only economically or politically undesirable, as Phyllis Schlafly argued; it was much worse, an attack on the principles that had guided their lives and a violation of deeply held religious beliefs. This was generally typical of participants in the pro-family movement during the 1970s and 1980s.

In response to a questionnaire I distributed to both Antis and Pros at the end of 1982, 56 percent of the Antis chose as their first reason for opposing the ERA, that it "was against God's plan." The choices in this questionnaire were those mentioned by activists in a smaller sample in previous interviews. Of those reporting that they gave the ERA campaign the highest priority in the last few months before the deadline, all chose "against God's plan." Closely tied for second were that "it would encourage an unbiblical relationship between men and women," and that it would "weaken families." It was precisely because of their belief that the ERA was "unbiblical" and would result in the destruction of "God's plan for the family" as set forth in the Bible that fundamentalists opposed it so vigorously.

Far down the list were the legal reasons that Phyllis Schlafly emphasized, such as the ERA's effect on Social Security (eighth), the increased power of the federal government that the ERA's enforcement would require (fourth), or even the possibility of drafting women (sixth). Given the salience of the religious reasons for the Antis opposition to ERA, it was not surprising that an overwhelming 96 percent of them said that religion was "very important in their lives." This compared with 53 percent of the Pros who give the same response.

FUNDAMENTALISM

> I'll be frank, I don't think that you can be knowledgeable of the ERA, and be a student of the Bible, and be for the ERA. I think it's very possible for Christians to be for the ERA, but I think they're very weak in their faith, and they're not very knowledgeable in the totality of the ERA. (young Oklahoma City businessman, 1980)

A nonfundamentalist reading the statement above might consider this devout church member arrogant. In the context of the entire interview, he did not seem arrogant, but like other fundamentalists, he was very sure of his beliefs. Three core beliefs of fundamentalism lead its believers to this assurance. The first, and the foundation of the others, is that everything the Bible says is true—"inerrant," to use their word. They are convinced of the second and third from their reading of the Bible and from the interpretations they hear from the pulpit every Sunday. The second is their belief that the end of this world could come at any time and that only those who have been saved will survive. The third is that it is the duty of a Christian to *save* as many others as possible before that time. "Saved" means to have a personal relationship with Christ, to accept the truth of the Bible, and to live one's life in accordance with biblical prescriptions about behavior. Convinced that the ERA is against God's plan, fundamentalists believe that to support the ERA is to jeopardize one's hope of eternal life.

To be sure, there is no verse in the Bible that says the ERA is wrong. That belief is based on a series of assumptions about what the ERA would require and a series of Bible passages about the proper roles for women, homosexuality, and abortion. If the ERA would require women to contribute equally to the family income, it is against God's plan as set forth by Paul when he writes to the Ephesians (Eph. 5:22–24) that women should submit to their husbands.[10] If the ERA would require equal acceptance of homosexuality and heterosexuality, it violates the biblical assertion in Lev. 18:11 (and in other passages) that homosexuality is "abomination."[11] If the ERA would require abortion on demand, that also violates God's plan, although the biblical support is less direct. It rests on Jer. 1:5,[12] and other verses in which God recognizes an unborn fetus as part of his creation.

ERA proponents, however, disagreed both with what Phyllis Schlafly claimed the ERA would require, and with what the Bible's message about women actually is. ERA supporters, who were likely to be members of non-fundamentalist churches or no church at all, could point to other passages in the Bible and other interpretations that would lead to other conclusions. In the Oklahoma hearings on ERA, a Catholic nun who was also a university professor presented her belief that Jesus' words in the Bible actually support the principles of the ERA. Nevertheless, the teaching in fundamentalist churches is remarkably consistent on these issues, and Phyllis Schlafly was remarkably adept at using arguments that resonated with it.

Schlafly's book *The Power of the Positive Woman*[13] was first published in 1977, but reissued in 1981 with only minor changes as *The Power of the*

Christian Woman.[14] It was a perfect example of what social movement theorists call "frame alignment," a not-so-subtle shift in the context of the anti-ERA argument so as to make it more appealing to fundamentalists. The first book was an appeal to secular women; the second, to religious women. The new first chapter in the second book is filled with biblical references to buttress Schlafly's argument against the ERA, and each of the succeeding chapters is headed by a biblical reference. The first version contains only a few Bible references. The only other changes in the text of the second book are the substitutions of "Christian Woman" for "Positive Woman" throughout.

Fundamentalists in the South are especially likely to be found in the Churches of Christ and Baptist churches. But not all Baptists are fundamentalists, and there are fundamentalists in other denominations as well, or in nondenominational churches. Even the Methodist church, generally considered one of the liberal churches, has a significant fundamentalist membership in the South.

Researchers have tried in vain to determine the exact number of fundamentalists, evangelicals, and other faith groups in the American population, but they have been unable to do so because of the different ways those terms can be defined. Several indicators have been tried as a way of identifying fundamentalists, but there is no consensus on the best one. The various ways of defining fundamentalism do, however, produce similar results—no more than one-third of the population is fundamentalist. The strictest definition produces an even smaller percentage.

Sometimes church membership is used to define fundamentalism, but it is an inexact method because so many denominational groups include members with a variety of beliefs. Even within the churches called liberal, or mainline—Presbyterian, Episcopal, Methodist, and Disciples of Christ—there are still conflicts about biblical interpretation. Each of these churches has a dissident minority pressuring official church bodies to return to the orthodox interpretation of the Bible as literally true and applicable in its entirety to the modern world.

Fundamentalists have no doubt about the truth of the creation story in Genesis, the virgin birth of Jesus, his miracles, and his death and resurrection. If they begin to question the literal truth of the Bible, they are no longer fundamentalist. One expert on fundamentalism has suggested that a good test of fundamentalism would be a belief in "a historical, six-day creation."[15] While that test has not been used to measure fundamentalist adherents, the General Social Survey, a standard public opionion resource, found slightly under one-third of the population believing that the Bible is the actual word of God and is to be taken literally.[16]

The percentage of respondents who will choose fundamentalist when asked to identify their own Protestant faith tradition hovers around one-third if the other choices are moderate and liberal.[17] To consider another possible dimension of Christian conservatism, "born-agains," those who can point to the time that they were "saved" or accepted Jesus Christ as their Savior, range from one-quarter to one-third of white respondents,[18] depending on the way the surveys are conducted. Gallup found in 1989 that about 31 percent of the population reported having had a "born-again" experience.[19]

The publishing houses of conservative churches turn out books supporting the fundamentalist interpretation of the Bible, preachers preach it every Sunday, and weekly Bible study groups in the churches analyze it. The pastors of their churches, like Jeremiah in the Old Testament, prophesy the wrath of God's judgment against the people "for all their wickedness in forsaking me" (Jer. 1:16). The belief that God would punish America for her sins, preached in so many churches, primed fundamentalists to join a movement promising to "turn it around."

But fundamentalist teaching also includes some obstacles to taking up a political cause. God's plan, as they interpret it, means that women should limit themselves to the roles of wife and mother.[20] The Churches of Christ do not even allow women to lead mixed-sex Sunday School classes, a policy based upon the writings of St. Paul.[21] Lottie Beth Hobbs's career was in teaching Bible classes of women only. Some of those active in the pro-family movement encountered opposition to their political involvement from their pastors, fellow church members, and their husbands. Although some may have been deterred, those who persisted argued that the stakes for the future of the family were sufficiently high to justify at least a short-term commitment to the pro-family movement.

> My husband wants me to quit this. He says, "when am I going to see your happy face again?" and when I showed him how important it is, he said, "well for a little while more, but when it is all over, I want to see you happy again." (Bunny Chambers, December 1981)

Another obstacle to fundamentalist involvement was the long-standing tradition in the conservative churches of avoiding direct involvement in politics. In years of attending their services, I never heard a pastor "overstep the bounds" by recommending a candidate or a political issue from the pulpit, and respondents, both pastors and laypersons, said they disapproved of it. Only once did one of my respondents report such an event, and he strongly opposed it. That does not mean it never happened, but it was rare and frowned upon. Fundamentalists' withdrawal from the political arena dated back to the time of the Scopes trial in 1925, and H. L. Mencken's unflattering portrayal of them at that time.

On the other hand, their inexperience meant that for many, political activism was a new and exciting role, and the depth of their beliefs about the dangers of ERA added to their commitment. One of the most impressive findings from my campaign questionnaire, which was sent to both Antis and Pros, was that 73 percent of the opponents reported giving the ERA campaign a high or highest priority, but only 29 percent of the proponents gave it a similarly high priority. The opponents reported spending an average of about one full day during the ERA campaign, while proponents spent only several hours, on average, during the same period.

Although the Antis were novices, they were neither stupid nor incompetent. Many of them had talents they had not been aware of, and they welcomed the opportunity to exercise them. Their inexperience also meant that they were not easily discouraged. Experienced political activists know how difficult it is to change the direction of government policy, but these new activists did not. Besides, they were convinced that God was on their side. As Beverly Findley said to me, "They're [the Pros] not just fighting us, they're fighting God!" The Antis turned out in large numbers to lobby at the capitol, to attend rallies, to sign petitions, and to write letters and make telephone calls to Congress. All of these consequences of inexperience, both positive and negative, were in evidence in the course of the anti-ERA campaign.

Because fundamentalists had largely refrained from political activity of any kind for many years, the phenomenon of their activity against the ERA was one of the first indications of what has since been recognized as a significant relationship between religiosity and conservatism in American politics. It had been recognized before the ERA campaign that regular church attendance was correlated with high civic participation of all kinds, including voting, but the additional correlation with conservatism was not so well known. It was confirmed by a study of political contributors to the candidates running for president in 1988. The study's authors found that "Within almost all groups, religious commitment increases turnout, intensifies Republican identification, bolsters the GOP share of the vote, and enhances social issue conservatism."[22]

THE CHURCHES OF CHRIST

The Churches of Christ furnished 43 percent of the anti-ERA activists in Oklahoma, 45.1 percent in North Carolina, and 59.7 percent in Texas. The influence of Lottie Beth Hobbs's leadership was largely responsible for the members' activism. In each state, members of those churches were greatly overrepresented among the Antis. Those who were members of the Churches of Christ were the most active in the anti-ERA campaign, more likely to have strong opinions on the pro-family issues, but also more likely to have fewer years of education and to have been recruited through their churches.

The Churches of Christ adhere strictly to the biblical model of church polity, with autonomous congregations and no church hierarchy. While such determined independence might seem to make it difficult for such churches to coordinate their political efforts, there are channels of communication, even in the Churches of Christ. The channels are horizontal rather than vertical. There is no central office sending communications to each church, but there is church-to-church communication. Each local church has a list of the other churches, which can be used by an individual member or a pastor to notify others of an event or a cause. This is what Beverly Findley did to organize the Four Ws in Oklahoma.

Despite the absence of formal hierarchies, there appeared to be more uniformity of belief among members of the Church of Christ than among, say, members of the United Methodist Church, which does have a powerful church hierarchy. Members of the Church of Christ attend church three times a week, United Methodists in most cases only once. The social life of a Church of Christ member is more closely circumscribed by church activities, so that there is less opportunity to develop ideas independent of the church. Twenty-five percent of the pro-ERA activists in Oklahoma were United Methodists, but so were some of the prominent

Anti leaders, whereas only 1.5 percent of the Pros were Church of Christ members, and none was a Pro leader. Some of the members remained active in other such organizations, but Church of Christ members did not have as prominent a position in the movement after Pro-Family Forum was disbanded in 1984 as they had before.

THE MORMONS

Members of the Church of Jesus Christ of Latter-day Saints, popularly called Mormons, were another group whose principles and beliefs resonated with the beliefs of the Antis so that they were easily mobilized against the ERA. Although not fundamentalists, Mormons found common cause with the fundamentalist churches on family values and on opposition to abortion. They went even further by discouraging (but not actually forbidding) artificial birth control. But they did not insist on biblical inerrancy and orthodox fundamentalism as did the Churches of Christ and the Baptist churches. For instance, they were willing to have evolution taught to their children in public schools, while the fundamentalists insist that their children be taught creation, or "intelligent design." Therefore Mormons were somewhat of an anomaly in the anti-ERA movement, and fewer of them were active in the Christian conservative movement after the ERA was defeated.

Mormons also share the fundamentalist opposition to the worldly vices of alcohol, tobacco, and gambling. They are encouraged to abstain not only from alcohol and tobacco, but from coffee and tea. My Mormon respondents offered me orange juice when I came for interviews, instead of the coffee that was the most common offering. (Fortunately, I did not feel deprived, for I have never liked the taste of coffee.) Like the evangelical and fundamentalist churches, Mormons also hold to the traditional view of sexual morality. To them, the "sexual revolution" or "new morality" is nothing more than the old immorality, a symptom of moral decline.

Because of their agreement on some of these issues, the Mormons were easily mobilized. Mormons were 9 percent of my 1980 sample, a percentage almost twenty times as large as their share (.5 percent) of the Oklahoma population. Their church was the only conservative church to adopt an official position against the ERA. Unlike other conservative churches, the Latter-day Saints had an official church hierarchy with the power to make such a decision. The influence of the church was generally credited for the decision of the Utah legislature not to ratify the ERA. The church was especially influential there because of the location of its headquarters and its university in that state. The church was also influential in Idaho, and possibly in Washington State.

The Mormon church, perhaps even more than the evangelical churches, emphasizes the importance of family. Women are encouraged to care for their children at home rather than having careers. The church goes so far as to plan its local schedules so as to leave room for its Family Home Evening, something that the church has recommended since 1915.

INTERDENOMINATIONAL DISTRUST

Although fundamentalists among the anti-ERA activists (mostly Baptists and members of the Churches of Christ) welcomed the support of the Catholics and Mormons on the issues, they would have denied the label of "Christian" to them in the past. Some of those I interviewed still had the mind-set common to their faiths during the previous years of fundamentalist separatism. One woman told of her church's project to send Bibles to Poland. When I expressed surprise at this, commenting that the Poles were known as especially devoted Catholics, she answered. "Yes, but *some* of them are Christians." Another told me that she had been raised a Catholic, but had been converted to Christianity after she was married. One of the Mormon respondents, in turn, told me, "I have almost begun to hate the word 'Christian' because so many people say they are Christians and then start running down other churches."

This seemingly intolerant attitude also stems from the fundamentalist beliefs that Catholicism is "unbiblical" and that Mormonism is a "cult." Fundamentalists believe that Catholics have misplaced their veneration by giving a central place to Mary rather than to Jesus.

Even as late as 1995, I met a Texas woman at the national convention of Concerned Women for America (CWA) who said she had not joined Eagle Forum (Schlafly's organization) because Schlafly is a Catholic. At the same convention, a CWA leader in Utah told me that the Mormons in her state *prefer* to work with Eagle Forum because they do not like to be associated with the fundamentalists in CWA or in the Christian Coalition. These incidents underscore the value to the movement of having different organizations with leaders from different religious groups. Despite these lingering traces of suspicion, the disparate groups have been able to form a remarkably united front on the issues important to them.

Because the pro-family movement and later the Christian Right depended so heavily on the religious fervor of the fundamentalists, their movement could not have mobilized successfully without overcoming these interfaith suspicions. Phyllis Schlafly did not recruit the fundamentalist women directly—that was Lottie Beth Hobbs's contribution—but Schlafly welcomed Hobbs and her constituency into the anti-ERA movement, thus bringing together groups that had for so long distrusted one another. When Eagle Forum was formally organized in 1975, Hobbs and two other well-known Church of Christ women, Shirley Curry and Tottie Ellis, joined the board of directors.

In later decades, the Christian Coalition and the pro-life organizations have managed to integrate people of different faith traditions in their political activities,[23] but it began with the opposition to the Equal Rights Amendment. In 1996, during the national convention of the Christian Coalition, I asked Schlafly how she was able to overcome the fundamentalists' long tradition of separating themselves from other Christians.

> Our movement brought together . . . Protestants of all denominations, Catholics, Mormons, and Orthodox Jews. . . . At our meetings, I taught them that, although they might be sitting next to someone who might not be saved, we could nevertheless work together in behalf of a political/social goal we all shared.[24] (September 13, 1996)

Between the well-known leaders, like Phyllis Schlafly and Lottie Beth Hobbs, and the grassroots participants were the women who were leaders in a region of their states, or at the state level. Although some of them had been active in other organizations, others were previously inactive women who saw the importance of defending their beliefs and volunteered to take on demanding roles. Their roles are described in the next chapter.

NOTES

1. Kent L. Tedin, David W. Brady, et al., "Social Background and Political Differences between Pro and Anti-ERA Activists," *American Politics Quarterly* 5 (July 1977): 397.

2. Interview with Lottie Beth Hobbs, Fort Worth, 24 April 1998.

3. Richard Fly, "How 'Rights' Letter Came to Houston," *Houston Chronicle*, 9 November 1975, reprinted in *Congressional Record—Senate*, 94th Cong., 2d sess., 17 February 1976, p. 3385.

4. Connie Marshner wrote a different and more coherent analysis of a similar bill in 1971.

5. Telephone conversation with spokeswoman in the Oklahoma office of Sen. Dewey Bartlett (R-Okla.), November 1975.

6. After corresponding with Marshner (e-mail, 1 May 1997), I still cannot be sure whether the incident she refers to was in 1971 or 1975. The description fits what happened in 1975 perfectly, but in her interview quoted in William C. Martin's *With God on Our Side: The Rise of the Religious Right in America* (New York: Broadway Books, 1996), p. 175, she said it was in 1971. After twenty years, memories fade.

7. Estimates of church membership in the various states are from C. W. Jacquet, ed., *Yearbook of the American and Canadian Churches* (Nashville: Abingdon, 1981); and Douglas Johnson, et al. *Churches and Church Membership in the United States, 1971* (Washington, D.C.: Glenmary Research Center, 1974), p. 11.

8. Kent L. Tedin, "Religious Preference and Pro/Anti Activism on the Equal Rights Amendment Issue," *Pacific Sociological Review* 21, no. 1 (January 1978): 60.

9. Carol Mueller and Tom Dimieri, "Oppositional Consciousness and ERA Activism in Three States," Paper presented at American Sociological Association Meetings, San Francisco, California, September 1982, using data for South Carolina collected by Theodore Arrington and Patricia A. Kyle.

10. "Wives, submit yourselves unto your own husbands, as unto the Lord. For the husband is head of the wife, even as Christ is the head of the church" Authorized (King James) version (AV).

11. "Thou shalt not lie with mankind, as with womankind: it is abomination" (AV).

12. "Before I formed thee in the belly I knew thee; and before thou camest out of the womb I sanctified thee, and I ordained thee a prophet before the nations" (AV).

13. New Rochelle, N.Y.: Arlington House, 1977.

14. Cincinnati, Ohio: Standard Publishing, 1981.

15. Nancy T. Ammerman, "Comment: Operationalizing Evangelicalism: An Amendment," *Sociological Analysis* 43 (summer 1982): 170–71.

16. James Allan Davis and Tom W. Smith, principal investigators, *General Social Surveys, 1990–1996* (Chicago: National Opinion Research Center). Analysis performed on MicroCase Analysis Software created by Microcase Corporation, Bellevue, Washington. The question was not included in surveys before 1990.

17. Davis and Smith, *General Social Surveys*. The percentage who chose fundamentalist actually increased from 27.4 percent in 1972 to 30.5 percent in 1996.

18. As religion has become a relevant category for political activity, researchers have found it expedient to limit their analysis to white Christian conservatives, because African Americans, although generally fundamentalist, do not usually support the Christian conservative political goals.

19. George Gallup Jr. and Jim Castelli, *The People's Religion: American Faith in the 90's* (New York: Macmillan, 1989), p. 92.

20. Margaret Lamberts Bendroth, "Fundamentalism and the Family: Gender, Culture, and the American Pro-family Movement," *Journal of Women's History* 10, no. 4 (winter 1999): 42–45.

21. "Let the woman learn in silence with all subjection. But I suffer not a woman to teach, nor to usurp authority over the man, but to be in silence," I Tim. 2:11–12 (AV).

22. James L. Guth and John C. Green, *The Bible and the Ballot Box: Religion and Politics in the 1988 Election* (Boulder, Colo.: Westview, 1991), p. 220.

23. Mark Rozell, Clyde Wilcox, and John C. Green, "Religious Constituencies and Support for the Christian Right in the 1990s," *Social Science Quarterly* 79, no. 4 (December 1998): 815–21.

24. Interview with Phyllis Schlafly at Christian Coalition convention in Washington, 13 September 1996.

4

SAVED PEOPLE
CAN SAVE THE COUNTRY

I had just finished an interview with a quiet motherly woman in a dilapidated farmhouse. She had seemed shy and ill at ease throughout most of the interview, yet there were flashes of humor. She felt serene and confident in her role as a wife and mother, but she was not accustomed to commenting on issues in the larger society. As I turned to go, she put her hand on my arm and said earnestly:

> It says in the Bible that God has given us this beautiful land, and as long as we are faithful, it will not be taken from us, so Russia can do her worst [she was speaking in 1980], and we will be safe, as long as we are faithful to the Lord. But if we're not—and I'm really worried about the way things are going now—we don't have the promise. (farmer's wife, Mormon, 1980)

A week later, in Tulsa, a more sophisticated woman, the wife of a lawyer, said "If America is to be saved, it has to be saved by saved people. People of the world don't care. They're happy with the way things are going."

As I read through my interviews, I found this theme again and again, in different forms. America was in danger of being destroyed from within by a decline in moral standards. The only hope of saving it was for Christians to work together. It was all in the context of God's covenant, according to which our faithfulness to his commands would fulfill the requirements for his continued blessings. Some were more optimistic

81

than others about the likelihood that the nation could actually be saved, but all agreed that the situation was grave.

> We've become a hedonistic society. . . . Personally, I believe our nation is very much comparable to the Roman empire. . . . Rome became a hedonistic society, where there was self-gratification and self-pleasure, no thought of tomorrow, no thought of the consequences, no commitment to others or to marriage. . . . They became dependent on government, became a welfare state. Everything that makes a decaying civilization was there. (suburban housewife, Baptist, 1980)

This was another recurring theme. Respondents often referred to Edward Gibbon's *The Decline and Fall of the Roman Empire*. They heard the "immorality of Rome" theme from their preachers, along with its corollary, that America will go the way of Rome if she does not mend her ways. When I asked both the Antis and Pros if they thought things were really worse than before, the typical answer of a pro-family activist was this:

> Yes, they are getting worse. There is a breakdown of the home. Women are working and not caring for children. There is immorality, dishonesty, and people are more interested in themselves than in others. And the worst thing of all is that now immorality is accepted, whereas it used to be frowned upon. (urban wife of a physician, 1980)

In contrast, two typical answers of women's movement activists were these:

> No, I think people who say that just don't know their history. There have always been problems, but now we've started becoming more aware of them and are trying to do something about them, so I think things are actually better now than before. (pro-ERA leader, 1981)

> Well, there are a lot of problems, of course, but they are caused by changes in technology and industrialization. I certainly wouldn't want to go back to washing on the washboard, so I think we will just have to go to work to solve the new problems that come with social change. (wife of a professor, 1981)

Whether optimistic or pessimistic, these women recognized that modernization and urbanization make upholding traditional moral standards more difficult. Because conservative Christians are more likely to emphasize the difficulties than the challenges, it was common in the 1970s for analysts to say that there was a conflict between "traditionalists" and "modernists." The implication was that right-wing protest was centered in rural areas, among older and less-educated people, who were likely to be fundamentalists.[1]

In the early years of the ERA ratification struggle, the association of fundamentalists with traditional rural culture was more accurate than it was later. The Pros were likely to be urban in origin and to be employed professionals. Only 23 percent of the Pros I interviewed were from rural areas and 61 percent of them were professional. The Antis, on the other hand, were more likely to have been reared in rural areas (40 percent). Thirty-eight percent of them were homemakers, and only 22 percent professional.[2] They were nostalgic for a simpler time when fathers earned the bread; mothers baked it; families were close; communities were small; values were held in common and reinforced by home, school, and church; crime was almost nonexistent; and the government was very far away.

> There was a time when sons followed in their father's footsteps, and learned a trade. We are no longer a rural society. We have large farms today, and just a few people can produce food for the whole nation. Somewhere along the way we lost our values, we became success-oriented, and from there we seem to have come to rely on government for everything. (suburban housewife, Baptist, 1980)

But the vestiges of a vanishing rural culture are not enough to explain the vitality and persistence of the Christian conservative movement. Although most of them are no longer rural, the religion of their rural origins is still important to them. As the second part of this book will show, the strength of Christian conservatism at the end of the twentieth century was precisely where modernism meets tradition, in the suburbs.

When those who believed that "things are getting worse in this country" were asked if there was any group that might be able to reverse the trend, some said that individual Christians and churches should try to teach their own children the old values. Others believed that Christians as a group had an obligation to "turn it around."

Well, it may be a faith more than a hope, but I really believe that the moral majority type of organizations, the fundamentalist Christians—all of us working together, not any one organization, but all the Christian people— might be able to turn it around. After all, we can't expect anyone else to do it. If you are a godless person, of course you won't be concerned about the moral standards of society. (farmer's wife, Church of Christ, 1981)

Christians are the only hope to turn things around, and it's just in the Lord's hands what the eventual outcome is. Things won't get better unless the Lord intervenes. But if all Christians work together, we could change it. I'm just not sure it's going to happen. (urban wife of a physician, Missouri Synod Lutheran, 1980)

To many of these fundamentalist respondents, it was not simply a matter of conditions getting worse, but of the danger that God would destroy our society for its wickedness. For others it was a matter of each individual's salvation.

God-fearing and Bible-believing people may have a chance of saving society. It's in God's hands. God can save us if man's choices are different, but even if that doesn't happen, each individual's outcome will be different if they make the right choices. (small-town housewife, Baptist, 1981)

These quotations refer to another important belief of some fundamentalists—*dispensational premillennialism.* Believing that this world will end abruptly with the second coming of Christ, they are driven to convert others to their faith. When Christ returns, he will take up with him, or "rapture," all those who have been "saved," while the others will be left behind. Tim LaHaye's best-selling fiction series, *Left Behind,* is based on this premise.[3]

The Christian conservatives felt obliged to convert others wherever possible in order to combat the general trend of moral decline, and also to tackle a list of specific problems that were "getting worse." The lists varied with the individual. They included violence, students attacking teachers, drugs, alcoholism, one-parent families, bad language in movies, loose morals, materialism, permissiveness, divorce, teenage pregnancy, abortion, homosexuality, and socialism.

THE SALIENCE OF THE SEX-RELATED ISSUES

For many of the Antis, the most frightening aspects of the "new morality" were those related to sexuality, particularly homosexuality, teenage pregnancy, abortion, and pornography. They were convinced that feminism, the ERA, sex education in schools, and the increased openness of homosexuality were all part of the same phenomenon. It was these issues that were the most appalling.

The lesbian issue was first raised in connection with the Equal Rights Amendment by Sen. Sam Ervin (D-N.C.) in the 1972 debate on submitting the amendment to the states. He reasoned that the ERA's ban on "discrimination on account of sex" could be interpreted to mean that any two persons, regardless of sex, could legally marry and claim the same rights as traditional married couples, such as income tax exemptions and adopting children. Other legal experts denied that this would be the result, but as long as the ERA had not become law and been tested in court, both sides could claim they were right.

Phyllis Schlafly repeated the substance of Ervin's arguments and some other testimony in her *Report* for September 1974, but did not dwell on it further. Neither Pros nor Antis paid much attention to it until the National Women's Conference in 1977. By then, news coverage of a conflict over homosexuality in Dade County, Florida, had brought the issue to public attention.

Anita Bryant, a former Miss America and a former Oklahoman then living in Miami, had a lucrative career as a spokesperson in TV commercials for Florida orange juice. Her high profile allowed her to earn still more with records, books, and public appearances. But after she led a public campaign early in 1977 to repeal a Dade County (Miami) ordinance banning discrimination against homosexuals, she was the target of protests and boycotts. As a result, her bookings dropped dramatically.[4]

Homosexuality became one of the hottest issues at the National Women's Conferences, described in detail in chap. 5. It has been a frequent topic in Christian conservative radio and television broadcasts and in their direct mail and publications ever since. Polls have consistently shown that conservative Christians are more opposed to homosexuality than the general public. For instance, when the 1984 General Social

Survey asked its respondents "Is homosexuality always wrong?" there was a differential of 20 percentage points (71.8 percent versus 91.8 percent) on that question between those who also believed that the Bible is the actual word of God and is to be taken literally, and those who did not. In 1994, fewer believed that homosexuality was always wrong, but the differential was about the same (63.5 percent vs. 84 percent).[5]

The relationship also held among those who answered my questionnaires in Oklahoma in 1980. Attitudes of fear and disgust toward homosexuals, and unwillingness to join organizations in which homosexuals were members or to have one's children taught by homosexuals were all significantly related to activity in the pro-family movement, and to agreement with pro-family positions on the issues.

The connection between opposition to homosexuality and the fundamentalist belief in the literal truth of the Bible was not a coincidence. For fundamentalists, if the Bible calls homosexuality an "abomination," that settles the question. Mormons, however, another religious group that furnished activists to the pro-family movement, while agreeing that the Bible calls homosexuality a sin, were not so quick to pass judgment.

> I know that according to the Good Book that there are a few things that are worse, like an incestuous father. . . . Personally, I believe they're all God's children, and sent here for a purpose, and maybe we're just not smart enough to know what the purpose is. (retired businessman, Mormon, 1981)

The Connecticut Mutual Study of American Values, a random sample survey of the entire U.S. population conducted in 1980, found that 87 percent of those with the highest degree of religious commitment believed homosexuality to be morally wrong. Among those with the lowest degree of religious commitment, 54 percent believed it morally wrong. In the general population, only 71 percent believed it to be wrong.[6] The belief was held by a strong majority among all groups.

Pro-family movement leaders were able to use the unpopularity of homosexuality to good effect as a recruiting tool in their fight against the ERA. Bunny Chambers, who replaced Beverly Findley as leader of Oklahoma Women Who Want to be Women, said to me in a rare moment of candor:

To me, the most important issue about ERA is states' rights, but you can't get people to listen by talking about states' rights, so I begin with the emotional issues. I have been criticized for that, but it doesn't make me any difference. (1981)

When I asked what emotional issues she was referring to, her response was: "Homosexuality. I really do believe the ERA will legalize homosexual marriages, and that upsets people."

Sex education was another threat to the family, according to pro-family activists. Forty-seven percent of my respondents believed that sex education should not be in schools at all, compared to 87 percent of the Pros who favored it. They believed that sex education in schools actually encourages sexual experimentation on the part of young people. Several believed that sex education had caused the increase in births to unmarried women and girls because that increase had come after sex education was available in more schools.

Pro-family meetings often featured two books calculated to appall the members. The first was *Our Bodies, Ourselves*, a product of the early years of the feminist movement.[7] The book's sponsors argued that male gynecologists for too long had dictated the management of women's reproductive systems, and that women should take control of their own bodies. Pro-family members were offended by the frank discussion of lesbianism and abortion, and by the drawings depicting sexual intercourse. The second was a European sex education book called *Show Me*.[8] It had been prepared for young children, but conservatives thought it much too explicit for that age group.

They also objected to sex education movies shown to school-age children. Oklahoma STOP-ERA purchased a film used by Planned Parenthood and made it available to chapters for showing during their meetings. Another film shown at local chapter meetings was narrated by Margaret Mead. It suggested that sexual mores tend to change along with other changes in society. Said one woman who saw it: "When they teach it in school . . . I think that is terrible. I nearly fell to the floor [at the meeting when the film was shown] and there wasn't anybody in there but women" (civil service retiree, 1980).

FEAR AS A MOTIVE FOR ACTIVISM

The forty years or so of fundamentalist separation from the world of politics was reflected in the lack of political experience among the Antis in those early years. In North Carolina, about one-half of the Antis had not been involved in a political issue before the ERA. A study of those lobbying at the state capitol in Texas in 1975 found the Pros to have been more active in politics[9] before the ERA campaign than the Antis. Among my Oklahoma Anti respondents, less than 15 percent had engaged in any political activity other than voting until the ERA became an issue.

The combination of their inexperience and the willingness of Anti leaders to use sex-related appeals as ammunition against the ERA led to behavior that sometimes seemed overemotional. In the early years of the ERA campaign, legislators noted that anti-ERA lobbyists were likely to burst into tears while telling of the consequences they feared if the ERA should be ratified. Several legislators told me, "The Antis were too hysterical at the beginning." However, it should be noted that the same legislators also told me that "NOW had the wrong people in Oklahoma in 1973, and it left a bad impression."[10] Legislators agreed that both sides were calmer and more professional in later years than they had been at the beginning.

Two legislators allowed me to examine their mail on the subject of the ERA from the 1975 session of the legislature. Some enclosed copies of the "pink sheet," some referred to and some repeated the substance of its arguments, that is, that America might become like Russia if the ERA were passed. Just over half of the letters, twenty-two of the forty-two, were clearly motivated by fear. Some excerpts follow, with spelling and punctuation exactly as in the originals:

> It seems to me that Russia's women's utopia is not for us in Oklahoma. They have Communism. We have a democracy with a voice in our government.

> A lady lawyer gave a group of us in AAUW [American Association of University Women] the good and bad points concerning the measure. It was frightening in its possible scope.

> First, I am the mother of three young children. I do not ever want to be forced to make at least fifty percent of our family income. Neither do I

want my daughter to ever be put in that position. Neither do I ever want our daughter to ever be forced to join the armed services, nor do I want my boys to have to use shower and bathroom facilities with the ladies.

We were given some papers telling about the equal rights amendment it is shocking to think women want to be like men. God never intented for us to be equal to them. We tought our children they were different and tought our sons to respect women but when I think about our grandchildren being put in school to use the same bathrooms and then all go into the armed services to live in the same rooms it just don't make sense.

By 1977, out of fifty letters to the same legislator, only five were so clearly motivated by fear. But even in 1982, during the last tense weeks before the final vote, there were reports of groups of women crying and praying on the front porches of legislators in some areas of Oklahoma.

The "responsible" leaders of the pro-family movement in Oklahoma were somewhat embarrassed by this kind of behavior. Nearly all of the Mormons were careful to dissociate themselves from it. Phyllis Schlafly was constantly at work to rein in the most extreme of her followers, and to train them to be more effective. Nevertheless, those who were responsible for guiding the anti-ERA campaign recognized that the intense commitment of these frightened women was an important element in their ability to mobilize lobbyists and workers in the campaign. As one legislator told me:

This is the closest thing to a groundswell that I've ever seen—a genuine grassroots movement—people coming out of their private lives who have never been active in politics before. . . . The Presbyterians on the other hand, and the other churches that are taking a stand for it, are doing so at the upper level, not the congregational level. They get the ministers in meetings to endorse it, but the people do not agree with it and they do not write the letters in support of it, which would carry more weight with me.[11]

POLITICAL NOVICES AS LEADERS

Betty Grogan, who has been quoted frequently in this book, dropped out of school in the eighth grade to marry an itinerant construction worker. Her daughter, Sandra Grogan Jeter, said she had lived in forty-three states during her childhood and had attended as many as seven schools in one year. By the time I interviewed them in 1980, they were settled in a small Oklahoma town. Sandra was married, with children of her own. The two women told me they had knocked on 3,107 doors during the election campaigns in 1980. Their efforts, along with others in other states, had helped to elect Ronald Reagan and a Republican majority in the U.S. Senate. One of the new senators who benefited from the work of the Anti women was Don Nickles of Oklahoma, who later became Republican majority whip in the Senate.

Betty's husband, John, was a staunch union member, and the Grogan family, like most southern whites, had been registered Democrats for as long as they could remember, but as John said, "Carter reformed us!" Because of their disappointment with the born-again President Carter, who turned out to be too liberal for their tastes, they had changed their voter registration. Comparing the platforms of the two parties had only confirmed their decision.

Members of the family were active in the Church of Christ. They attended three times a week, and Betty described herself as "Very active—I try to be," although she admitted that "I haven't been as active as I should have been, since I've been involved in politics. I feel like that's still the Lord's work. I'm doing what I can to save the country, and try to protect our religious freedoms." Betty and Sandra together taught a class for women on Wednesday nights, and Sandra worked on the "Joy Buses" which brought 150 to 200 children to the church each week for the morning service.

Betty had first heard of the ERA when a friend picked up copies of Lottie Beth Hobbs's "pink sheet" at the state fair. It did indeed say that women would be forced to go to work if the ERA were adopted. After reading it, Betty was convinced that the ERA had to be stopped. She started by sending out letters to people in states where the ERA had not yet been ratified. She used the list of the Churches of Christ, the churches to which most members of Women Who Want to be Women belonged. She sent copies of the "pink sheet," urged them to work against the ERA, and also notified them of a bill in Congress to draft women. After that, "I had quite a few that wrote to me and asked if there was other legislation to work on, so instead of doing all this with personal letters, I decided to start sending out a little newsletter, so that's how I started it." The newsletter went out once a month, and continued until after the final defeat of the ERA in 1982.

Betty also belonged to right-to-life groups and the newsletter covered other bills pending in Washington on abortion, domestic violence, and anything else that she thought important. Her list grew until she was sending out two thousand copies to addresses all over the United States and even to some foreign countries. She also became active in Republican politics, attending precinct and district meetings and campaigning for candidates for the state legislature and Congress.

I asked her how much time all of this political activity took, and again Betty and John answered jointly:

Betty: You should ask my husband!

John: I sleep with it, eat with it.

Betty: You know, once he said "You just live with ERA, you're always on the phone, sending out newsletters, if you're not talking about it, you're thinking about it." So the next morning when I fixed his lunch, I folded one of these pink sheets and stuck it between two sheets of bread and put it in a baggie, and when he came in that night, I asked him if he was surprised, and he said "Nothing you do surprises me."

John: You talk about equal rights, if anyone has 'em, she has! (September 12, 1980)

It was the ERA that had caused Betty to become active politically, and she in turn had encouraged her daughter, Sandra. Neither Betty nor her daughter had been active in politics until the ERA came along, although they had always voted. Sandra said she would go on with it even if her mother quit. "She said this would be her last campaign, but I'm just getting started. I love campaigning, I love politics. I like the phone calling, I like going door to door, I like the conventions, I like calling and talking to people" (September 12, 1980).

THE REGIONAL STARS

Betty Grogan and others like her were regional "stars," disseminating information and directing political activity. I became aware of these "stars" when I tried to set up interviews with respondents and many said: "Well, I'm just an ordinary person. If you really want to know about it, you should ask _____. She can tell you a lot more about it than I can." As I moved from one part of the state to another, I heard different names in each area. Some of the regional stars were the experienced women from the Farm Bureau, the John Birch Society, or the Republican Party, but others, like Betty Grogan, were new to politics.

Both Phyllis Schlafly and Lottie Beth Hobbs had a relatively nonbureaucratic leadership style. And the local and state organizations were not formal in structure. There were formal positions like president, secretary, or treasurer, but they were more often appointed than elected, and others, like the regional stars, simply took it upon themselves to fill leadership roles.

The entry of the relatively inexperienced activists into political activity was nurtured by the regional stars. The regional stars, all of whom were energetic and outgoing, were the ones who had the bright ideas, who put out newsletters and spoke to church and civic groups. On Bread Day, the women who were unwilling to speak to a legislator by themselves would go along with one of the stars. Sometimes they found it easier than they had feared, and they would have the courage to do it alone the next year. Bunny Chambers, who took over the leadership of Pro-Family Forum after Beverly Findley resigned, told me about her first experience at Bread Day:

> It seemed to me like there were two hundred or three hundred women at the capitol that day, and it was so exciting to talk to all of them, and I talked to my legislator for the first time. I hadn't known him, I had to find out who he was, and I went in there with my knees knocking and told him I opposed the ERA, and he says, "I do too," and I breathed a sigh of relief. I didn't know what I was up against. (interview at capitol, November 10, 1981)

Betty Grogan was one of the political novices. Gerry Lowe was another. Lowe was a Mormon who had first heard of the ERA while living in Illinois. After she moved to Oklahoma, she called Phyllis Schlafly, who gave her Ann Patterson's phone number. She called Patterson and then organized a group in her town with a name similar to Patterson's statewide group: Citizens for Responsible Legislation. Lowe had small children, but she did not let that keep her at home. She took her children to the meetings and was outraged when a local reporter featured her crying baby prominently in a newspaper story. "She made it sound like she cried the whole time" and "wrote a really nasty story about it." But Lowe was undeterred. She believed that she eventually won respect not only in the town, but in the legislature. She described herself as "really naïve" about lobbying at first, but she learned through experience.

Lowe's group started with only about twenty women, but eventually her newsletter went to about six hundred addresses. She spoke to classes at the local university and to other groups in the community, she contacted a wealthy conservative family in her church for money, and she distributed literature wherever she could. One of her more successful ventures was sponsoring a booth at the county fair. True to her Mormon faith, she believed that the most important role for a woman was to raise a family, but the church also encouraged women to take a leadership role in organizations whose aims were compatible with and reflected the church's policies. Her motivation for working against the ERA was "my three daughters. . . . I want them to have the same freedoms I have— freedom to be a homemaker, and the freedom not to join the military if there was a draft."

Although many of the regional stars produced newsletters, they did not limit themselves to these impersonal methods of communication. They began each morning by making and receiving telephone calls. A regional star in eastern Oklahoma was Myrtle Kelly, another whose first involvement in politics was in the pro-family movement. Her participation was sparked by her own child's bad experience with a values clarification program in her local schools. She found herself being asked for advice about other children who were having difficulties in school, as well as about legislation. Although she resorted to newsletters on occasion, most of her contacts were by telephone. She made friends all over the country as she talked to people in other states about similar problems.

TWO TYPES OF LEADERS

The leadership in Oklahoma during the ERA campaign was a microcosm of the national Christian conservative leadership. Two groups—those with experience in conservative politics and the inexperienced recruits, mostly from conservative churches—came together with a common goal. I was able to identify twenty-six women who had taken a leadership role at some time in the STOP-ERA in Oklahoma. Eleven had been leaders on the local level, nine had written newsletters or traveled within a specific region of the state, and six had been active at the state level. An analysis of the backgrounds of these leaders revealed the nature of the volunteer leadership resources available to the anti-ERA and pro-family movements.

Sixteen of those leaders had been active in politics before the ERA became an issue, and thirteen of those sixteen had either belonged to or received literature from the John Birch Society, the Cardinal Mindszenty Foundation, Liberty Lobby, Pro-America, or George Benson's National Education Program and Citizenship Seminars—all organizations of the old anticommunist Right. One woman told me that she and her husband had thought the John Birch Society was a "far-out" organization but had joined enthusiastically after actually attending a meeting.

> We kept hearing about this radical extremist group that had been organized, and they were really fanatics, so . . . [when they announced a local speaker] my husband said he'd go just to see what he looked like. He thought he might have horns and a tail and a pitchfork, and when he came home, he said, "you won't believe this, but that guy talked just like we feel. Not only that, but he belongs to a national organization that feels that way." (urban woman, 1980)

Even some of those who had not belonged to the John Birch Society had a positive attitude toward it. Leaders in the anti-ERA movement were more likely than rank-and-file members to approve of the John Birch Society. Many of those who were not leaders had a negative opinion of it.

Of the ten leaders who had *not* been active in politics before the ERA became an issue, all but three were members of the Church of Christ. Of those three, one was Baptist and two were Mormons. Five of the ten had been recruited to political activity by a friend who was active in the movement, three had been recruited through their churches, and two had become involved because of a personal experience in which their children had been exposed to something that they saw as objectionable in the public schools. Those in the first group, active before the ERA, were more diverse in their church memberships. Some actually belonged to liberal churches but had become discontented with them, or had recently changed their membership to a newer nondenominational and more conservative church.

An analysis of leaders for and against a referendum on a state ERA in Massachusetts in 1976[12] showed that the Antis in Massachusetts were predominantly Catholic rather than fundamentalist. This difference reflects the difference in the church affiliations of the Massachusetts population as compared to the southern states. Massachusetts was also different in that it, like other northeastern states, was less receptive to the Antis' cause. Massachusetts both ratified the national ERA and adopted a state ERA. Anti leaders in southern states were less likely than the Pro leaders to have had previous political experience. By contrast, Massachusetts leaders on both sides had identical histories of voting and contributing to political campaigns.

The early leaders and organizers of the pro-family movement, on both the state and national levels, were continuing a longtime interest in right-wing causes. On the other hand, the rank and file and the leaders who joined during the ERA crusade were, for the most part, recruited through churches or by friends, many of whom had, in turn, been recruited through their churches.

POLITICAL VETERANS

I drove into the yard of Buddy's Ranch on a warm fall afternoon. The rambling house seemed to be sprawling against the landscape. A back porch was enclosed with canvas screens, the steps worn from many feet. Dogs immediately circled my car, barking furiously. Just as I was wondering how I could get out of the car, a large hearty woman with coal black hair and an infectious laugh came out of the house and waved the dogs away, saying, "You must be Mrs. Brown!" She led me through the cluttered back porch into an equally cluttered kitchen, where she scooped enough things off the kitchen table so that I could put down my notebook and tape recorder. What followed was not so much interview as monologue.

She started talking, even before the tape recorder was turned on, about the telephone calls she received in her position as a voter registrar

for the upcoming November election. She continued until past supper-
time, interrupted occasionally by my questions, more often by the ringing
of her telephone, or as she jumped up to stir the food she was preparing.
When I left, she insisted that I take along some special cucumbers.

Carol Ellison was the driving force behind the STOP-ERA/Eagle
Forum in her county. She was one of those experienced in politics and one
of the few Catholics among the Antis in Oklahoma. She had moved to
Oklahoma from Illinois thirty-seven years before I spoke with her.

> Well, I'll tell you what, I was discriminated against at first. I was a
> Catholic and a Republican, and that's about as discriminated as you can
> get. At that time, everybody around here was partial to the Methodists.
> But now they call me from every church. And people say, "You can ask
> Carol, and if she don't know, she'll find out." (October 24, 1980)

Ellison was a long-time political activist, a member of Pro-America,
and a contributor to the Cardinal Mindszenty Foundation, founded by the
Schlafly family to fight Communism.

> It seems like I've been involved forever. I'm a precinct leader, on the
> ward committee, I'm district committeewoman for the county Repub-
> lican Party, and I'm not just one of these that goes to fund-raising func-
> tions. I go door-to-door, call people, get literature out. I do all that work,
> which I think it really takes to elect a candidate. (October 24, 1980)

Her energies were not exhausted even by all this political work in her
own county. As a farm wife, she was also active in the Farm Bureau. "I
also go down to the capital for the ERA or for Farm Bureau bills. They
laugh at me and say, 'that old Pontiac, she just turns it on and it heads
down to the capital.' Sometimes I'm down there two or three times a
month." Although a local organizer, her considerable talents were available for statewide activities as well.

In summer 1981, just before the last legislative session in which the
ERA would be considered, the members of her STOP-ERA/Eagle Forum
chapter talked about what they could do to "keep our girls' motivation up."
They decided to start a petition campaign in the county, urging legislators
not to ratify the ERA. Later in the summer, she presented the idea at the

Farm Bureau Women's Committee meeting and talked about it to Ann Patterson. Patterson endorsed the idea, the Farm Bureau approved it, and before long it was a statewide project of both the Farm Bureau and STOP-ERA.

With the help of STOP-ERA/Eagle Forum and Farm Bureau members in her home county, Carol Ellison mailed the petitions all over the state. Those who received them were urged to copy them, get signatures on as many as possible, and mail them back by December 1, so there would be time to put them in order before the opening of the legislative session the first week of January.

> We didn't even know Christmas came and went. They kept coming in all through December, and we finally had to stop doing anything with the new ones, because we wanted to tape them all together by counties into one long scroll. We had petitions from sixty-eight [of the seventy-seven] counties. Some people did sixteen or twenty pages, and they came from all kinds of churches, Baptist, Church of Christ, Mormon, and Methodist. A lot of people signed in the churches. (October 24, 1980)

There had been no public announcement when the petition drive began, and no media coverage of the petition's progress, but that long scroll with its twenty thousand signatures got plenty of media attention when it was brought to the capitol on STOP-ERA's regular Bread Day. It reached down the stairs of the capitol from the fourth floor to the outside steps. The pro-family movement had surprised the opposition as well as the legislators and captured the evening headlines with an innovative campaign idea.

The use of innovative advocacy tactics is a hallmark of a young social movement. Social movements begin as "outsiders." They have not yet been recognized as part of the organizational structure of politics, so they are forced to seek other means of getting their message out. In a media-driven age, the spectacular petition was a sure attention getter.

Carol Ellison was not the only anti-ERA'er who was also a member of the Farm Bureau. Some members of its Women's Committee who were also members of the John Birch Society had read and heard about humanism in textbooks, and about the ERA. They persuaded the state director of the Farm Bureau to emphasize those issues. He told me that "We were very reluctant to get into it, but the women have caused us to see the need."

Anti-ERA activists holding a long petition running from the fourth floor to the sidewalk outside the Oklahoma state capitol, January 10, 1982. (*Copyright 1982, the Oklahoma Publishing company*)

Another regional star whose influence extended across the state boundaries was Dianne Edmondson, one of the more experienced ones, whose work will be described more in detail in the next chapter. A former member of the John Birch Society, she grew up in Oklahoma, moved to Texas, then returned to Oklahoma when her second husband's work brought him to Tulsa.

Some of the original volunteers made the transition to paid work. Two of those who had served as state coordinators of Women Who Want to be Women became secretaries to very conservative legislators who shared their views. Like Sandra Grogan Jeter, they were women who had always believed that they should be stay-at-home wives and mothers rather than career women. But they also had talents they did not use, and perhaps did not even know they had, until they were pulled into the fight against the ERA.

SUBMISSIVE WOMEN AS LEADERS?

First these women had to overcome their reluctance to be involved in politics, or to play a public role of any kind, a reluctance they had learned in their churches. Some of them struggled with this contradiction between their ideal role and their actual one.

> Always, when there's a void, it's going to be taken up. I think one of the things wrong with society is that men have left the leadership roles. They did not take it for some reason, whether or not the woman made them feel too dominant, or whatever, they left their role, and the void was filled by the women. I really would like to see men take over the chapters, I still do. Women have been pushed into the role. (Bunny Chambers, 1980)

In one case, I sensed from the interaction between the woman I was interviewing and her husband that he resented her work against the ERA. When I asked her how much time she spent on anti-ERA work, she said, "My husband worries about that too. He said, 'I wish you'd keep track of how long you're on the phone.'" When he came home later in the interview, he said, "Well, she's up twelve hours a day, so I'd say maybe ten hours a day she works on it."

Others were criticized by some of their fellow church members for their political activity, and several told me that Lottie Beth Hobbs was criticized within the Church of Christ for her leadership of Pro-Family Forum. But, encouraged by leaders like Lottie Beth Hobbs and Phyllis Schlafly, they had come to see their campaign against ERA, abortion, homosexuality, and other issues as "the Lord's work."

Feminists who had expected the ERA to be ratified easily felt obliged to explain their failure. One of the reasons offered, that in the beginning the Pros did not have a good organization in the states, was true, but the Antis were no better organized at first. In Oklahoma, at least, the Pros were simply outworked, and that was the case in other states as well. The Antis spent less money, but put in many more hours and were far more dedicated to their cause.

Even though many of the anti-ERA campaigners, especially the older ones, did not continue their political activity after the ERA was finally defeated, they had set an example for their younger counterparts to continue the fight on other issues. Without the work of these pioneering women and their leaders in breaking down the opposition to conservative churches' political involvement, the political power of the Christian conservatives in the 1980s and 1990s would not have been possible.

NOTES

1. James Davison Hunter, *American Evangelicalism: Conservative Religion and the Quandary of Modernity* (New Brunswick, N.J.: Rutgers University Press, 1983); Seymour Martin Lipset and Earl Raab, *The Politics of Unreason: Rightwing Extremism in America, 1790–1970* (New York: Harper and Row, 1970).

2. These figures are the combined totals of those I interviewed from among participants in the Oklahoma Conference on Families and participants in the ERA campaign.

3. Tim LaHaye and Jerry Jenkins, *Left Behind* (Wheaton, Ill.: Tyndale House, 1995).

4. *New York Times*, 9 June 1977, 1:3.

5. James Allan Davis and Tom W. Smith, principal investigators, *General Social Surveys, 1972–1994* (Chicago: National Opinion Research Center). Analysis performed on MicroCase Analysis System, created and sold by Micro-Case Corporation, Bellevue, Washington.

6. *The Connecticut Mutual Report on American Values in the '80s* (Hartford: Connecticut Mutual Life Insurance Company, 1980), p. 96.

7. Boston Women's Health Collective, *Our Bodies, Ourselves: A Book by and for Women* (New York: Simon and Schuster, 1976).

8. Fleischaur-Hardr, *Show Me.*

9. Kent L. Tedin, et al., "Social Background and Political Differences Between Pro- and Anti-ERA Activists," *American Politics Quarterly* 5 (July 1977): 403. "Active" was defined as voted in last election, displayed campaign button or bumper sticker, or donated money to campaigns.

10. Interview with Rep. Jim Townsend at his office in the Oklahoma State Capitol, 29 February 1979.

11. Interview with Sen. Jeff Johnston, at his office in the Oklahoma State Capitol, 12 February 1979.

12. Carol Mueller and Thomas Dimieri, "Structure of Belief Systems among Contending ERA Activists," *Social Forces* 60 (March 1982): 657–75.

5

FROM STOP-ERA TO PRO-FAMILY: THE WOMEN'S CONFERENCES

The National Women's Conference in Houston in November 1977 was planned to be the climax of a series of state conferences marking International Women's Year. Feminists had envisioned that women of all ages, races, and occupations would come together at the conference, make new friends, and discuss common problems. Instead, after the conferences were over, the plans of the feminists were in tatters while the antifeminists of the pro-family movement, who had opposed the conferences, were stronger than ever.

The feminists hoped for a harmonious conference in the belief that all women faced similar problems and needed similar solutions. But even when they had similar problems, not all women interpreted them the same way. One of the workshops in the Oklahoma Women's Conference in the summer preceding the national conference in 1977 clearly demonstrated those different interpretations.

In the workshop on "The Legal Status of the Homemaker," one of the Antis, young, attractive, wearing a long red dress, sobbed as she told her story. Her husband, having decided that he preferred his secretary to her, had divorced her. Her lawyer had not represented her well, and now she was struggling just to make ends meet. The feminists in the workshop told similar stories, but none quite as sad as hers. Amid sympathetic murmurs from the audience, the "expert" panelists tried to suggest some ways that she might seek redress.

Then it was time to vote on resolutions. With near-unanimous votes, the group approved calls for stronger efforts to enforce payment of child support, for pension and retirement benefits to be included in dividing property upon a divorce, and for consideration of women's contributions to an estate in writing inheritance tax law. After specific resolutions were approved, the workshop leader suggested that the Equal Rights Amendment would take care of all of these problems at once. The harmony disappeared in an instant, as all participants snapped back into their predetermined positions. Ann Patterson, the head of the STOP-ERA forces in Oklahoma, spoke for the antifeminists.

> This new idea of no-fault divorce, which is what ERA would bring about, has been a disaster for women. In the states where they have it, they are finding that women are even worse off than they were before.

INTERNATIONAL WOMEN'S YEAR

International Women's Year (IWY) was originally proclaimed for 1975 by the United Nations, which also sponsored the IWY Conference in Mexico City. The UN's involvement alone was enough to arouse the suspicions of some of the conservatives who believed the UN to be part of a sinister international conspiracy. The U.S. Commission on the International Women's Year, appointed by President Ford, adopted a list of recommendations for removing the "barriers to the full participation of women in our nation's life." These recommendations, called "The Plan," were to be the basis for the work of fifty-six state and territorial conferences: to discuss resolutions and elect delegates for a National Women's Conference.

The International Women's Year Conference bore some similarities to previous official "White House conferences," although it was not so designated. Just as in White House conferences, the president called the conference with an official proclamation, and it brought citizens together to discuss a particular range of issues. The important difference was that women, the group that the commission and the conference purported to represent, were far from homogeneous in viewpoint. When White House conferences dealt with small business or libraries, to take two other examples from the late 1970s, the group represented was so small that almost no one else was even aware of the conference. Nor were there any countermovements within the constituent group.

Planners of these other conferences did not need to worry about "balanced representation," for there was apparent consensus on the goals of the conferences. The feminists who controlled the IWY Commission and persuaded the Congress to appropriate funds for it operated on the assumption of consensus also, but Phyllis Schlafly and her supporters quickly demonstrated that assumption to be false. The unexpected result was that the conferences transformed the STOP-ERA movement. From a mostly southern group with a limited agenda of opposing the ERA, it evolved into a well-coordinated national pro-family movement with a much broader agenda.

By the time commission members had actually been appointed and the appropriated funds made available early in 1977, the Antis and the Pros had already survived numerous confrontations in the state capitals. Each group had learned something about the other, if only in caricature. Many of the Antis were homemakers with little previous experience in politics. The Pros saw them as unwitting tools of their experienced right-wing leaders. Reflecting media coverage at the time, the Pros found it difficult to credit that these people were not just mouthpieces for someone else's agenda. The Pros were generally more accustomed to public roles, but their naïve assumption that all women—if they were adequately informed—would naturally support the ERA struck the Antis as sheer arrogance. Phyllis Schlafly's biting rhetoric, describing the Pros as "radical feminists" and "notorious women's libbers," infuriated them. That same rhetoric predisposed the Antis to read hostility into every move of the Pros. In hindsight, it seems inevitable that the women's conferences would be all but destroyed by conflict.

OPPOSITION FROM PHYLLIS SCHLAFLY

In January 1976, Schlafly declared war on the IWY Commission and all its works. Her *Report* for that month urged her readers to write their congressmen calling for defeat of the $5 million appropriation for the conferences. If that failed (as it did), she wanted her readers to demand that

Traditional women opposed to the feminist movement identified themselves by wearing "Majority" streamers at the National Women's Conference in Houston, November 1977. (*National Archives*)

a majority of the staff, speakers, delegates, time allocation, resolutions, press coverage, and money be given to the anti-ERA forces. In June 1976, her Eagle Forum newsletter included this charge to her followers:

> Because we represent the majority of women, we must take over these conferences and make sure they project a pro-family, pro-homemaker, pro-morality, pro-life image. If you do your job right, you can make the libbers sorry they ever decided to have state conferences! It is your job to make sure that (1) our Federal money is NOT spent to project radical lib, anti-family, anti-homemaker, pro-ERA propaganda, and (2) that the libs do NOT use these conferences as a vehicle to rip off more Federal funds to give themselves useless Federal jobs to make the taxpayers provide them with a free babysitting service so they can be out agitating to destroy homemakers' rights, and to rewrite our textbooks to conform to their radical demands.[1]

The commissions, both state and national, were balanced as to racial and ethnic background, age, income, and occupation, but not, as Schlafly's supporters repeatedly complained, as to their position on the ERA. A typical state commission had only token representatives, two or three at the most, from the anti-ERA camp. Despite the feminist protests that the conferences were about all aspects of women's lives, not just the ERA, Schlafly insisted that her supporters actually represented a majority and that they should therefore have at least equal representation on the commissions. Having failed in this, her supporters set out to harass the state commissions at every turn.

In order to do so, Schlafly appointed Rosemary Thomson of Morton, Illinois, as national chairman of the International Women's Year Citizen's Review Committee. Thomson then began to recruit similar committees in the states. According to Thomson's book about the women's conferences,[2] the Citizen's Review Committee distributed several thousand copies of an audiotape prepared by Dianne Edmondson of Oklahoma throughout the nation. The tapes were another example of the pro-family strategy of "appealing to the appalled." They attributed the most outrageous, usually sex-related, goals to the feminists. They explained the "evil that is inherent within the so-called women's liberation" and showed "how as Christians we must do good as the Lord commands by opposing this evil." The evil that she referred to was the series of IWY Conferences. The tapes were instrumental in enabling the antifeminists to elect all or part of at least fourteen state delegations to the Houston conference. An excerpt from the tape follows:

> The IWY is currently chaired by Bella Abzug, former Representative from New York City. . . . Bella is the one who first introduced, when she was in Congress, the Gay Rights Bill. . . . If this bill had passed that Bella introduced, it would mean that homosexuals could teach our children in schools, could be counselors in city, state, or federally supported camps.

Although their numbers were not great, the radical feminists and lesbians were colorful and unusual enough to attract a great deal of media attention, peaking in the early 1970s. Edmondson had gathered a rich collection of shocking quotations to buttress her claim that the feminist movement was promoting radical goals. For example, she tried to show that a goal of the feminist movement was to promote immoral behavior by influencing sex education courses. According to one Edmondson tape:

> They want your child taught that there is no right or wrong, nor normal or ideal circumstances for sexual intercourse, such as, you might be

teaching your child the ideal place for sex is within marriage. This would not be taught. . . . I can't even share with you some of the language in some of the books that they recommended.

The "core" list of resolutions, called the "National Plan of Action" which had already been announced by the National Commission for the IWY Conference, was comprehensive in scope, including child development, homemaker issues, women in employment, women in governmental positions, and rape, for example. But it also called for "Reproductive Freedom" (abortion rights) and for ratification of the ERA.[3] That the resolutions were published in advance seemed to the Antis to be proof that the whole conference system was rigged to achieve a prearranged outcome. The content of some of the resolutions, especially those about abortion and the ERA, was offensive to the conservative women. They also disagreed with the resolutions calling for more day care services and public financing of political campaigns.

In the states where the IWY Citizens' Review Committees were well organized, the state conferences were acrimonious. The suspicion and mistrust that had developed as the two groups lobbied for and against ratification at the state capitols poisoned the atmosphere at the women's conferences as well. Phyllis Schlafly had set a confrontational tone when she announced the formation of those committees. Throughout the conference cycle, her advice on strategy continued to urge confrontation. Her attorney-husband even filed lawsuits against the commission, alleging that it would use federal funds for interest-group lobbying.

Although some states avoided serious conflict, there were noisy confrontations in New York, New Jersey, Florida, Oklahoma, Kansas, Washington, and to a lesser degree in other states. The general pattern was that the IWY sponsors planned the conferences as if the Antis did not exist and then were evasive and suspicious when the Antis asked for representation on the planning committees or on the lists of speakers. That only made the Antis more determined to be included. One of the Antis inadvertently left the notes of a telephone call from Schlafly after a committee planning meeting in the Oklahoma State capitol. The notes included detailed instructions, listing hostile questions to ask of the Coordinating Committee and telling how to create bad publicity if they did not get satisfactory answers.[4]

THE STATE CONFERENCES

The conferences themselves got underway early in 1977 with a relatively harmonious meeting in Vermont in February, and another in Alaska in May. The worst fears of the Antis were confirmed when the Vermont conference adopted a resolution calling for the rights of lesbians, which had not even been on the original list of "core" resolutions. Nellie Gray, president of March for Life, had gone to Vermont to observe the convention, expecting it to endorse abortion and the ERA. But she had not expected gay rights. She and the local Antis reported that "parliamentary procedures were ignored," "rules fluctuated at the whim of the committee," and the election process was unfair.[5]

Phyllis Schlafly's summary[6] of the state conferences noted that there was only one anti-ERA person on the IWY Coordinating Commission for Georgia, the state which held the second conference, although the summary in the IWY official report[7] claimed that the coordinating committee was carefully balanced. Such contradictory accounts were to be found in the aftermath of many of the state conferences. In any case, there were enough Antis in attendance in Georgia to elect some of the delegates and to defeat some of the core resolutions.

In Missouri, Ann O'Donnell, the leader of the right-to-life group in that state, served on the coordinating committee. Although some right-to-life individuals had been active in the anti-ERA groups' campaign, they had not been visible as a group until the Missouri conference. A large contingent of anti-ERA and antiabortion participants came to the conference on Saturday, doubling the number of registrants. After electing an all-conservative delegation to the Houston convention, they went home, leaving the remaining attendees to pass the "core" resolutions without dissent on Sunday.

There were also large numbers of late-registering voters on Saturday in Kansas, Oklahoma, and Hawaii, for Saturday was the most convenient day for the religious conservatives to attend. Their men were available to drive buses or cars—and in some cases, to direct the delegation's activities—without taking off work, and they could all be back in time for Sunday services.

The Ohio conference, also held in June, was another in which Antis elected a strong majority of delegates to the Houston conference. Forty of the state conferences were held in June, sixteen on one weekend alone. The fast pace of the June conferences may have prevented the Antis from controlling more conferences than they did. But they had a string of victories when nine of the ten states meeting in July elected all- or part-conservative delegations. By this time, they could benefit from the experience gained in the states that had already met.

The pattern in those states was similar to the one in Missouri. Large contingents of church members overwhelmed the meetings. In Hawaii, Washington, Montana, Idaho, and Utah, Mormons were the most visible group, outnumbering other participants by about ten to one in Utah. A spokesman for the Mormon Church told the *New York Times* that the Relief Society, the women's organization of the Mormon church, had sent information to its members in other states about the conferences along with statements about the Church position on the issues.[8] In the southern states, contingents from the Baptists and the Churches of Christ were the largest.

In Hawaii, New York, Missouri, Oklahoma, and Kansas, nearly twice as many participants showed up as the organizers had expected. The unexpected numbers meant scrambling to duplicate registration forms, programs, and ballots and to find larger meeting places. The delays occasioned by the influx were always interpreted by the Antis as a plot to deprive them of voting privileges. When fire regulations made it impossible to accommodate everyone, announcement of the limitation was met with disbelief. That, too, was interpreted as a strategy to limit the Antis' participation. The Citizen's Alert Committee in Kansas claimed that the fire marshal's limit for the meeting hall was actually larger than the organizers had announced. In New York and New Jersey, some meetings were held outdoors to avoid the risk of fire.

Among the charges and countercharges, it was impossible to determine who was actually at fault. Antis accused the Pros of not giving timely notification of the time, date, place, and rules for the conferences; of conducting elections unfairly without allowing pro-family monitors to watch ballot counting; of refusing to schedule Anti speakers; of shutting them out of meetings whenever possible; and of being rude. Pros insisted that the problems were caused by the unexpectedly large number of attendees overwhelming a volunteer staff. They in turn accused the Antis of using men as floor managers in Ohio, Mississippi, Alabama, Hawaii, and

Indiana (although this was not illegal); of coming in to affect delegate voting without participating in the entire conference; of precipitating conflict; and of being rude.

THE HOUSTON PRO-FAMILY RALLY

By the time of the conferences, Lottie Beth Hobbs had become a vice president of Schlafly's Eagle Forum. Hobbs's Four Ws, by then called Pro-Family Forum, had joined with Eagle Forum, some right-to-life groups, and other smaller conservative organizations in a Pro-Family Coalition. The coalition, soon to become the pro-family movement, had been able to elect only about 20 percent of the delegates to the Houston conference. Rather than depend on what little impact they might have on the main conference, Lottie Beth Hobbs and some of the others in Pro-Family Forum decided to organize their own rally in Houston. They considered having it in a nearby church, but Hobbs feared that a gathering of only four or five hundred would simply be "showing our weakness rather than our strength." So instead they reserved the Houston Astrodome and set out to fill it up.

Hobbs planned the rally and made arrangements for the speakers, the hotel rooms, and the Astrodome itself. The expenses were covered by contributions that came in the mail, augmented by a freewill offering taken up at the rally. In order to have representatives from every state at the Pro-Family Rally, she made contacts: "all over the U.S., from Florida to California, to Denver, the Senate of Colorado, to Virginia, West Virginia, not in every state, but in every state in the South. That's where we had to fight it. We had somebody from everywhere, Hawaii and Alaska, even."

In September the *Phyllis Schlafly Report* included a copy of a petition, prepared by Lottie Beth Hobbs and Nellie Gray of Right-to-Life, opposing "ERA, Abortion, Federally-controlled Early Child Development Programs, and the Teaching or Glorification of Homosexuality, Lesbianism, or Prostitution." The petitions were to be signed and sent to Houston, along with a contribution for the expenses of the Pro-Family Rally. There were so many contributions that just opening the envelopes, counting the money, and taking it to the bank was a major undertaking.[9]

Dianne Edmondson of Oklahoma prepared another cassette tape

urging listeners to attend the Pro-Family Rally in order to make a statement to the nation that the "radical goals of the feminists" were not supported by the majority of the American public. Whereas the delegates at the women's conference were to be paid "with your tax money," participants at the Pro-Family Rally would come at their own expense. The tapes were distributed throughout the nation through the networks built up by Eagle Forum, Pro-Family Forum, and other cooperating organizations.

The tape went on to describe the state women's conferences, which had preceded the planned National Women's Conference:

> At least twelve IWY workshops in Colorado pertained to lesbianism. At the Virginia IWY conference, there was a workshop on witchcraft, conducted by witches. Free literature distributed in Minnesota included copies of the *Militant*, a radical Communist publication. . . . In Hawaii, the entertainment culminated by a dance showing how lesbians make love in a pay toilet.

It is easy to imagine the outrage this tape generated among fundamentalist Christians. Appalled all over again, they responded with massive support of the rally at the Astrodome. At the official National Women's Conference in the larger coliseum, the galleries were seldom more than half full, but the Astrodome was packed. Rosemary Thomson[10] reported that the Astrodome held 12,000 and that several thousand more were turned away. The *Houston Post* estimated 20,000, a figure that was picked up and repeated in subsequent accounts of the rally.[11]

On the Saturday of the rally the weather was warm and sunny, and the parking lots at the Astrodome were crowded with buses and cars. Some were church buses, others were chartered. One bus driver said that he had counted 250 chartered buses. Some had driven all night the night before the rally. They planned to drive all night again on Saturday in order to be back home for church services the next day.

The crowd was mostly middle-aged, but there were also young people, many with small children. Most wore casual clothes; women were in skirts or polyester pantsuits, and a few younger people wore jeans. I could see only three African Americans in the audience, while there were two on the platform. Sensitive to the charge of being a movement for whites only, pro-family leaders were careful to include at least one African American person on each public program, or better still, a choir from a African American church. They were less successful in attracting the rank and file, for I never saw more than a handful of African Americans in the crowd at any of the rallies and conventions I attended. African Americans, who are likely to be Democrats, are wary of the Republican leanings of the conservative pro-family movement, but many of them are members of fundamentalist churches. They often shared the views of the pro-family movement on abortion, homosexuality, and traditional values. At this rally, an African American Texas legislator, Clay Smothers, delivered the most interesting speech.

> Some of my black friends ask me why I am working with this movement, when most of the blacks are on the other side of town. I have enough civil rights to choke a hungry goat. I ask for public rights, Mr. Carter. I ask for victory over the perverts of this country. I want the right to segregate my family from these misfits and perverts.

Smothers, who had introduced a bill in the Texas legislature that would have barred homosexuals from college campuses in Texas, began his speech in a fairly calm voice, but as he warmed to his subject, he began to sound more and more like a tub-thumping preacher. In the tradition of African American preaching, he increased his tempo and volume as he went along. As he continued talking about the misfits, perverts, and baby killers, the crowd began to respond: whistling, stomping, cheering, and saying "A-A-men!" Finally, he stopped, wiped his brow, and exulted, "I am overcome. I feel like I'm in a black Baptist church!" The crowd responded with more cheers and whistles.

Lottie Beth Hobbs opened the rally by asking for a show of hands from each state's delegation. Then she presented the four pro-family resolutions, a total of 300,000,[12] filling the boxes piled on the stage, that were to be sent to Congress to contrast with the "anti-family" resolutions of the women's conference. There were also speeches by Nellie Gray, president of March for Life; by Mildred Jefferson, a black female surgeon and the president of Right-to-Life; and finally, by Phyllis Schlafly.

Schlafly opened with her favorite line, always good for a laugh and applause: "First of all, I want to thank my husband Fred, for letting me come—I always like to say that, because it makes the libs so mad!" Her speech, entitled "ERA: An Attack on the Family," listed the reasons for opposing the ERA, for example: "The libs want ERA to give an equal right for women not to be pregnant, just like men. . . . If you don't like the fact that women are the ones who have babies and nurse them, you will just have to take it up with God!" She also asserted that the ERA would benefit homosexuals. In the next *Phyllis Schlafly Report* after the conference, she saluted Lottie Beth Hobbs, "a great lady who saw her 'impossible dream' crowned with the glory of success."[13]

THE WOMEN'S CONFERENCE

The word "polarization" was applied to the Houston conference so often that it became a cliché. Those of moderate views on both sides who might have been more comfortable somewhere in the middle were forced to align themselves with one or the other of the opposing groups, just as iron filings line up at the two poles of a magnet. This was particularly so with the two most controversial resolutions, the ones dealing with abortion and homosexuality.

Those resolutions were euphemistically named "Reproductive Freedom" and "Sexual Preference," thus putting them near the end of the alphabetical list of resolutions. That there were differences of opinion, both within and between the two contending groups, was evident from listening to the debate and from talking to the delegates. It was confirmed by Alice Rossi's study of the Houston delegates.

Rossi, a member of the IWY Commission and a professional sociologist, sent questionnaires to all delegates both before and after the conference. So few of the Antis answered her questionnaires that she could not draw firm conclusions about their attitudes, but she found that among the Pros

> Many women defined themselves as strong feminists who have reservations about abortion, worry that the lesbian issue may do more harm than good to the women's movement, and reject the view that opposition to [these issues] is sufficient to deny the label of feminist to someone like themselves.[14]

Similarly, some of the Antis recognized the necessity of abortions in some circumstances, but they felt obliged to close ranks on all of "their issues." Thoughtful pro-family leaders like Myrtle Kelly told me of their reservations.

I support some things I don't really agree with, because I'm just determined that the other side won't get its way! I know there's a danger of
going too far, but I wouldn't want some people to hear me say that. (1980)

Kelly and some other conservatives hesitated to support antiabortion
laws because they recognized that government involvement in such a private matter as abortion was inconsistent with their conservative philosophy of government. But pro-family members could unequivocally
oppose sex education, access to contraceptives for teenagers, and inclu-
sion of abortion in federally funded health programs—all of which were
in the Reproductive Freedom plank.

Two members of the right-to-life–dominated Missouri delegation
spoke against the Reproductive Freedom plank, Ann O'Donnell saying,
"It is the antithesis of the feminist movement to oppress the less powerful
[referring to the unborn fetuses]." During the debate on the plank, posters
and signs expressing both points of view were raised in the hall, including
color photographs of aborted fetuses. The resolution was adopted, as
expected, but there was less jubilation among the Pros after this victory
than after some of the others.

Feelings were similarly mixed on the Sexual Preference plank, which
had been added in response to resolutions at thirty state meetings. Betty
Friedan, the founding mother of feminism, although she had long
believed that lesbians were using the women's movement for their own
purposes and had opposed making sexual preference a part of the feminist program,[15] finally spoke for it this time:

As someone who has loved men too well, I have had trouble with this
issue. Now my priority is passing the ERA. And because there is
nothing in it that will give any protection to homosexuals, I believe we
must help the women who are lesbians.[16]

But a feminist delegate from Georgia called the issue "an albatross
around our necks as we try to pass the ERA." And further, it is "not a
unique women's problem." The pro-family delegates were unanimous in
opposing this question. When the plank was approved, they turned their
backs to the podium. But lesbians in the gallery cheered and released pink
and yellow balloons that said "We are everywhere."

Pro-family delegates had complained at the state conferences that the resolutions, although dealing with problems that all could agree needed attention, recommended expenditure of tax dollars rather than private-sector solutions. Indeed, all but four of the resolutions adopted did call for government funding of new programs, additional funding for existing programs, additional enforcement of existing laws, or additional kinds of record keeping and statistics, all of which would cost money. With "Pro-Plan" delegates in the majority, most of the proposed resolutions passed easily.

Those pro-family delegates who were willing to talk about the issues and about themselves always turned out to be experienced in politics, while the others were reluctant to speak at all. One of those who was experienced in politics was from a small town in Texas. She was only an observer, not an elected delegate. A Democratic county chairman and a state executive committee member in Texas, she had gone to the Texas Women's Conference, and had been "appalled [her word!]" at the open agitation of the "lesbians, with Levis on and hair on their legs." She went home and told some of her friends about it; they immediately reserved their airplane tickets and hotel rooms in Houston.

She and her friends had been refused space in the hotel although they had made reservations months in advance. The conference had begun with the most massive booking foul-up that anyone could remember. Pro-family delegates blamed the "libs," and the Pros blamed the "Antis." But since both Pros and Antis encountered this difficulty, it was more likely that it was just an unfortunate occurrence rather than a conspiracy on anyone's part. It simply added to the anger and paranoia that many on both sides felt throughout the conference.

Mrs. Blake, the experienced politico from Texas, did not belong either to the Four Ws or to Eagle Forum, and neither she nor her friends knew of anyone else who belonged. "Certainly I have no connection with the John Birch Society," she said. At this point, she was not a part of the pro-family movement, but she was ready to be recruited. Her involvement was entirely spontaneous, sparked by her personal conviction that the women's movement was offensive to her moral values. Although she was concerned about other issues, it was the lesbian issue that had brought her to Houston.

Q: What is your main concern about lesbians?

A: I think it's a serious threat to family life!

Q: How exactly is it a threat to family life?

A: Well—lesbians can't set up families. Don't you think it is a threat to family life?

Q: What then do you think is the solution to the problems of families in the United States today?

A: Well, I certainly don't think the government needs to be involved in it. I believe in equal rights, certainly, but I don't like the homosexuals coming out of the closet. They should stay back in the closet where they belong. And I don't believe in abortion on demand, although I would support it for medical and psychological reasons. I am concerned with family and marriage and a personal relationship with the Lord. If everyone had a right personal relationship with the Lord, we wouldn't have all these troubles with the family. (November 1977)

The lasting significance of the Houston conference was that it brought the issues separating the Antis and the Pros before a nationwide audience, resulting in recruitment of additional activists like Blake. It was the catalyst for the creation of the Pro-Family Coalition, uniting anti-ERA, antiabortion, and pro-morality groups together. It gave some of the Washington groups like Conservative Caucus an opportunity to help with some local organizations.

EMERGENCE OF THE HOMOSEXUAL ISSUE

Another important consequence of the Houston conference was that Christian conservatives were so outraged at open lesbian politicking and their success with the resolutions that they were willing to go to almost any lengths to fight "this great evil." Bunny Chambers told me later: "It's the best recruiting tool I've ever had. I just spend twenty minutes reading it [the Houston resolutions] to them. That's all I have to do."

Dianne Edmondson asserted on her recruiting tape that half of the delegates at the Houston conference would be lesbians. Jean O'Leary, the lesbians' chief spokeswoman, who might have had reason to exaggerate, said that there were 130 lesbian delegates, less than 10 percent of the total of 1,403.[17] But to the pro-family delegates, it seemed that the lesbians really were everywhere, just as their motto said.

The exhibit room at the Houston Women's Conference held about two hundred exhibit tables in a room as large as the proverbial football field. Exhibit space was available to any group that applied and paid the $50 fee. Included among the exhibitors were forty-five states or territories, twenty government agencies, twelve occupational associations, five religious groups, and six long-standing women's organizations such as AAUW, YWCA, and the League of Women Voters. Businesses advertised their wares: art galleries, sports groups, political and health groups were all represented. There were five exhibits sponsored by groups associated with the pro-family or pro-life movements, and there was Women Against Violence Against Women, a feminist group opposing pornography.[18]

But there were also lesbian advocacy groups, some businesses advertising lesbian products, and some avowedly Marxist groups. These latter categories, by the broadest possible definition, constituted no more than 10 percent of the exhibits, but it was from these tables that the women from Oklahoma collected several boxes of materials and prepared a display filling more than sixty sheets of posterboard. An Oklahoma woman—a member of the Farm Bureau, the John Birch Society, and Eagle Forum—took what they called the "display" to show at the Oklahoma Farm Bureau Convention in December, the month after the women's conference. Her husband, a farmer in western Oklahoma, told me about it in their home while she was out shopping.

> There was between 600 and 800 people went through that room and some of them was just stunned. There was a chair down there at the end and sometimes they just had to sit down and catch their breath.
>
> Well, when they saw what a reaction they got out of it, they decided to put it together in a more permanent form. Well, Phyllis wanted it for some kind of meeting in Atlanta on Thursday. . . . Well, this was a Monday, so they spent that week putting it together and got it on the plane and took it down there and took it the next day to Charlotte, South Carolina. They found they had dynamite. (September 12, 1980)

The "display" became famous nationwide. It was shown in thirty states, after a notice in Phyllis Schlafly's Eagle Forum newsletter told of its availability:

The display of the pro-family movement in the exhibit hall of the National Women's Conference in Houston, November 1977. (*National Archives*)

It will shock you to know that this kind of material is financed with $5 million of YOUR money. You should be informed about the radical and lesbian forces that are waging war on the American family.[19]

It is not quite accurate that the material was financed with taxpayer money; it was sponsored by private organizations that had paid for the exhibit tables and furnished their own materials. Feminists were not convinced even that the materials had all come from the conference exhibits. "I think they went out and bought that at an adult bookstore!" said one. Pro-family activists, however, insisted that this was not the case. And a few of the items were indeed financed with taxpayer money, for there were some informational pamphlets about lesbianism issued by the Civil Rights Commission. To those who saw the "display," the message was clear and appalling: feminists, homosexuals, and socialists were allied in working for passage of the ERA.

On the whole, the conference cycle did little for the feminists, but it was good for the pro-family movement. The individuals involved remembered it as a dreadful experience, however. Those I interviewed in 1980, whether Pros, Antis, or those in the middle, were unanimous in their condemnation of it.

It was a dreadful conference. The only good thing about it was that I found out that there are a lot of people all over the state who feel the same way about things that I do. (prominent Anti leader and Republican Party activist)

It took me several years to get over it. It was the worst experience of my life. (feminist member of the Coordinating Committee)

I just went to find out what it was all about. I thought I would meet a lot of neat women and talk about women's problems. And there I was in the middle of a fight! (ordinary citizen who responded to the newspaper publicity)

Conflict with an outside group can often serve to unify the members of a group. That principle could have worked for both the Antis and the Pros, but it did not for the Pros. The Pros in Oklahoma, only about one-fifth of the total registrants at the state women's conference, withdrew to another room to hold their own session, in which they vowed not to lose the spirit of cooperation that was developing at the conference. "Out of this disaster we can bring something good, if we form a strong politically active group." But it never happened. The Pro organizations competed among themselves for money and attention throughout the ERA ratification battle and became almost invisible in the state after it was over.

The Antis, on the other hand, motivated by their religious convictions, reinforced by their fellow church members, and inspired by Phyllis Schlafly's hot rhetoric and her steady stream of new issues and new ideas for promoting them, remained united and active until the ERA's final defeat. The feminists on the IWY Commission did a favor to the conservative Christians by giving them a national forum in which to air their disagreements with the feminist movement. The press, ever sensitive to charges of bias, gave them more press attention than their numbers warranted. And the Antis adroitly took advantage of the opportunities for publicity and recruitment. The conferences also served as a catalyst for the formation of coalitions among their organizations. Best of all, in an ironic way, it furnished them with a superb recruiting tool which they used to good advantage in the months following the conference.

Only two years later, the Pro-Family Coalition was doing its best to thwart the planners of another set of state conferences intended as preparation for the White House Conference on Families, explained in chapter 7. This time the coalition was augmented by other activists. A whole host of new organizations joined the fray. By 1980, the year that Ronald Reagan was elected president, the Pro-Family Coalition had attracted enough media attention to establish itself as a player in the making of domestic policy.

NOTES

1. Eagle Forum newsletter, distributed with the June 1976 *Phyllis Schlafly Report*.

2. Rosemary Thomson, *The Price of LIBerty* (Carol Stream, Ill.: Mansions 1978), p. 131.

3. National Commission on the Observance of International Women's Year, *To Form a More Perfect Union* (Washington D.C.: GPO, 1976), pp. 139–319.

4. *Oklahoma Women's Conference, Report of the Chair, Oklahoma IWY Coordinating Committee to National Commission for IWY,* 15 July 1977, pp. 32–34.

5. Thomson, *Price of LIBerty*, p. 93.

6. *Phyllis Schlafly Report* 11, no. 1 (August 1977): 3.

7. National Commission on the Observance of International Women's Year, *The Spirit of Houston* (Washington, D.C.: GPO, 1978), p. 103.

8. John M. Crewdson, "Mormon Turnout Overwhelms Women's Conference in Utah," *New York Times*, 25 July 1977.

9. From the interview with Lottie Beth Hobbs.

10. Thomson, *Price of LIBerty*, pp. 138–47.

11. Carol Barnes, "NWC Foes Termed Inspired," *Houston Post*, 21 November 1977, p. 1.

12. *Phyllis Schlafly Report* (December 1977): 2.

13. Ibid.

14. Alice Rossi, *Feminists in Politics: A Panel Analysis of the First National Women's Conference* (New York: Academic Press, 1982), p. 195.

15. Betty Friedan, *It Changed My Life: Writings on the Women's Liberation Movement* (New York: Random House, 1963), pp. 158, 373.

16. National IWY Commission, *Spirit of Houston,* p. 166.

17. Mary Lu Abbott, "Women's Factions Preparing for Fight," *Houston Chronicle,* 19 November 1977, p. 8.

18. National IWY Commission, *Spirit of Houston*, "Appendix: Exhibitors," pp. 298–99.

19. Eagle Forum newsletter, distributed with *Phyllis Schlafly Report*, January 1978.

6

PROLIFERATION AND COORDINATION IN THE 1970s

T he pro-family movement, the first phase of the Christian or Religious Right, evolved in just five years from Ann Patterson's first effort to "slow down" the Equal Rights Amendment, to the Pro-Family Coalition with organizations in almost every state and a high-profile leader, Phyllis Schlafly. By the time of the National Women's Conferences in 1977, the ERA was only one of several issues of concern to the movement. Phyllis Schlafly had always had a broader range of interests, especially national defense and foreign policy. Lottie Beth Hobbs's concern about traditional morality had not changed, but during the ERA campaign, she came to believe that feminism was only a part of a much greater threat to that morality. That greater threat was "humanism," which she understood as an anti-God atheistic philosophy being taught in public schools.

During the second set of national conferences, which will be described more fully in chapter 7 of part two, education became one of the top issues for the pro-family movement. But in the meanwhile, there had been local protests about education and a variety of other issues. These spontaneous local actions did not always attract national attention, or at least not for very long. Some of them resulted in permanent organizations, others did not, but all of them pointed to issues that would became part of the pro-family movement's agenda. During the 1970s, perhaps emboldened by the publicity about the anti-ERA and antiabortion movements, six other smaller protest movements began to call for changes in the moral climate of the nation.

ANTI-ERA AND THE RIGHT-TO-LIFE MOVEMENT

The first two protest movements were the longest lasting. While the Protestant anti-ERA movement objected to what its activists saw as government interference in family decisions, the Catholic right-to-life movement urged government control of family planning decisions. The two movements were separate at first, but eventually joined forces after about 1980.

The anti-ERA movement in 1972 was the first protest movement to call for changes in the moral climate. It was also the first to create a permanent national organization with a base of fundamentalist and conservative Christians. Just one year later, the pro-life movement came into being in opposition to another action of the national government: the Supreme Court decision in *Roe* v. *Wade*, the landmark ruling that legalized abortion. The two movements were similar in that their memberships were based in a religious communities, Protestant or Catholic. There was a difference, however. The Protestant movement did not want government interference with family decisions, while the Catholic movement wanted government prohibition of a family decision. Each of these initial protest movements resulted in a lasting social movement with several enduring organizations.

The National Catholic Bishops' Conference responded to the Supreme Court decision legalizing abortion in 1973 by renaming their existing Committee on Family Life the National Right-to-Life Committee. A few months later, the National Right-to-Life Committee voted to become independent of the Bishops' Conference, although the church continued to fund it and to provide space and equipment.[1] As the right-to-life movement developed, other right-to-life organizations were created, in some cases as a result of a leader or faction becoming disenchanted with the National Right-to-Life Committee.

At the time of the *Roe* v. *Wade* decision, the conservative Protestant fundamentalists had given little thought to abortion. But pro-life and pro-family leaders cooperated in planning for the counterrally to the National Women's Conference in Houston. The two movements, one largely Catholic and one largely Protestant, remained organizationally distinct.

HUMANISM

The third protest action for the Christian Right began in Kanawha County, West Virginia, in 1974. It focused on school curriculum, objecting to a textbook series that some parents though was too explicit about sex, while others thought it not explicit enough about patriotism. Others joined in objecting to textbooks at other locations in the nation, but because educational administration is so decentralized in the United States, they never coalesced into a major national movement. At about the same time, national legislation about education in the form of government child development programs also sparked objections. By this time, national conservative organizations, especially the Heritage Foundation, were hoping to organize a national movement about education, but were unable to do so. A mom-and-pop organization in Texas also tried to lead such a movement.

The protest against school textbooks in West Virginia foreshadowed the later Christian Right crusade against humanism. Alice Moore, the wife of a Church of Christ minister and a member of the school board in Kanawha County, West Virginia, announced her opposition to a new language arts series the board was considering for use in kindergarten through high school. She had not yet heard of humanism, but she saw the government, in the form of the local school board, as interfering with the prerogatives of parents to direct the moral training of their children. She had objected to a sex education curriculum a few years earlier; this time she objected to "nonstandard English," profanity, and a frank discussion of sexual intercourse.[2] Others joined her protest, which to her dismay soon spiraled out of control. The controversy over the books continued through much of 1974 and into 1975, escalating to window smashing, fire setting, explosions in the schools, and even shootings.

This protest, although it received national publicity, did not result in a permanent organization. The Conservative Heritage Foundation in Washington, D.C., sent a lawyer to the area and tried to jump-start an organization to deal with the issue, but it failed. A local compromise finally allowed the community to return to normalcy, although Moore was not satisfied with it. She refrained from further protest,[3] but the issue did not die.

Mel and Norma Gabler of Longview, Texas, with their own non-profit organization, Education Research Analysts, offered advice and textbook evaluations to the protesters in Kanawha County. They were ready to help with written evaluations, or even to travel to consult with local activists anywhere in the country, as they did in Kanawha County. In view of the widespread influence they had on textbooks and the number of local groups that called on them, it is probable that they could have created an action organization, but they never did. Phyllis Schlafly, however, took up the textbook issue later when she issued her own transcripts of a set of congressional hearings on textbooks.[4]

The 1971 and 1975 defeats of a child care bill in Congress as a result of a massive grassroots protest against it has already been described at length in chapter 3. It is listed here to place it in chronological context. Despite the widespread response to the bill and the massive protests that representatives and senators received about it, no permanent organization resulted on this issue either. The memorable battle cry in that protest campaign was that "government would interfere with parents' right to ask children to take out the garbage." The response against the bill was so overwhelming that it not only defeated the bill at that time, but assured that it would not come up again.

HOMOSEXUALITY

The fourth issue to inspire protests, homosexuality, first surfaced in 1977 in Florida when Anita Bryant urged the passage of the antihomosexuality initiative. Later others took up the issue in California. Bryant, a former Miss America and the TV spokeswoman for Florida orange juice, felt that she was divinely inspired to testify against an ordinance prohibiting discrimination against homosexuals in Dade County, Florida, thus firing the first shot in what became a major battle for Christian conservative organizations in later years. Christian conservatives believed that heterosexual couples and their children would be threatened if government allowed any discussion of homosexuality in schools or provided any protection specifically for homosexuals against violence or discrimination. Bryant formed an organization called Save Our Children, calling for defeat of the ordinance. In June 1977, the voters of Dade County did in fact defeat it.[5] Bryant was anathema among supporters of gay rights, but a heroine to Christian conservatives. The crowd at the Pro-Family Rally in the Houston Astrodome passed a resolution supporting Bryant after hearing a taped message from her.

If not for a tragic turn in Bryant's personal life, the traumatic breakup of her marriage, she might have become the leader of a permanent organization. She certainly had strong support among Christian conservatives. However, one of those who offered to help during her crusade in Miami was John Briggs, who in the following year put Proposition 6, an initiative making it easier to fire homosexual teachers, on the ballot in California. The proposition failed to pass, but three years later the Reverend Lou Sheldon, who had worked with Briggs, organized the Traditional Values Coalition specializing in opposing homosexuality.[6] In 1998 the coalition moved into new offices near Capitol Hill,[7] and Sheldon's daughter Andrea became its chief lobbyist.

TV PROGRAMMING

A fifth protest, organized by a Methodist minister in Tupelo, Mississippi, was the next flurry of Christian Right activity in defense of "Christian morality." Rev. Don Wildmon tried unsuccessfully to pressure television advertisers to withdraw support of television programs that he though objectionable. Wildmon looked for a TV program for his family to watch during Christmas week in 1976. Not finding anything he thought suitable for children, he asked his congregation to join in a "Turn off the TV Week." Two months later, he started the National Federation for Decency to campaign against immoral television fare. Later renamed the American Family Association, it published lists of objectionable programs and encouraged its members to write the sponsors and boycott the programs.[8]

Wildmon's protest was unique in that it targeted media corporations and advertisers rather than the government. Perhaps for that reason, the American Family Association never had high visibility in the media, although it was mentioned favorably by most of my respondents. It did succeed in persuading some advertisers to withdraw their support of certain programs, but it is not clear how much effect it had on the overall "moral tone" of television programming. It was still in operation but less visible in the year 2000, under the direction of Wildmon's son, Tim.

RACIAL SEGREGATION

The sixth protest movement opposed a government initiative to withdraw funding from private schools formed to avoid racial desegregation. In 1978 the IRS announced its intention to cancel the tax exemption of Christian schools that remained segregated. The decision was predicated on the fact that some Christian schools had originally been founded as "segregation academies." To head off the action, Bob Billings, the head of an organization called National Christian Action Coalition (NCAC), coordinated a massive letter-writing campaign augmented by television announcements on Pat Robertson's *700 Club* and Jim Bakker's *PTL Club*, and radio announcements and publications by such fundamentalists relgious personalities as James Dobson and Jerry Falwell. The campaign generated so much mail to the White House, the IRS, and congressional offices that Congress called hearings, and the IRS agreed to halt its enforcement plans.[9] This government plan was pounded so thoroughly that it was never resuscitated.

Bob Billings turned NCAC over to his son when he (the elder Billings) became executive director of the Moral Majority. Although NCAC was listed in a directory of traditionalist organizations as late as 1995,[10] it has not been especially visible. The elder Billings, who died in 1996, probably deserves recognition as a leader in the formation of the Christian school movement, however.

SOUTHERN MORALITY AGAINST GOVERNMENT INTERFERENCE

All of these protests originated from and every new organization except Right-to-Life was headquartered in the South—Miami in Florida, Kanawha County in West Virginia, Tupelo in Mississippi, Oklahoma, or Texas—or in southern California, where the culture and religion of the South had taken root after the dust-bowl migrations of the 1930s.

Of the seven protest actions, including anti-ERA, all but one were in response to some threatened or completed government action. Only Don Wildmon's National Federation for Decency had a different target; it was a protest against popular entertainment media as a source of immorality. William Bennett, a popular conservative who held several different positions in President Regan's administration including national drug czar, chairman of the National Endowment for the Humanities, and secretary of the Department of Education, was a regular speaker at national gatherings of the pro-family organizations, and also a harsh critic of the entertainment media. But neither Wildmon nor Bennett succeeded in attracting a large following. The other activists blamed the government. Although the organizations at this point were not openly partisan, their objection to big government was compatible with traditional Republican ideology.

Religious conservatives, either in a single community or as part of a national constituency, objected to all of those attempts as violations of their moral and religious beliefs. In each case, they responded with protest actions, and all of the issues involved became part of the pro-family agenda. In two cases, a constitutional amendment and a Supreme Court decision, permanent organizations resulted. One was nurtured by a skilled and experienced leader, Phyllis Schlafly. The other thrived under the sponsorship of the National Conference of Catholic Bishops.

STOP-ERA was disbanded after 1982, but Eagle Forum, its Siamese twin, remained a part of the pro-family movement. The right-to-life movement came to include organizations with no Catholic connection. Only a few of my respondents mentioned the abortion issue in the 1980 interviews, but by 1997 almost every one listed it as one of their primary concerns. The pro-family organizations themselves eventually included abortion in their lobbying efforts, radio broadcasts, publications, and direct-mail appeals.

Two protests which did not result in a permanent organization were those against the child care bill and the IRS attempt to punish segregated schools. In both of those cases, the proposals to which they objected were so overwhelmingly defeated that there have been no serious attempts to reintroduce them. During the administration of Bill Clinton, he and his wife, Hillary, convened a conference on child care, but once again there was a strong negative response to it, and it went no further. These two examples suggest that a single protest, if dramatic enough, may sometimes dispose of the issue, with no need for a long-term social movement.

The Anita Bryant campaign against antidiscrimination laws for gays is a case that falls between an ongoing social movement and a single successful protest. In the years since 1977, there have been many similar attempts to pass local or state discrimination laws applying to gays. In almost every case, some local or state organization has been mobilized, either to oppose such antidiscrimination laws or to pass a law forbidding them permanently. Some have been successful, some not. Colorado's Proposition 2, forbidding such laws, was supported by Colorado for Family Values and was approved by the voters, but was declared unconstitutional by the Supreme Court.

The issue is still very much alive in the pro-family movement, with all the major organizations opposing gay rights laws. They are particularly likely to emphasize it in direct-mail appeals for funds because it still attracts responses and contributions. Although Lou Sheldon's Traditional Values Coalition claims to be concerned about pornography and abortion as well, its direct-mail and lobbying efforts are devoted primarily to the homosexual issue. The issue is no longer purely local, since the 1992 controversy about gays in the military and the attempts in Congress to ban marriage between two persons of the same sex. The pro-family movement mobilized massive telephone and letter-writing campaigns opposing the first and urging adoption of the second of those proposals.

There is no well-known national organization with textbooks or curricular reform as its main issue, despite the efforts of the Heritage Foundation to unite the Kanawha County protest and other similar educational protests into a group called the National Congress for Educational Excellence. That organization soon dissolved because of personal conflicts among its leaders.[11] But Christian conservatives still support school reform and oppose much about public education in general. Christian conservative parents are especially upset and angered when they perceive that government-supported schools, where their children spend so many hours of the day, are undermining their own moral authority over their children. Robert Simonds's Citizens for Excellence in Education in California and Peg Luksik's National Parents' Commission in Pennsylvania are just two of the organizations active on that issue. Although neither has attracted much attention from the national media, they have succeeded in encouraging Christian conservatives to run for local school boards and to lobby state legislatures for their preferences in school curricula. The lack of powerful national organizations pushing curriculum reform may be due to the great number of local school districts and the consequent decentralization of decisions. But each time the national government proposes a regulation applying to all districts, the Christian conservatives can be counted on to oppose it.

1974: THE NEW RIGHT

While the grassroots activists organized against moral decline in local communities, a group of Washington, D.C.–based conservatives began to build an infrastructure for conservatism they called the New Right. It differed from the pro-family movement in that it focused on research and advocacy of conservative ideas, coordination of other organizations, and electoral politics. The leaders of the New Right facilitated issue-oriented action by others, rather than directing it themselves.

The acknowledged leader of the New Right was Paul Weyrich, a sometime journalist who came to Washington in 1966 as an aide to Sen. Gordon Allott (R-Colo.). Weyrich was not a southerner, but had grown up in Wisconsin. He was a master of strategy, anticipating what conservatism would need in the long run, beyond the immediate tasks of campaigning or governing. After watching liberals in action, Weyrich concluded that the secret of their success was coordination among their various groups. He was able to persuade Joseph Coors, the beer magnate from Colorado, to fund his ideas. His first project was to found the Heritage Foundation in 1973 as a tax-exempt think tank to develop conservative policies. In 1974 he founded the Committee for the Survival of a Free Congress to encourage and train conservative Republican candidates. As it took more of his time, Ed Feulner, who had been a trustee of Heritage, became its head.

Just as Phyllis Schlafly, who was eighteen years older than Weyrich, had roots in the old anticommunist Right, Weyrich and his colleagues had roots in Young Americans for Freedom (YAF), which in turn, had been founded by William F. Buckley Jr. in 1960 as a way of training young conservatives who would be future leaders. In 1975 when journalist Kevin Phillips first used the term "New Right," he meant to differentiate their movement from the Old Right.[12] Both Schlafly and Weyrich were devout Catholics, but unlike the conservative Protestants that Schlafly welcomed into the pro-family movement, the New Right did not focus on moral decline, at least not at first. That emphasis came from those in the anti-ERA organizations, and later from Jerry Falwell and James Dobson.

Paul Weyrich is sometimes called the "father" of the Christian Right. Here he is shown beside a display advertising National Empowerment Television, his cable television outlet for conservative causes and ideas. (*Joseph Conn/Church and State*)

The Heritage Foundation publishes papers on economic issues like taxation and regulation, and also on family issues. In 1975 Weyrich hired Connie Marshner, another veteran of YAF, as education director at the Heritage Foundation. In 1979 she joined the Committee for the Survival of a Free Congress (CSFC) because of her interest in education issues. She chaired the Pro-Family Coalition at the White House Conference on Families, but left the CFSC in 1983 to spend more time with her own family.

In the early days of CSFC, when its main activity was to support candidates, it supported only challengers, not incumbents, on the grounds that incumbents ought to be able to take care of themselves. Free Congress support went beyond the usual campaign contributions, providing its protégés with rigorous training courses on campaign techniques and tactics. Weyrich himself conducted the early training sessions. After Connie Marshner became a staffer at Free Congress, she joined him in the "seminars," as they were called. I heard them at a rally in Dallas, where they joked that they had appeared together so often that people thought they were husband and wife.

Weyrich also tried on several occasions to form a coordinating structure for all of conservatism encompassing all the various issues, organizations, and movements. He invited Phyllis Schlafly and Lottie Beth Hobbs to join one of these, the Council for National Policy, as representatives of the pro-family movement. Hobbs soon resigned because she felt that little was being accomplished, but Phyllis Schlafly remained a member.

Other New Right attempts at coordination were the Conservative Caucus and the Religious Roundtable. Howard Phillips, a Harvard graduate and a Jew, had been an ardent right-winger in his student days, had worked in the Nixon administration, then registered Independent, then Democrat, and finally became the candidate of the Taxpayers' Party. During his Republican phase in 1974, he was chairman of the Conservative Caucus, possibly the first attempt to coordinate the various local conservative protest groups around the country.

Ed McAteer was a marketing specialist at Colgate-Palmolive and a prominent Baptist layman who joined the Christian Freedom Foundation and then worked with Phillips at Conservative Caucus. In 1979 he organized the Religious Roundtable, intending to sponsor a series of briefings to educate both laymen and pastors about the threat of secular humanism. Like so many others, he hoped to bring the political moralists and the religious conservatives together in a common enterprise. He did not succeed in that goal, but he did have one moment of glory when Ronald Reagan appeared at the National Affairs Briefing for conservatives in Dallas during the 1980 presidential campaign and made his famous comment: "I know you can't endorse me, but I endorse you."

The Council for National Policy, the only coordinating organization that survived into the new millennium, tries to avoid publicity. It hires guards to keep nonmembers away from its meetings, but enterprising reporters who hang around the meeting rooms, especially Skipp Porteus of the Institute for First Amendment Studies, have managed to learn a few things about it.[13] One of its most important functions may be managing financial resources, for it includes representatives of some of conservatism's wealthiest foundations.

SOURCES OF FUNDS

By 1997, after the CFSC had created its own foundation in addition to the Heritage Foundation, the two foundations created by Weyrich were among the top five conservative think tanks, receiving funding from various other foundations based on corporate fortunes. The favored think tanks of Richard Mellon Scaife and the Bradley, Olin, and Koch families were the conduit for the "funding stream that currently supports the conservative policy infrastructure."[14]

Richard Viguerie of the New Right was responsible for the successful development of another source of funds. He took the new and relatively unsophisticated technology of direct mail and perfected it as a way of bringing in small contributions from a large base of donors. His contribution to the conservative infrastructure was well timed because the campaign finance laws of 1974 limited the amount of money large donors could contribute to candidates. He was so successful that Republicans quickly surpassed Democrats in bringing in small contributions, although Democrats had always boasted of depending on the "little people."

Viguerie's database of 25,000 names started with the 1964 Goldwater campaign list.[15] The technology was eventually adopted by the Democrats as well, but Republicans had a head start of several years. Viguerie's innovation was to include notations in the computerized database about the particular appeals that appalled each person sufficiently to bring a response. With that information, the mail could be more precisely targeted.

Direct mail requires a heavy dose of appalling examples to convince recipients of a threat great enough to justify loosening their purse strings. The language in direct mail is always more heated than that in the regular periodical literature from the Christian conservative organizations. In turn, the organizations opposing the Christian Right must turn up the heat in *their* direct mail. This use of rhetorical weapons of mass destruction gives credence to the assertion of some politicians and even some noncombatant observers that Americans are in the midst of a "culture war."[16]

Direct-mail technology, which was fairly new in the 1970s, is one of the factors in the success of the pro-family movement and the Christian Right, but the new technology may have passed its peak sometime during the 1990s. My respondents, all of whom were receiving mail from several different organizations, were getting tired of it by 1997, as were other citizens who were not Christian conservatives. I was receiving it myself, and I noticed that the frequency of mailings began to decline in 1999. It may be that the new "hot" technology will be the Internet.

Weyrich's organizations were among Viguerie's clients, and for a time they prospered together. But Viguerie was forced to declare bankruptcy when his clients discovered that his company's percentage of the take was unacceptably large, and began to withdraw from their contracts with him.[17] He then gravitated to other conservative organizations and even started one of his own. It is the Seniors Coalition, which seems to exist only to raise money, having no visible program, doing so with regular warnings of possible catastrophe in the Social Security system.[18]

By 1979 Weyrich and his colleagues had created a direct-mail business and a tax-exempt research foundation, and had made several attempts to create coordinating structures for all of conservatism. The success of their efforts should be measured by the long-term impact of their fund-raising, think-tank products, and candidate training, rather than by the action or coordinating organizations they helped create, most of which were short-lived.

THE MAP OF MODERN CONSERVATISM

Jerome Himmelstein,[19] another analyst of conservative movements, sees the entire spectrum of conservative activity as a single social movement, encompassing the old John Birch Society, Christian Anti-Communism Crusade, other organizations of the Old Right as well as the New Right, and all the organizations discussed in this book. But Weyrich himself, as well as Alan Crawford and Kevin Phillips, others who were involved in the New Right in the early years, all claimed that the new conservatism was different from the old in that it was more populist and less intellectual.[20]

The New Right was not the first manifestation of the Christian Right, although some have claimed that it was, usually because of its role in encouraging the formation of the Moral Majority.[21] That role was consistent with the New Right's function of facilitating all kinds of organizations to advance the cause of conservatism, and it came seven years after the beginning of the anti-ERA campaign.

Although Weyrich himself was a religious conservative, he and his colleagues did not at first focus on the moral issues. The New Right facilitated both economic and social conservatism. Its member organizations were able to support candidates, something which the religion-based organizations could not do unless they gave up their tax-exempt status. When Phyllis Schlafly began working with Christian conservatives to defeat the ERA, Weyrich thought she was "on a fool's errand." He did not disagree with her, but thought it was a hopeless quest.[22] He soon recognized the political potential of the Christian conservatives mobilized against the ERA, however, and Connie Marshner of his staff began working with them in 1979.[23]

Like a river system fed by tributaries, the Christian Right began in the 1970s as several different conservative social movements. The earliest of the Christian Right movements, or streams, to attract a grassroots constituency and to make an impact on government policy was the pro-family movement; the second was the pro-life movement. Along with the Christian Right river system, another river system centered on economic issues, but the two have remained independent, despite some attempts to join them.

The conservative infrastructure that was the New Right supported both economic conservatism, libertarian and free-market policies, and social conservatism, the moral agenda of the Christian Right. For instance, the New Right's Heritage Foundation published position papers on economic policy, and Weyrich encouraged Jerry Falwell to found the Moral Majority. But the prickly relationship between the social-issues conservatives of the Christian Right and economic conservatives of the free-market right continued to plague the Republican Party as it sought to unite them in a quest for electoral victories. Not until the 2000 election were they able to submerge their differences in a united campaign for George W. Bush.

The anti-ERA campaign and the pro-family movement, the early stages of the Christian Right, were interesting to observe because they had not yet settled into a predictable routine. New leaders, even those with no previous experience, can make a noticeable impact; it is an exciting time for them. Because a new movement does not yet have credibility in the political system, it is forced to devise unexpected strategies to get attention. In the television age, getting space on the evening news is essential. Phyllis Schlafly's charismatic leadership style was well suited to the early stages of a movement. But as the newness wears off, there is a tendency for movements to become more bureaucratic—to replace the innovative strategies with formalized procedures and to replace enthusiastic volunteers with paid professionals. At some point, the political arms of the movement begin to resemble other interest groups as they try to secure support for their agenda in state legislatures and in the three branches of the national government: the Congress, the presidency, and the Supreme Court.

NOTES

1. Dallas Blanchard, *The Anti-Abortion Movement: References and Resources* (New York: Prentice-Hall, 1996); Connie Paige, *The Right to Lifers, Who They Are, How They Operate, Where They Get Their Money* (New York: Summit Books, 1983).

2. William C. Martin, *With God on Our Side* (New York: Broadway Books, 1996), pp. 119–23.

3. James Moffett, *Storm in the Mountains* (Carbondale: Southern Illinois University Press, 1982).

4. Phyllis Schlafly, ed., *Child Abuse in the Classroom* (Alton, Ill.: Pere Marquette, 1984).

5. B. Drummond Ayres Jr., "Miami Votes 2 to 1 to Repeal Law Barring Bias against Homosexuals," *New York Times,* 9 June 1977, A1.

6. David W. Dunlap, "Minister Brings Anti-Gay Message to the Spotlight," *New York Times*, 19 December 1994.

7. *Traditional Values Coalition Report* 16, no. 1 (summer 1998).

8. Tim Stafford, "Taking on TV's Bad Boys," *Christianity Today*, 19 August 1991.

9. Martin, *God on Our Side*, p. 172.

10. Robert W. Klous, ed., *The Traditional Values in Action Resource Directory* (Lynchburg, Va.: Christian Values in Action Coalition, 1995).

11. Alan Crawford, *Thunder on the Right* (New York: Pantheon Books, 1980), p. 38.

12. Richard A. Viguerie, *The New Right: We're Ready to Lead* (Falls Church, Va.: Viguerie Company, 1981), p. 53.

13. Edward Ericson Jr., "Behind Closed Doors at the CNP," reprinted from *Orlando Weekly* in *Church and State* 49, no. 6 (June 1996): 4; Jim Yardley, "Bush's Words to Staunchly Conservative Group Remain a Mystery," *New York Times*, 19 May 2000, A20. For funding of the conservative organizations, see Jean Stefancic and Richard Delgado, *No Mercy: How Conservative Think Tanks and Foundations Changed America's Social Agenda* (Philadelphia: Temple University Press, 1996).

14. David Callahan, *$1 Billion for Ideas: Conservative Think Tanks in the 1990s* (Washington, D.C.: National Committee for Responsive Philanthropy, 1999).

15. Crawford, *Thunder on the Right*, p. 48.

16. James D. Hunter, *Culture Wars* (New York: Basic Books, 1991). The theme was picked up by Pat Buchanan at the 1992 Republican National Convention. For another point of view see Christian Smith, et al., "The Myth of Culture Wars: The Case of American Protestantism" chap. 9 in *Cultural Wars in American Politics*, Rhys Williams, ed. (New York: Aldine deGruyter, 1997).

17. Ben A. Franklin, "Money Magic to Money Misery" *New York Times*, 14 January 1986.

18. Erik Eckholm, "Alarmed by Fund-Raiser, the Elderly Give Millions," *New York Times*, 12 November 1992, A1.

19. Jerome Himmelstein, *To the Right: The Transformation of American Conservatism* (Berkeley: University of California Press, 1990), chap. 3.

20. Paul Weyrich, "Blue-Collar or Blue Blood: The New Right Compared with the Old Right," in *The New Right Papers*, R. W. Whittaker (New York: St. Martin's, 1982); Kevin Phillips, *Post-Conservative America* (New York: Vintage, 1982), pp. 31–52; Crawford, *Thunder on the Right*.

21. Robert C. Liebman, "Mobilizing the Moral Majority," chap. 3 in *The New Christian Right*, Robert C. Liebman and Robert Wuthnow (New York: Aldine, 1983); Richard V. Pierard, "Religion and the 1984 Election Campaign," *Review of Religious Research* 27, no. 2 (December 1985): 98–114; Kenneth D. Wald, *Religion and Politics in the United States* (New York: St. Martin's, 1987); Clyde Wilcox, *God's Warriors* (Baltimore: Johns Hopkins, 1992); Matthew C. Moen, *The Transformation of the Christian Right* (Tuscaloosa, Ala.: University of Alabama Press, 1992); Michael Lienesch, "The Origins of the Christian Right: Early Fundamentalism as a Political Movement," chap. 1 in *Sojourners in the Wilderness*, Corwin E. Smidt and James M. Penning (Lanham, Md.: Rowman and Littlefield, 1997).

22. Interview with Paul Weyrich, Washington, D.C., 18 September 1996.

23. Connaught (Connie) Marshner edited the CSFC's Family Protection Report and was chairman of the Pro-Family Coalition for the 1979 White House Conference on Families. Rosemary Thomson, *Withstanding Humanism's Challenge to Families* (Morton, Ill.: Traditional Publications, 1981), p. 22; Martin, *God on Our Side*, p. 175.

PART II

"CHRISTIAN NATION"

RESTORING THE VISION
OF THE FOUNDERS

The story of the Christian Right in part two, therefore, is the story of nationally based bureaucratic organizations in transition. Although they had local affiliates, the national level drew more media attention and had more influence on local activity. But first there was the transitional year of 1979. In that year, the White House Conference on Families attracted the attention of new organizational entrepreneurs. New organizations were created, although many had relatively short lives. The 1980s were a time for the new organizations to sort themselves out. Individuals moved from one to another as they sought their niche in the crusade. Political strategies pioneered by one organization were later picked up by others. By the end of the 1990s, the movement was more centralized and bureaucratized, and the focus was more clearly on attempts to redirect the legal interpretation of the religion clauses of the First Amendment.

7

THE WHITE HOUSE CONFERENCE ON FAMILIES

The peak year for creation of new organizations in the pro-family movement was 1979. By the end of that year, the transition between the first antifeminist phase of the movement and the second anti-secularist Christian America phase had begun. The prospects for ratification of the Equal Rights Amendment were dim, but in 1979 Congress allowed an unprecedented extension of the ratification deadline for another three years and six months because the decline had not been included in the original submission of the amendment.

The national Pro-Family Coalition was gearing up for a second set of state and national conferences, the White House Conference on Families. Paul Weyrich appointed a staff member, Connie Marshner, to work with them in the Pro-Family Coalition, with Tim and Beverly LaHaye, a California fundamentalist pastor and his wife, as honorary cochairpersons. Two new organizations became part of the pro-family movement as a result of their founders having been involved in the White House Conference. One was Beverly LaHaye's Concerned Women for America; the other was James Dobson's Focus on the Family.

The Oklahoma City newspaper cartoon showed the ERA as a bride left waiting at the church after the failure of the state legislature to ratify the Equal Rights Amendment. (*Copyright 1979, the Daily Oklahoman*)

WHITE HOUSE CONFERENCE ON FAMILIES

During the 1976 presidential campaign, Jimmy Carter had promised a Catholic audience that his administration would sponsor a White House Conference on Marriage and the Family. In fact, there were three White House conferences during Carter's four-year term. Two more conferences planned by his administration took place in 1981, after Ronald Reagan had become president. But because of the contentious atmosphere at some of these conferences, Reagan was unwilling to call any more during his presidency.

The controversy surrounding the White House conferences was partly due to the inherent contradictions of the White House conference format. The first and most basic contradiction is that, although they were promoted as being open to everyone, they were nevertheless called at the behest of a particular interest group, and that interest group expected to dominate them. In earlier conferences, it had been a "win-win" situation; the interest group had a showcase for its agenda, and the president gained the goodwill of the interest group.

For example, until the 1960s the decennial White House Conferences on Children and on Aging had been dominated by the social work establishment. But after that, the vocal and increasingly politicized organizations of minorities and other interest groups began to challenge the social workers' "prescriptions for treatment," and by 1980 the outcomes pleased no one.

Early in the planning process for the 1979–1980 Conferences on Families, three different groups had organized coalitions to demand representation. There was a broad coalition of social service agencies, the traditional constituency of White House conferences. There was also a Catholic coalition, representing those to whom Carter had first promised the conference, and there was the Health, Education, and Welfare Department's coalition of black groups, which demanded that at least 30 percent of the National Advisory Committee and staff be African American. In addition, there was the Pro-Family Coalition, organized in 1977 for the National Women's Conference, and now augmented by Weyrich's group.

Phyllis Schlafly, who had been so visible in mobilizing opposition to the 1977 women's conferences, said relatively little about the White House Conference on Families. She delegated one of her Illinois colleagues, Rosemary Thomson, to coordinate Eagle Forum's activities at the White House conferences, and to serve as liaison with the National Pro-Family Coalition.

Connie Marshner, the New Right specialist on family issues and director of the Family Policy Institute at Paul Weyrich's Free Congress Research and Education Foundation, was to be chairman of the Pro-Family Coalition. She was doing what Weyrich had envisioned for the New Right: coordinating and facilitating conservative organizations. Tim and Beverly LaHaye, well known among fundamentalists and evangelicals—the larger category of conservative Protestants of which fundamentalists are the most conservative component—agreed to serve as honorary cochairs. The Reverend Mr. LaHaye was pastor of the large Scott Memorial Baptist Church of San Diego.

First of all, the Pro-Family Coalition objected to the proposed name—White House Conference on Families. According to the planners, the word "Families" in the title had been chosen to recognize the diversity of family types—divorced and widowed parents, as well as two-parent families, employed as well as stay-at-home housewives and mothers, young as well as old families, and minority as well as majority families.[1] Conservatives protested that "diversity" was in reality a code word for homosexual couples. From their point of view, the government was deliberately downgrading the only kind of family that was approved by the Bible. In response, the planners left the term undefined, but did not actually remove it from the title. The coalition was not to be so easily put off. They held out for their own definition: families are "persons who are related by heterosexual marriage, blood, or adoption."[2]

After numerous delays occasioned by the disagreement among various interested groups, the National Advisory Commission began work in 1978 with a membership that was 30 percent minority, although not 30 percent African American. The Pro-Family Coalition objected that there was only one avowedly "pro-family" representative, and she (Barbara Smith, president of the Mormon Relief Society) was counterbalanced by Eleanor Smeal, president of the National Organization for Women (NOW). Further, half of the commission members represented minority groups or social work agencies that might be expected to favor expanded government services, the very thing the pro-family coalition opposed.

The commission hoped to avoid further controversy, or at least to avoid a national media spotlight on it, by scheduling three regional conferences instead of one large national one. A committee would compile the final report from the results of the three conferences, which because of the organizational delays, would not be held until the summer of 1980. The so-called White House Conference on Families was actually to be a whole series of conferences, the fifty state conferences in 1979 and the three regional conferences in 1980. Unfortunately for the committee, having to choose three conference locations meant three more controversial decisions.

Coretta Scott King suggested that one of the regional conferences be held in the South, perhaps in her home city of Atlanta, in President Jimmy Carter's home state. But feminists on the commission insisted that Georgia be rejected because of its failure to ratify the Equal Rights Amendment. The centrally located cities of Chicago in Illinois and St. Louis in Missouri were out of the question for the same reason. The conferences were finally scheduled in Minneapolis, Baltimore, and Los Angeles, with vertical regional boundaries instead of the more usual North, South, and West divisions. This meant that the southern and western regions, where the pro-family movement was strongest, were divided among the three conferences, potentially diluting their impact.

The decisions, bowing to NOW's boycott in locating the conferences, splitting of the South, and the presence of the NOW president, were taken by the Pro-Family Coalition as evidence that the "anti-family" forces of the feminist movement were to have undue influence on the conferences. Meanwhile, the social workers who had dominated such conferences in the past were to be allowed no more than half the delegates.

The conferences were advertised as an opportunity for ordinary people from all walks of life, all ethnic and racial groups, and all income levels to come and speak out about families. Previous White House conferences could claim legitimacy on that basis without actually having to put it into practice, because ordinary people, with few exceptions, do not respond to such general invitations. As long as the interest group dominating the conference is the only one that makes a real effort to mobilize its members, there is little danger of its being challenged by another group. But in this case, large numbers of pro-family participants exposed the contradiction between rhetoric and practice.

The method of delegate selection was still another contradictory aspect of the conferences. In earlier conferences, delegates had been appointed directly by the president, following the advice of the relevant interest group. But by the end of the 1970s, there was pressure for a more democratic process, and also pressure to have more diverse delegations, goals which were not necessarily compatible.

The White House Conference on Families guidelines called for 30 percent of each state's delegates to the regional conferences to be appointed by the state's governor as a means of ensuring representation of all points of view. But to preserve the appearance of democracy, a minimum of 30 percent and a maximum of 70 percent could be elected. The most common solution to this mathematical puzzle, adopted in twenty-three states, was to elect one-third, and to have the governor and the state committee each appoint one-third. Only in Virginia did the state conference elect the maximum 70 percent of the delegates. Pro-family delegates won all the seats in that state, as they did in other states where seats were filled by election.

The Pro-Family Coalition charged that the twenty-three states electing only the minimum one-third were attempting to dilute the impact of the "real pro-family people of America" on the regional conferences. Kansas and Texas devised the ultimate conflict-avoidance strategy by choosing one-third of their delegates in a random drawing from among those who had sent in applications. The pro-family groups were able to win under this procedure as well, simply by encouraging large numbers of their adherents to submit applications.

The format of the White House conferences, chosen to reduce confrontation, also reduced the likelihood of attention from the national news media. Further, these conferences seemed at first glance to be merely a repetition of the state women's conferences, and thus less worthy of intensive scrutiny. They were significant, however, as an indication of the extent to which the pro-family movement had become nationalized, and as a glimpse of the issues that the pro-family movement would concentrate on in the future. The Oklahoma White House conference was typical of those held in states with strong pro-family organizations.

THE OKLAHOMA WHITE HOUSE CONFERENCE, 1979

Anti-ERA activists were in a heightened state of alert, expecting the Pros to pull the same "tricks" that they had in the previous set of conferences. The preliminary decisions at the national level did nothing to allay their suspicions. The coalition saw to it that its representatives in all the states knew as much about conference plans and procedures as did the state officials themselves. Taking advantage of the public meeting laws, pro-family representatives attended all the planning meetings and objected to almost every detail of the plans. Nothing escaped their notice, for they had copies of the national guidelines.

On the other hand, the director of the Oklahoma White House Conference on Families knew nothing about the earlier Oklahoma Women's Conference. She said later that if she had, she would never have accepted the job of directing the White House conference. But some of the committee members who had been involved in the women's conference knew about it all too well; the rules reflected the experience of that conference. Only at the opening and closing sessions would all conferees come together in one room. Those sessions would be tightly scheduled. No one who was not on the announced schedule would be allowed to speak. There would be no formal "resolutions." The conference report would simply summarize what was said in individual workshop meetings.

When the committee announced that the conference would be held in early December 1979, in the same city and the same building as the earlier women's conference, the pro-family leaders immediately sent one thousand letters to their mailing list, warning their readers that the state White House conference would be just like the IWY Conference. They saw reflections of the IWY Conference in every move of the committee. They charged that the conference had been scheduled in the middle of a week and only twelve days before Christmas on purpose to hold down the attendance of pro-family members, that the voting procedures had been devised to prevent a democratic election, that the $5 registration fee would be used to promote feminist causes, and that the "other side" had booked up all the hotels in advance so that pro-family supporters would not be able to attend.

The coordinating committee of the conference had arranged for newspaper announcements, a mailing to member churches of the Oklahoma Conference of Churches, and another mailing to voluntary organizations throughout the state. The Conference of Churches was generally thought to be the home of the liberal churches. The fundamentalist churches to which most members of the pro-family movement belonged did not agree with its theology and had not joined it. But the most effective recruitment for the conference was done by the pro-family organizations, with two mailings and the distribution of another audiotape.

An analysis of a random sample of the 849 persons who signed legible registration cards for the conference showed that about 45 percent were recruited to the conference by pro-family organizations or by churches sympathetic to the pro-family movement. Twenty-three percent were members of the "helping" professions: social workers, school teachers, state university extension personnel, or employees of agencies serving Indians or blacks.[3]

Pro-family activists complained that these public employees were able to come in such large numbers because they were allowed to take leave for the conference. While this was true, it was also true that they were allowed only a certain number of days of leave per year; the day that they spent at the conference was a day that would not be available for other purposes. The remainder of those attending were university faculty or students; represented community organizations such as Junior League, PTA, or Church Women United; or were helping with the conference as moderators, resource persons, or recorders. Almost none came in response to the general invitations.

When registration opened, the pro-family groups, with their literature, were in business near the end of the registration line, although conference rules forbade exhibit tables or distribution of literature. But Young Americans for Freedom, a registered student organization of conservatives, allowed the Antis to use their existing table permit. At the table, pro-family delegates could sign a petition opposing the ERA, consult a list of homes and church basements where they could spend the night, and obtain a copy of instruction sheets detailing the rules for nominations and balloting. They were instructed to follow the lead of pro-family leaders in each workshop, who would be wearing a SAVE THE FAMILY button with a red ribbon attached. Each instruction sheet was coded for certain workshops so that pro-family groups would be distributed among all of them.

The tightly controlled format prevented confrontation. The careful planning of the pro-family leaders prevented confusion. But there was also very little real dialogue, which some of the participants had hoped for. Most workshops were so large that there was just time for each person to make one comment, but no opportunity to respond to anyone else.

The emphasis of the White House conference was not on feminist issues, despite the fears of the pro-family organizations. In Oklahoma at least, the feminists had almost nothing to do with it. Without the feminists, the social workers and teachers were the only identifiable groups left to bear the brunt of pro-family hostility. The first comment in many of the workshops was a question: "How many of you in here are teachers or social workers, or employed by the government, and how many are representing families?" Protests from the professionals that they were also wives, mothers, and grandmothers were ignored.

As a matter of fact, many of the professionals would have agreed with pro-family positions on the issues if a vote had been taken. When I distributed a questionnaire to a random sample of the conferees after the conference, I found that, although only about half of them were consciously allied with the pro-family movement, agreement with pro-family positions ranged from 35 to 94 percent, and was above 50 percent on most issues. When I showed the results of this survey to pro-family leaders, they refused to believe it. They continued to insist that the "libs" had dominated the conference, and that their views had been shut out, both at the conference and in the written report.

Although the Report of the Oklahoma White House Conference did not rank issues, and there were no separate issue votes to indicate their relative strength, a simple count of the 229 statements in the report showed that 87, or 38 percent, embodied the pro-family or conservative philosophy of limited government, local initiative, and moral responsibility. The wording was milder than that found in the conference transcripts, but the ideas were there. Some examples were:

- No program changes which force women to work outside the home.
- A return to the principles and practices of Judeo-Christian ethic would foster caring for low-income people at local levels, eliminating the need for many federal programs.
- Parents must be consulted before any contraceptive or abortion counseling is available to minors.
- Inheritance tax should be abolished.
- Abstinence from all addictive substances, including tobacco, should be a part of (drug) rehabilitation programs.
- Educational programs should emphasize abstinence from sexual activities and not a "do your own thing" permissive attitude.[4]

There were only 38 statements, or 16.6 percent of the total, that represented the "liberal" view of greater government involvement. Examples were:

- Individuals should be free to decide whether to participate in family planning educational programs or services.
- Recommend incentives be provided to corporations to provide day care for employees' children.

And finally, 104 of the 229 statements, or 45 percent, could not be classified as either "pro-family" or "liberal." These statements called for evaluation or study, without indicating what goals should guide the evaluation, or called for families to spend more time together, a program with which both ideological groups could agree. Examples were:

- Examine government regulations for their effect on the economy and families with attention to farming and small business and to families with one parent only.
- Parents should become more involved with the education of their children.
- Parent/citizens should become more knowledgeable about existing programs and become involved in planning, implementation, and evaluation.

THE NATIONAL CONFERENCES, 1980

The Pro-Family Coalition was able to secure all or most of the elected delegates in nine state conferences, and in two of the lotteries.[5] That did not stop them from objecting to the eventual outcome, however, because so many of the states appointed more than two-thirds of the delegates. Unable to control the delegations, their only recourse was the one in which they were by now well versed: accusing the conference planners of violating the consensual rules of fair play and majority rule. In order to dramatize their cause, there was a confrontation of sorts at each of the regional conferences, held in June and July 1980.

In Baltimore, where pro-family delegates numbered about 40 out of nearly 700 delegates, Connie Marshner led a walkout in a dispute over the conference voting procedure. Following the style of the state conferences, the regional conference was to be divided into small work groups, each of which would vote and recommend three priority issues in its topic area. Intermediate-size groups voted on these proposals. Finally, the resolutions that had survived the first two stages were voted on by the entire conference membership. If the pro-family delegates had not walked out during the final vote, a multitopic resolution supporting access to abortion and family planning, ratification of the ERA, and elimination of discrimination based on sexual preference would have been defeated. The thirty pro-family delegates would surely have voted against this resolution, but without them, it was approved by just one vote.[6]

In Minneapolis, there were about 150 pro-family delegates, most of them elected, out of more than 500 altogether. In that conference, the conservatives' strategy was to request that voting figures be tabulated separately for elected and appointed delegates. They wanted to demonstrate that the pro-family positions were supported by the majority of the elected delegates. When their motion was defeated, pro-family delegates called for an "elected delegate caucus" and voted on all resolutions, then announced to the press the differences between their votes and the votes of the whole conference.[7]

The Los Angeles conference, with only about 50 pro-family delegates out of more than 500, nevertheless produced a report which, on the face of it, seemed to be less offensive to pro-family delegates than the reports of the other conferences. But to call attention to the lack of elected delegates and to the content of some of the resolutions, the pro-family delegates tore up their ballots in the final session and placed them at the foot of the flag in a symbolic protest.[8]

In all three conferences, the pro-family delegates chose symbolic protest when it was clear that they could not significantly impact the actual results, although in Baltimore they might have. The pro-family movement also took advantage of the media coverage of the regional conferences by staging alternate conferences at the same time in both Baltimore and Los Angeles, just as they had in Houston at the time of the National Women's Conference.

The final report of the White House Conference on Families listed the top twenty resolutions in terms of support at all three conferences. For the pro-family activists, the real problem was that it was not their agenda. Although the conservatives did not actually object to most of the goals embodied in the resolutions, they did not consider them important. On the other hand, none of the items that were important to them—opposition to the "hot-button" issues of homosexuality, abortion, the ERA, or federalized child care—appeared among the top twenty, although they did receive healthy margins of support.

The resolutions were couched in the vague language generally found in such reports, but there were at least eight that pro-family activists would probably have approved. They called for prevention of drug abuse, curbing media violence, and tax policies benefiting women who stay home and families caring for their elderly persons. Another five resolutions embodied goals the conservatives would have approved—but they did not envision government action—and the rest were on topics in which the pro-family movement had no particular interest.

On the whole, it was not a report that they would have written. Their efforts did not significantly affect the outcome of the conference, and they did not really expect them to when they began their monitoring efforts. Rosemary Thomson understood the situation well when she first began working with the Pro-Family Coalition, for she noted at one of the early meetings:

> Whether we win most of the delegates . . . or not, we win, nevertheless, because . . . they will be ready to register to vote, work for, and elect pro-family candidates next November.[9]

Her prediction came true when President Ronald Reagan was elected a few months later, in November 1980, along with a Republican majority in the Senate. That Don Nickles of Oklahoma was elected to the Senate surprised most observers in the state. No one had expected the obscure young state legislator to beat a popular prosecutor from Tulsa, and by a margin of almost ten percentage points at that. If they had sat in on my interviews, they might not have been so surprised, for almost everyone I interviewed during that autumn was working full time for Nickles. Several respondents put off their interviews with me until after the election because they were so busy campaigning. Mary and Ellen Weber had themselves made 3,107 campaign visits.

THE CONFERENCE CYCLES IN RETROSPECT

The first conference cycle, the state and National Women's Conferences, resulted in a direct confrontation in a very public setting between feminists and their opponents in the ERA campaign. Even as late as 1977, despite the trouble they were having in getting ratifications for ERA, most feminists believed that they represented the majority of Americans. They had the support of the national media, and polls showed that a narrow majority of Americans favored the ERA. They were confident that direct dialogue with their opponents would be a means of finding common ground on at least some of the issues. The Christian conservatives, on the other hand, were suspicious from the beginning, and the conferences only added to their suspicion. There was very little real dialogue, and they felt that they were not taken seriously.

The second conference cycle was not planned by feminists, and its agenda was broader. Potentially at least, there was more consensus between the two groups on general family issues than on women's rights. But the emotions generated by the first set of conferences inevitably colored the second, and the angry confrontations of the first influenced the procedures of the second, making them even less conducive to true dialogue.

With figurative chips on their shoulders, the Christian conservatives could not recognize the extent to which other participants were sympathetic to their views. For them, it was all or nothing. Their intransigence added to other participant's negative view of their movement. Perhaps the hope for dialogue was a vain one, but as it was, each side went away more convinced than before that their opponents were wrong and misguided, even evil.

Throughout the ERA ratification fight and the two national conferences, pro-family conservatives saw their chief enemies as "the libs and the fems." Perhaps the most important effect of the conferences was that national media coverage of the two conferences brought the conflict between two ways of seeing the family, women's roles, and the role of government into the nation's living rooms. Both sides attracted more grassroots activists as a result.

By the end of 1979, conservatives were creating new organizations at a dizzying rate and organizing more conferences and rallies. No one was checking credentials at these events; anyone who paid the entrance fee would have been welcome, but the only outsiders were reporters for the news media and researchers like me. The formats were unlike those of the two government-sponsored conferences. If there were "workshops" or "discussion groups," they were only to give tips on lobbying and campaigning. The main business was a series of speeches. There were no more direct confrontations. In view of the bitterness at the 1977 and 1979 conferences, this was probably just as well.

NOTES

1. Rosemary Thomson, *Withstanding Humanism's Challenge to Families: An Anatomy of a White House Conference* (Morton, Ill.: Traditional Publications, 1981), pp. 38–48.

2. *Phyllis Schlafly Report* 13, no. 10 (May 1980): Sec. 2. p. 4.

3. From analysis of a random sample taken from the registration list for the conference.

4. *White House Conference on Families: Focus on Oklahoma* (Oklahoma State Steering Committee for WHCF, December 1979).

5. They won the elections in Arkansas, Illinois, Michigan, Massachusetts, New Hampshire, Virginia, Nebraska, Oklahoma, South Dakota, and the lotteries in California and Texas.

6. *Listening to America's Families: A Summary for the Report to the President, Congress and Families of the Nation* (Washington, D.C.: White House Conference on Families, 1980), pp. 75, 90, 91.

7. Thomson, *Humanism's Challenge,* p. 104.

8. Russell Chandler, "Conference on Families Endorses ERA," *Los Angeles Times,* 13 July 1980, 3.

9. Thomson, *Humanism's Challenge*, p. 9.

8

JERRY FALWELL AND OTHER BAPTISTS

Jerry Falwell, born in the depths of the Great Depression in 1933, attended Baptist schools and was ordained a Baptist minister. He founded the Thomas Road Baptist Church in 1956 in his home town of Lynchburg, Virginia, beginning with a congregation of thirty-five members. Within twenty years, he was host of a television program, pastor of a church of 16,000—the largest in the nation according to *Conservative Digest*[1]—principal of an elementary school and president of his own Liberty Baptist College, later to become Liberty University.

After creating the same kinds of religious and educational institutions that other churches before him had produced, Falwell broke with the tradition of his fundamentalist upbringing. He admitted in his autobiography that it had been difficult for him to think of working with other churches and of being involved in politics.[2] He had been taught that "being 'yoked with unbelievers' for any cause was off limits." Therefore, he faced "a terrific problem: his own personal psychological barrier." The life and writings of Francis Schaeffer, a writer well regarded by evangelicals, helped him to overcome his separatist beliefs, as did his own hatred of "abortion, the drug traffic, pornography, child abuse, and immorality in all its ugly, life-destroying forms." He was willing to work with others if it would help in fighting these evils. He was particularly appalled by abortion and determined to fight it with all the means at his disposal.

In 1976 Falwell organized a series of road shows in connection with the nation's bicentennial. Called *America, You're Too Young to Die!*, the show traveled to 150 cities offering Falwell's call for a return to morality, speeches by local politicians, and music by a team from Liberty Baptist College. The road shows expressed publicly what many fundamentalists had long believed—that America was at risk of losing God's favor because it had departed from the righteousness of the founders. In his 1980 book, *Listen America!*, he explains why he embarked on the project:

> God has blessed this nation because in its early days, she sought to honor God and the Bible, the inerrant word of the living God. Any diligent student of American history finds that our great nation was founded by godly men upon godly principles to be a Christian nation. Our Founding Fathers . . . developed a nation predicated upon Holy Writ.[3]

While on these trips, Falwell met with local ministers and lay leaders who were committed to political action. With a list of possible associates, he would soon be ready to move into a new arena. Falwell was already a formidable figure among fundamentalists. His radio and television following had provided him with a large mailing list, and his Thomas Road church and Liberty Baptist College were well known. There was even a front-page feature about him in the *Wall Street Journal* in 1978.[4] Troubled about the moral decline in America, he thought about it, prayed about it, and discussed it with other pastors, including fellow Baptist Tim LaHaye.

THE MORAL MAJORITY

Already committed to forming an organization with broader goals, Falwell needed advice on how to go about it. In his capacity as the head of Liberty Christian Academy, founded in 1967, Falwell had met Bob Billings, a graduate of Bob Jones University, the leading Fundamentalist source of higher education. They had met because Billings had committed himself to encouraging private Christian schools. In May 1979 Falwell and some of his colleagues met with Billings, Paul Weyrich, Ed McAteer, and Howard Phillips to talk about his project. Weyrich suggested the name "Moral Majority" and recommended Bob Billings for executive director.[5] Timothy LaHaye's California organization, Californians for Biblical Morality, became that state's branch of the Moral Majority. Also loosely linked was a Pasadena organization, Christian Voice, which shared mailing lists with Moral Majority. Both mobilized through networks of local pastors.

The Moral Majority's first official act was to borrow $25,000 and send out a fund-raising letter. Another road show, called *I Love America*, went to forty-four state capitals in 1979 and 1980, focusing on abortion and helping to get state chapters organized. Within three years, the organization had a budget of $10 million.[6]

The pastors recruited for the Moral Majority were predominantly from Falwell's denomination, the Bible Baptists. Their

Falwell's "I Love America" rallies at state capitals in 1979 kicked off his drive to restore "A Christian America." (Bettman/Corbis)

theology was standard Baptist theology, but Bible Baptist churches were more inclined than some of the other Baptist groups to cooperate with other churches. Therefore, its rating on separatism, one of the criteria for fundamentalism, was relatively low. Falwell's own personal uncompromising stance was also beginning to moderate. As he became more willing to cooperate with others who did not share his radical separatist policy, he broadened his agenda and began to behave more like a moderate evangelical than like a fundamentalist. An example was his strategy on abortion.

Shortly after the 1980 elections, pro-life groups wanted to take advantage of the Republican Senate majority to push through a pro-life amendment to the Constitution, or perhaps a pro-life statute. But arguments about the exact strategy——whether or not to make exceptions for the life of the mother, and whether or not to let states regulate abortion—eventually stalled the campaign, and the issue never even came up for a vote. Falwell pleaded with the warring factions to compromise, arguing that something was better than nothing, but they remained intransigent and got nothing.

Falwell has also been more willing than many of the other Christian Right leaders to appear on television programs like CNN's *Crossfire* with those who oppose him, and even to invite opponents to speak at his church and his college, which became a university in 1985. For instance, he invited Sen. Ted Kennedy (D-Mass.) in 1983;[7] Jesse Jackson in 1985; and Mel White, a prominent homosexual activist, in 1999,[8] for all of which he was criticized by other conservative pastors.

Like other Christian Right entrepreneurs, Falwell had a tendency to exaggerate his accomplishments. Instead of the 30 million viewers he claimed for his *Old Time Gospel Hour*, a claim that was repeated even by publications and groups opposing him, the actual audience at its peak was closer to 1.5 million.[9] He claimed a membership for the Moral Majority of 2 to 3 million, when the circulation of the *Moral Majority Report* (as reported to the U.S. Postal Service) was only 482,000.[10] The standard procedure seems to have been to count as a member every person who has ever contacted the ministry, even if only once.

A Gallup Poll in 1982 showed that only about half of the population had heard of the Moral Majority. Among those who had, unfavorable opinions outweighed favorable ones by two to one.[11] The results were only slightly more positive among those I interviewed in Oklahoma, where the climate would be expected to be more favorable. Less than one-fourth of the respondents said they were members of the Moral Majority, and more than a third had not heard of it at that time. This was true even though most were Christian conservatives, and the interviews were conducted in fall 1980 when speculation about the Moral Majority's potential impact on the November elections was appearing in the news almost daily. Sixteen percent of the respondents were actually opposed to it. But some had a favorable view.

> I am not a member of Falwell's group, but I agree with the things they work for. I just don't agree with the denominationalism he represents. But we have an obligation to do something about the depths the country is sinking into. (real estate agent and part-time minister, 1980)

> I don't watch TV preachers a lot myself, but I really believe in what Jerry Falwell is doing. He's an answer to prayer. (suburban woman, 1980)

Among those pro-family conservatives, the direct influence of the Moral Majority was not great, but many of them were nevertheless doing what Jerry Falwell hoped they would do—campaigning for Ronald Reagan and for other conservative candidates. Their enthusiasm in campaigning suggested that they would have an effect on the 1980 elections out of proportion to their numbers. If so, it may have been true only in Oklahoma and a few other very conservative states. A Republican political consultant told the Republican Governors Club, a fund-raising group, that the Moral Majority's influence probably made the margin of difference for the election of Republican senators in Alabama, Oklahoma, and Idaho.[12]

What I learned from my interviews in Oklahoma led me to believe that the Republican margin was more likely attributable to a general mobilization of Christian conservatives, many of whom were either indifferent to, or even critical of, the Moral Majority. Falwell claimed that out of forty-three 1980 elections in which a Moral Majority chapter was involved, the morally conservative candidate won in forty.[13] The candidates associated with the Moral Majority in Oklahoma lost their elections, while Don Nickles, a Catholic enthusiastically supported by the activists of Eagle Forum and Pro-Family Forum, won.

It was true that evangelicals throughout the nation turned out in large numbers for the 1980 election, but that seems to have been because of a "general conservative backlash against the Carter administration."[14] The consensus of political scientists who studied the 1980 presidential election was that the Moral Majority made little difference, and that other issues were at least as important as those emphasized by the Moral Majority and other Christian conservative groups. A study in Muncie, Indiana, for example, concluded that "the Christian Right had virtually no influence at all."[15]

Interviewers for the National Election Study (NES) spoke to people as they left their voting places, while their vote was still fresh in their minds. In 1980 and 1984, the NES asked voters if they considered themselves evangelicals and if they had positive attitudes about the Christian Right. The 1980 voters were also asked about their voting participation in 1976. Using these data and making some assumptions that seem reasonable, Clyde Wilcox, a political scientist who studies conservative movements, concluded that white evangelicals probably were drawn into higher voting participation by Jimmy Carter's candidacy in 1976 and voted in high numbers again in 1980 (often against Carter), but that their voting turnout declined in 1984.[16]

Whether or how much influence the Moral Majority or other Christian Right organizations exerted in an election is probably less important in the long run than the unquestioned decline of participation by the citizenry in general. All indications of political engagement have been declining since the early 1960s—voter turnout, attendance at town meetings or school meetings, and basic knowledge about how government works.[17] The decline in voting participation provides an opportunity for any highly mobilized group to increase its influence, simply by showing up. Studies of the Christian Right find that its sympathizers are no more than 30 percent of the population, at most. But with total voting turnout less than 50 percent, a small but highly motivated group can still make a difference.

The two Baptist pastors among those I interviewed thought Falwell and the state chairman of the Moral Majority (also a Baptist pastor) were improperly mixing religion with politics.

> I don't think I need the Moral Majority. What do they do for me? They give me backgrounds of different candidates. If I was the least bit concerned, I could do that on my own. I have been told that the Moral Majority endorses candidates, although I've not seen that myself. To me, that's overstepping the bounds. In my job as pastor, political analysis is not my job. If I'm teaching the word of God to my people, they're going to be able to discern right from wrong, but if I fail in that area, then I have failed my own people. If a person in my church dies, Jerry Falwell doesn't bury him. I do. Jerry Falwell isn't there to give comfort to mom and dad when a teenager gets himself wrapped around a tree, but I am. (small-town Baptist pastor, October 1980)

Falwell never realized his lofty aspirations for a Christian influence in politics, but he was adept at getting free publicity in the secular media. As one indication, a count of stories in the *New York Times* from 1973 to 1997 showed that Falwell himself was the subject of 156 stories, and the Moral Majority of 202, for a total of 358. This was far more than the nearest competitor, the Christian Coalition, which had garnered only 234 stories in the same period, including those about its two prominent leaders, Pat Robertson and Ralph Reed.[18]

Falwell closed the Moral Majority in 1989, believing that his own church needed him to spend more time on it. But he continued to put out a monthly publication, to appear on talk shows, and to make news with startling pronouncements. He occasionally announced a new campaign to register Christian voters, and the *National Liberty Journal*, the successor to the *Moral Majority Report*, always devoted at least a page to political commentary.

After President Clinton took office, every edition of the *National Liberty Journal* denounced Clinton—for sexual impropriety, campaign finance irregularities, draft dodging, and even the murder of Vincent Foster, one of Clinton's Arkansas friends who had joined his administration. Falwell also advertised the *Clinton Chronicles*, a video dramatizing those charges. Even those who agreed with him on the issues thought he was too obsessed with attacking Clinton. Interview respondents in 1997 were even less favorable toward Falwell than those in 1980.

In April 2000 Jerry Falwell announced a new initiative to be called People of Faith 2000. The announcement was classic "Christian America" rhetoric, similar to the rationale for the Moral Majority of twenty-one years before. In his new announcement, Falwell accused President Clinton of driving the country to the "brink of moral collapse, and possibly Divine Judgment." He declared that "as a student of Bible prophecy, I tremble at what may lie ahead for America. . . . God is giving his people one last opportunity to take the lead in calling our nation to repentance," and that he (Falwell) was called to "sound the alarm." Ever enthusiastic and optimistic, Falwell promised to contact 50,000 pastors, increase the circulation of his *National Liberty Journal* to 1 million, register 10 million new voters, and get 25 million "God-fearing Americans" to the polls.

Although Falwell's accomplishments were less impressive than his claims, he did pave the way for other organizations of Christian conservatives by showing that interdenominational cooperation would not bring down the wrath of God on their heads. He also contributed to the Christian Right agenda by arousing the interest of Protestants in the abortion issue.

BAPTIST BATTLES

Baptists are the largest Protestant denomination, especially strong in the South. Baptists were also a significant proportion of activists in the Christian Right. In the states where the church affiliation of the anti-ERA crusaders was known, Baptists averaged about 20 percent of the totals. Pastors of the Southern Baptist Convention, the largest Baptist group, were among those participating in the mobilization phase of the New Right in the early 1980s. Adrian Rogers of Memphis; Bailey Smith of Oklahoma City; Jimmy Draper of Dallas; Charles Stanley of Atlanta; Greg Dixon of Indianapolis; James Robison, a television evangelist in Dallas; and Paige Patterson of Southeastern Bible Seminary in Wake Forest, North Carolina, were all active in the movement. Southern Baptist pastors spoke at rallies and sat on the boards of the American Coalition for Traditional Values, the Religious Roundtable, and Concerned Women for America (in the last case, it was the wives of the Baptist pastors who were enlisted). Jerry Falwell was not a member of the Southern Baptist Convention when he founded the Moral Majority, but he joined it later.

By one count, there were twenty-seven different Baptist groups in America in 1995, ranging from "hard-shell" separatist fundamentalists to relative moderates.[19] The Southern Baptist Convention resulted from a North-South split before the Civil War. Despite some wavering, the southerners have remained mostly fundamentalist, while their brothers in the North, the American Baptist Convention, are more liberal but still conservative enough to be described as evangelical.

The Southern Baptist Convention and the northern Baptists once had an agreement not to plant new churches or seek new members in each other's territory, but when southerners migrated in large numbers to California during the Great Depression, they found the California churches affiliated with the northern Baptists too formal and too liberal for their taste. After the Southern Baptist Convention accepted the California churches, the agreement began to crumble. The growth of Southern Baptist churches throughout the nation is one of the factors in the "southernization of America," for by the 1960s, there were Southern Baptist churches in every state.[20]

The Southern Baptist Convention, however, like other conservative churches in the past, had begun to suffer "creeping modernization" until some of the same men who were involved in the formation of the New Right also engineered a conservative takeover of the convention. Ed McAteer, a layman in Adrian Rogers's church, and Morton Blackwell, both of whom had worked with Paul Weyrich in the New Right, cooperated with the plan.[21]

The fundamentalists had noticed that pastors with seminary training were likely to be liberal, while those without it remained conservative. Their strategy was to change seminary teaching by electing conservative presidents of the convention. A president could influence church colleges, seminaries, and church agencies by his power over the nomination of trustees and the allocation of funds. Unlike the Churches of Christ, in which extrachurch agencies depend on contributions directly from individuals or churches, the Baptist Convention furnishes a significant part of the budgets of such Baptist institutions.

The insurgent conservative men were supported by Southern Baptist women who had learned their political skills in the anti-ERA campaign. In her account of the "Baptist battles," Nancy Ammerman, a sociologist of religion, noted that activists from Eagle Forum and the pro-life movement were among those speaking for the insurgents who sought, among other things, to stop the ordination of women.[22] Helen Blackwell, the wife of Morton Blackwell, one of the male leaders, later served as a state president of Eagle Forum.

By 1990 fundamentalists were assured of control of the Southern Baptist Convention. In 1996 the convention called for new efforts to convert Jews to Christianity. In 1998 Southern Baptists amended their faith statement to declare that "a wife is to submit herself graciously" to her husband's leadership—the very issue that had led conservative women to oppose the ERA twenty-six years before. In 2000 the leaders pushed through a revision of the denomination's basic statement of faith to say that the Bible qualifies only men to be church pastors.[23] After this decision, a number of churches threatened to withdraw from the Southern Baptist Convention.

Ever since the 1960s, church membership statistics have shown a consistent trend for strictly conservative churches to grow more rapidly than liberal or moderate ones.[24] Dean Kelley, a political scientist who studies religion and who first called attention to the trend in 1972, attributed the growth of the conservative churches to their "strictness" and their "strength." They expected their members to attend church regularly, to engage in Bible study, and to adhere to certain behavioral principles. When Kelley's book came out in 1972, that trend had lasted for a decade; by 2000 it had lasted three decades, although conservative church growth had slowed. The Southern Baptist Convention was the first denomination to stop growing *after* becoming more strict. The Southern Baptist growth rate in the decade after the conservative takeover did not even keep up with the growth in the U.S. population.[25]

NOTES

1. "Mobilizing the Moral Majority," *Conservative Digest* 5, no. 8 (August 1979): 16.

2. Jerry Falwell, *Strength for the Journey* (New York: Simon and Schuster, 1987), pp. 361–62.

3. Jerry Falwell, *Listen America!* (New York: Bantam-Doubleday, 1981), p. 25.

4. Jim Montgomery, "The Electric Church," *Wall Street Journal*, 19 May 1978, 1.

5. William Martin, *With God on Our Side* (New York: Broadway Books, 1996), p. 200.

6. Falwell, *Journey,* pp. 363–64.

7. "Ted Kennedy Begins LBC Debate Series," *Moral Majority Report* (November 1983).

8. J. M. Smith, "Scenes from an Unlikely Summit," *National Liberty Journal* (December 1999): 1.

9. William C. Martin, "The Birth of a Media Myth," *Atlantic Monthly* 247, no. 6 (June 1981): 11.

10. Jerry Hadden and Charles Swann, *Prime-Time Preachers* (Reading, Mass.: Addison Wesley, 1981), p. 165.

11. "Unfavorable Views of Moral Majority Outweigh Favorable by 2-to-1," *Gallup Report* 201–202 (June–July 1982): 72.

12. Adam Clymer, "Bush Says No Single Group Gave Reagan His Victory," *New York Times*, 18 November 1980, B10.

13. Falwell, *Journey,* p. 366.

14. Anson Shupe and William A. Stacey, "Public and Clergy Sentiments toward the Moral Majority: Evidence from the Dallas-Fort Worth Metroplex," in *New Christian Politics*, David G. Bromley and Anson Shupe (Macon, Ga.: Mercer University Press, 1984), pp. 69–90.

15. Stephen D. Johnson and Joseph B. Tamney, "The Christian Right and the 1980 Presidential Election," *Journal for the Scientific Study of Religion* 21, no. 2 (1982): 123–31.

16. Clyde Wilcox, "The New Christian Right and the Mobilization of Evan-

gelicals," in *Religion and Political Behavior in the United States*, Ted Jelen (New York: Praeger, 1989), pp. 139–56.

17. League of Women Voters of the U.S., "Charting the Health of American Democracy," National Report, Washington D.C., 1997.

18. Although Falwell began making news before Robertson did, there was a long period in the 1990s when he was out of the spotlight.

19. Frank S. Mead and Samuel S. Hill, *Handbook of American Denominations* (Nashville, Tenn.: Abingdon, 1995), pp. 49–80.

20. Nancy Tatom Ammerman, *Baptist Battles* (New Brunswick, N.J.: Rutgers University Press, 1995), pp. 50–52.

21. Sidney Blumenthal, *Pledging Allegiance: The Last Campaign of the Cold War* (New York: HarperCollins, 1990), p. 100.

22. Ammerman, *Baptist Battles*, pp. 95–96, 218.

23. Gustav Niebuhr, "Southern Baptists May Rule Women May Not Be Pastors," *New York Times,* 19 May 2000

24. Dean M. Kelley, *Why Conservative Churches Are Growing* (New York: Harper and Row, 1972).

25. *The 2000 Almanac and Book of Facts* (Mahwah, N.J.: Primedia Reference), pp. 385–86.

9

THE LaHAYES
AND JAMES DOBSON

F alwell was not the only Christian Right issue-entrepreneur to create
    a new organization in 1979. Although not new to the crusade
against moral decline, Beverly LaHaye, her husband Tim, and James
Dobson were all drawn into deeper involvement in the movement by the
two series of conferences in 1977 and 1979–80.

THE LaHAYES

Beverly LaHaye, wife of Baptist pastor Tim LaHaye, was living a quiet
life in San Diego when a friend told her what she had seen at the 1977
Women's Conference in Houston. LaHaye was upset about it but put it
out of her mind until a few months later when she saw a Barbara Walters
television interview with Betty Friedan. Friedan had written the popular
1963 book *The Feminine Mystique,* for which she was credited with being
the "mother" of the feminist movement. LaHaye resented Friedan's claim
in that interview to represent all American women and decided she would
do something about it.

   After thinking it over, she organized a series of coffee hours in the
San Diego area with some of her friends, inviting Christian women to
come to discuss the ERA, feminism, and humanism. With the support of
the women who had attended the coffee hours, LaHaye and her friends

organized a rally in San Diego. Twelve hundred people, far more than they had expected, came to the rally.

Beverly Ratcliffe was only eighteen when she married Tim LaHaye. They had met while students at Bob Jones University. She followed him as he pastored Baptist churches in small towns in South Carolina and Minnesota, and then in San Diego at the larger and more prestigious Scott Memorial Baptist Church. She was a submissive housewife and mother of four; by her own admission, she lacked self-confidence. Unlike other pastors' wives, she did not play a public role in her husband's ministry. Finally, under the tutelage of a psychologist, she began to overcome her shyness and to risk speaking in public on occasion. To Tim's credit, he supported her in her new public role. The LaHayes' mutual support of one another and cooperation in their careers is one that feminists would applaud, although the LaHayes recommend women's "submission" to their husbands rather than the egalitarian model the feminists prefer. In 1971 the LaHayes jointly founded Family Life Seminars, traveling around the country to speak about family relationships, and starting a mail-order tape ministry on family life. At its peak, the ministry had thirty-five to forty employees and a budget of $1 million.[1]

In 1970 Tim LaHaye had founded and become president of a private school system, San Diego Christian Unified School System, and also a college, Christian Heritage College. When his church was denied a zoning variance, he realized, as he put it, that "men and women largely hostile to the church controlled our city."[2] Like the pastors who banded together to defend their Christian schools from the IRS, LaHaye's decision to enter politics was sparked by a conflict between his church and a governmental entity. The second incident that pushed the Reverend Mr. LaHaye toward politics was the Briggs Initiative in California in 1978. LaHaye was criticized because of his church's support of the Proposition 6 initiative to make it easier to fire homosexual teachers. The organization he founded for that campaign, Californians for Biblical Morality, later became a chapter of Jerry Falwell's Moral Majority.[3]

The experience of Beverly and Tim as cochairs of the Pro-Family Coalition for the White House Conference on Families only whetted their interest in taking political roles. The organization growing out of the San Diego coffee hours and rallies several years before, Concerned Women for America, was incorporated in 1979.

Two years after the founding of Concerned Women for America, Tim gave up his posts in San Diego as head of American Heritage College and as pastor of Scott Memorial Baptist Church to devote himself full time to his writing and to his political activities. He was the first president of the Council for National Policy based in Washington, D.C. In September 1982, Concerned Women for America (CWA), which by that time was claiming over 235,000 members, moved its headquarters to Washington. Tim LaHaye's office in the building that housed CWA was shared with both Christian Voice and the American Coalition for Traditional Values (a short-lived organization, not to be confused with Lou Sheldon's more durable Traditional Values Coalition).

For the next five years, Tim and Beverly presided over CWA, Christian Voice, and the American Coalition for Traditional Values, producing publications on family life and politics. During that time the LaHayes themselves moved to Washington. By 1990 after Tim's political organizations had disbanded, he devoted himself full time to writing, while Beverly continued to lead CWA.

CONCERNED WOMEN FOR AMERICA

When Concerned Women for America was founded in 1979, the campaign against the ERA was still in progress. One year later, there were 655 members.[4] Beverly LaHaye said she intended to support Phyllis Schlafly, not to compete with her. LaHaye's connections in the Baptist church, like Lottie Beth Hobbs's in the Churches of Christ, attracted a different constituency than Schlafly's. At first, the Eagle Forum and the CWA were almost indistinguishable in the issues they dealt with, but they began to diverge in later years.

CWA's first newsletter contained information about the upcoming Year of the Child, sponsored by the United Nations, and suggestions for action. In the 1980s, CWA lawyers defended parents who objected to what they viewed as humanism in school textbooks. Later LaHaye was involved in fighting Communism in Central America, and then in opposing United Nations initiatives such as the International Year of the Child. She also continued work on the standard Christian Right issues of abortion and homosexuality.

The heart of the Concerned Women organization is in the Prayer-Action chapters on the local level. As the name implies, they combine telephoning and writing legislators with praying for them to see the light. The CWA members believed that the power of prayer, and the divine help it accessed, was the secret of their success. But CWA was less successful in finding human help on a consistent basis. There was a CWA Prayer-Action chapter only if someone organized it, and the degree of activity it sustained also depended on the local members and leaders. The area representatives, also volunteers, were responsible for an entire state or for a smaller area in the more populous states. It was not always easy to find leaders as Jodie Williams, who served briefly as Oklahoma area representative, discovered.

Instead of self-selected and self-directed workers like Betty Grogan, described in chapter 4, the state leaders in CWA were thoroughly trained to make sure they did not violate the policies of the organization. The recruitment and training of leaders in CWA followed the model of Phyllis Schlafly's STOP-ERA/Eagle Forum chapters. To become a chapter leader, a woman was required to fill out an application, have references, and attend training conferences.

While this was undoubtedly necessary to ensure that leaders did not embarrass the organization with unwise actions, it made it more difficult to find leaders. Jodie Williams explained that she had a year of training before she was appointed to be an area representative. Some of it was done by telephone, but there was also a required four-day leadership conference, held in a different state each year. As one of the former leaders complained, they had to pay their own transportation to attend the training conferences, and young mothers often had neither the time nor the money to attend.

> There were classes on how to have a prayer chapter, classes for your specific duty, like how to keep the records, how to be your area representative, how to speak to the press. One of the big things that we do is we have media classes. We practice interviews, so if we get called, we know how to handle ourselves. We videotape it, then they critique you and it's really good. (Jodie Williams, 1997)

They also learned about current issues and heard reports from CWA's legislative liaison in Washington about bills in Congress. While she was area representative, Jodie Williams traveled at least two weekends a month, going to about twenty communities where someone had asked her to come and talk about CWA. But she found it discouraging. Women were willing to attend meetings if somebody else took the lead, but were reluctant to take the responsibility themselves. Williams finally succeeded in getting ten chapters organized, only to have two of her most active and capable leaders resign within a year.

Despite Oklahoma's leadership in the anti-ERA campaign, it was one of the states in which CWA's area representative post was filled only sporadically. It was hard to recruit leaders, and they often resigned after only a short time in the position. Most were young mothers who resigned when they became pregnant, adopted a child, started home-schooling their children, or moved away. Some were pastors' wives who saw the responsibility as part of their husbands' ministry. One such woman had a chapter with four or five members for about three years, but when her husband moved to another church, she did not continue with CWA work. Another woman headed the CWA chapter as part of her duties as head of women's ministries in her church.

In general, the Christian Right organizations of the 1990s depended on paid professionals in each state rather than on volunteer leaders. CWA was an exception to this rule, but judging from the experience in Oklahoma, as well as from the rapid area representative turnover in other states,[5] it has not been uniformly successful. It also depends on volunteer lobbyists in its 435 Project, so named because there are 435 congressional districts. These volunteers, living near Washington, D.C., undertake to represent the legislative interests of areas in other parts of the country.

In 1999 CWA announced the creation of state directors' posts. These positions carried about the same responsibilities as the former area representatives. One of their duties was still to recruit local leaders, and they were still volunteer positions. As of June 2000, the CWA Web site[6] listed state directors for only twenty of the fifty states. Apparently, the problem of volunteer recruitment has not yet been solved. In contrast to other Christian Right organizations, CWA was not particularly strong in the South. Only half the southern states had state directors, although two other southern states had at least five local chapters a year earlier. The other state directors were in the Pacific West or in the Midwest, but both Connecticut and Massachusetts each had one.

CWA'S POLICY AGENDA

After the end of the ERA campaign in 1982, CWA differentiated itself
from Schlafly's Eagle Forum, as Schlafly returned to the issues of foreign
policy and defense which had always been her chief interests. Phyllis
Schlafly had never considered herself an advocate for women or women's
issues, although she gained national prominence because of her efforts
against the ERA, and later took up the abortion issue as well. Beverly
LaHaye, on the other hand, had always been an advocate for traditional
women, although she also took on a church-state issue and a foreign
policy issue.

The annual indexes of CWA's magazine, *Family Voice,* indicate that
abortion and homosexuality, the chief issues on which the pro-family
movement believes government policy is undermining biblical morality,
still predominate. During the five years from 1995 to 1999, abortion was
by far the most frequent topic, with 69 listings. Population issues, which
are of interest to the writers in *Family Voice* chiefly because population
control often means birth control and abortion, had 10 listings. Absti-
nence/sex education, also closely related, was listed 29 times, making a
total of 108 abortion-related listings. The second most frequent topic, also
a biblical morality issue, was homosexuality, with 51 listings. Issues
arising out of the recent agenda of the Christian Right—concern for governmental infringement of Christians' right to public religious observances and to political or legal activism—totaled 58.[7]

During the 1980s Michael Farris, a young man from Spokane who
had been director of the Moral Majority in Washington State, was CWA's
legal counsel. He filed a number of high-profile court cases supporting a
schoolgirl who was not allowed to enter a nativity scene in a poster contest; a mother who left the state rather than letting her homosexual ex-
husband have custody of their son; a Nebraska pastor who refused to have
his Christian school inspected by the state for compliance with safety regulations; and, in *Mozert et al.* v. *Hawkins County Schools* in Tennessee,
defending parents who wanted their children excused from reading certain texts which they believed promoted humanism. In these cases, CWA
was challenging the interpretation of the church-state separation as it
affected school policies.

President of Concerned Women for America, Beverly LaHaye, standing with Michael Farris, who was the CWA attorney in cases in which parents objected to school curriculum policies. (*Karl Schumacher/TIMEpix*)

After Farris left CWA to run for office, and then to head the Christian School Legal Defense Association, Beverly LaHaye led the CWA in supporting the Nicaraguan "Contras." It was President Reagan's support of the Contras that led to congressional accusations that he had unconstitutionally disregarded congressional policy. In 1986 Oliver North, a major figure in Reagan's relationship with the Contras, spoke at a CWA national convention. In 1987 LaHaye visited Nicaragua and met Violeta Chamorro, the woman who was elected president of Nicaragua in 1990 in the first free elections after the Contra victory. The CWA also sponsored a refugee camp in Costa Rica. In a speech at the 1987 CWA national convention, President Reagan himself thanked the organization for its help to the Contras.

In the 1990s the CWA's agenda again centered on women and family issues, but with the addition of an international angle. Her concern for women's issues led LaHaye to attend a series of United Nation Conferences, some specifically on women's issues, others on related issues impacting women. In objecting to the UN conferences, CWA was extending the Christian Right's fear of governmental policies detrimental to biblically prescribed family relationships from the national level to the international one, and raising the additional specter of a loss of national sovereignty. Phyllis Schlafly, who often criticized the UN on other grounds, had relatively little to say about the UN conferences. The publications of both Focus on the Family and Family Research Council referred to them occasionally, but the CWA was more active than other Christian Right organizations on this issue.

At the 1998 national convention of the CWA, Beverly LaHaye announced the formation of the Beverly LaHaye Center for Traditional Women's Studies, "to represent women whose views are biblically based" and to counteract the liberal-dominated academic field of women's studies. In 1999 Janice Shaw Crouse, holder of a Ph.D. from an unnamed Christian college, became the senior fellow of the institute. Her experience included working with the UN Women's Conference in Beijing in 1995 and also with the U.S. Department of Health and Human Services.[8]

Although the CWA is organizationally weak in Oklahoma, about half of those I interviewed in 1997 listened to Beverly LaHaye's daily radio program, *Beverly LaHaye Live*, or subscribed to the CWA magazine, *Family Voice*, making CWA the third most popular Christian Right organization with these respondents. The Christian Coalition was in first place, and James Dobson's Focus on the Family, the other organization that was inspired by the National Women's Conferences, was second.

JAMES DOBSON

James Dobson first became known to Christian conservatives as the author of *Dare to Discipline*, published in 1970, while he was an assistant professor of pediatrics at the University of Southern California School of Medicine in Los Angeles. The book's endorsement of spanking was seen by Bible-belt conservatives as a needed corrective to what they believed was permissive child-rearing advice in the sixties. By 1995 3 million copies had been sold.[9]

Born in Louisiana, the son of a traveling evangelist in the Church of the Nazarene, Dobson received a Ph.D. in psychology from the University of Southern California in 1967. After the National Women's Conference in Houston, he created the nonprofit, tax-exempt Focus on the Family in 1977 to "teach scriptural principles of marriage and parenthood and to help preserve and strengthen families."[10] One of its first projects was a video about Christian family relationships, called *Focus on the Family*. Many of those I interviewed in 1980 had seen it in their churches; Dobson claims that the video has been seen by from 60 to 70 million people.[11] Other books, several magazines about family relationships and a radio program featuring Dobson's advice to families were also produced by the new organization.

Dobson had attracted little attention outside of fundamentalist and evangelical churches until he was appointed by President Carter to the steering committee of the White House Conference on Families. He had asked his radio listeners to nominate him for the committee, and they responded 80,000 strong.[12] In the meantime, Jerry Regier, a native Oklahoman and a minister in another evangelical organization—Bill Bright's Campus Crusade for Christ and Christian Embassy—had approached John Carr, the executive director of the White House conference, to request that Christian conservatives be placed on the conference planning committees. Carr, following President Carter's instructions to include all points of view in the conference planning, arranged for Jim Guy Tucker, chairman of the conference, to meet with Regier's group, including Dobson.

Regier and Dobson attended the Baltimore conference of the White House Conference on Families, where they unsuccessfully tried to dissuade Connie Marshner from walking out to protest the conference voting procedures. When she left, accompanied by the pro-family delegates, she assured that a multipart resolution they had opposed—on homosexuality, abortion, and the ERA—would pass.

An article in the *Wall Street Journal* in 1988 reported that Focus on the Family had a staff of more than 550, a new $14 million headquarters in Pomona, California, and a budget of $42 million. By that time, Dobson and his board had adopted a new mission statement with a more explicitly evangelical Christian emphasis: "To cooperate with the Holy Spirit in disseminating the Gospel of Jesus Christ to as many people as possible, and specifically, to accomplish that objective by helping to preserve traditional values and the institution of the family."[13] In November 1988, his newsletter announced a series of new policy initiatives.

The first was the reorganization of the Family Research Council, which Dobson and Regier had created in 1980 as an independent unit.

James Dobson in his radio studio. His *Focus on the Family* print and broadcast media reach a larger audience than any other Christian Right leader's. (*Los Angeles Times photo by Steven Dykes*)

Gary Bauer, who had been a policy adviser to the president and undersecretary of the Department of Education in the Reagan administration, was to be its president. The Family Research Council was free to lobby, but as a tax-exempt organization, it could not participate in partisan campaigns.

Second, *Citizen* magazine, then in its first year, would continue to inform its readers about family issues and encourage them to be active in the political arena. At the time, *Citizen* had 135,000 subscribers. Sent only to those who specifically subscribed to it, *Citizen* was the only political magazine among at least ten others produced by Focus. Its circulation was far below the 2.2 million circulation of the nonpolitical flagship magazine, named simply *Focus on the Family*.

Third, Dobson started a new radio program, *Family News in Focus*, specifically for political issues. But, mindful of Focus on the Family's tax-exempt status, Dobson assured readers that less than 5 percent of the Focus budget would go for political work.[14] Just as *Citizen* was only one of many magazines, *Family News in Focus* was only one of the ministry's eight radio programs, and not the most popular one.

Finally, Focus on the Family planned to encourage the formation of pro-family coalitions in each of the fifty states. They were already in operation in six states, and eleven more were almost ready to open.[15] They were to be completely independent—associated, not affiliated. Right-to-life and antipornography organizations, public education critics, and gay rights opponents would all be invited to join. In March 1998, ten years after the announcement of state coalitions, Focus's Web site listed state coalitions in thirty-two of the fifty states.[16] In June 2000, there were thirty-three; some had been added since 1988, but others were no longer listed.[17]

Dobson's books, magazines, and broadcasts, even the political ones, are relatively low key, far less strident than the output of the other Christian conservative organizations. Focus on the Family's only regular mailings to everyone on its list are the *Focus on the Family* magazine, with heart-warming stories illustrating marriage and family issues, and the monthly newsletter *Family News from Dobson*. Of forty-eight newsletters from 1996 to 2000, only seven could be classified as political. Even *Citizen*, specifically designed for readers interested in political issues, is less strident than the magazines of the CWA or the Christian Coalition, and far less so than Jerry Falwell's output. The writers for *Citizen* leave no doubt about where they stand on the issues, but they are less inclined to use inflammatory adjectives like "radical" and "extremist" and more likely to give a thorough explanation, citing research, original resources, and even in some cases, the evidence for a contrary view. *Citizen* also features articles about developments that are positive from the conservative point of view, like the trend for divorce education as a way of preserving marriages, an admired congressman, and an organization called Feminists for Life.

Unlike Jerry Falwell and Pat Robertson, neither James Dobson nor Gary Bauer is an ordained minister. Dobson has a Ph.D. in psychology from one prestigious university, and Bauer has a law degree from another (Georgetown). It may be that Dobson's and Bauer's academic credentials have moderated their rhetoric. In addition, Dobson at least, does not need to use direct mail as a means of raising funds, for he has a fine income from his books and radio programs, some of which he donates to Focus on the Family.

Dobson is unbending in his moral principles, however, in keeping with the strict "holiness" codes that were part of his Nazarene upbringing. "Wesleyan perfectionism," or "holiness" doctrines, largely abandoned by the Methodists who adopted them in their early years, are alive and well in the Church of the Nazarene, which broke off from Methodism at the beginning of the twentieth century. Nazarenes strictly prohibit illicit sexual activity, insist on marital fidelity, and disapprove of frivolous entertainment. Dobson's "holiness" views were evident in his work on the 1986 Commission on Pornography and the 1996 Commission on Gambling, where he vigorously opposed both. He joined Donald Wildmon's American Family Association in calling for boycotts of the sponsors of television programs it judged to be pornographic. Dobson also cooperated briefly with Susan Baker—the wife of President George Herbert Walker Bush's secretary of state James A. Baker—and Tipper Gore—the wife of Al Gore—on their project of requiring warning labels on rock music and rap music that promote violence.

THE FAMILY RESEARCH COUNCIL

The Family Research Council (FRC) severed its ties with Focus on the Family in 1992 in order to be more independent, although Dobson and Gary Bauer, head of the FRC, continued to serve on one another's boards. Bauer's attitudes were shaped by a childhood in a low-income family in Kentucky. He is more of a populist than a traditional Republican conservative. He opposed free market solutions for health care and Social Security, for instance. In a 1997 op-ed piece for the *New York Times,* Bauer criticized the proposal to privatize Social Security as detrimental to working families.[18]

In 1996 Bauer founded his own political action committee, Campaign for Working Families, which by 1998 was larger than either the National Education Association or the United Auto Workers.[19] Bauer resigned from the Family Research Council in 1999 to seek the Republican presidential nomination. During the campaign he took some positions that displeased Dobson, and he did not return to the FRC after his campaign collapsed. Kenneth Connor was brought in as head of Family Research Council in fall 2000.

Bauer had placed the FRC on a firm foundation during the years that he directed it. A 1999 report by the Committee for Responsible Philanthropy called the FRC one of the fastest growing and most influential of the conservative organizations, with a 1997 budget of $14 million.[20] The FRC benefited from the foundations created by Betsy and Richard DeVos, the founders of Amway. At the end of 1996, the Prince Foundation of Betsy's family, and the DeVos Foundation of Richard's family provided funds for the FRC to build a fine, new six-story headquarters in Washington, D.C.[21] In 1998, the FRC had a membership of 455,000.[22]

True to its name, the Family Research Council sponsors research and conducts forums with expert speakers. It claimed to have provided the research used by those opposing the Employment Non-Discrimination Act (ENDA) sponsored by Sen. Ted Kennedy (D-Mass.), which would have added "sexual orientation" to federal civil rights workplace laws. According to the Family Research Council, it would also have "threatened the freedoms of religion, speech, and association of millions of people."[23]

The FRC's publication is *Washington Watch*, a glossy sixteen-page monthly with reports on legislation and articles presenting the FRC's point of view. Its articles are heavily weighted toward the "Christian America" theme, but abortion and homosexuality are also frequent topics, and there are some articles about taxes and the budget as well. *Washington Watch*, like *Citizen,* avoids using inflammatory adjectives and concentrates more on educating its readers about history, about the actual provisions of the Constitution, and about the background of current legislative proposals.

Focus on the Family moved its entire operation from California to Colorado Springs, Colorado, in 1991. It is the only major Christian conservative organization with no office in Washington, D.C.; the Family Research Council serves as its Washington outpost. Focus on the Family depends on its state associates to extend its influence throughout the country. The political influence of the Focus on the Family empire varied from one part of the country to another because its associates were more active in some states than in others. The regional strength of Focus on the Family was similar to that of Christian conservatives in general, with state associates in all the southern states and in California. The seventeen states lacking a Focus associate were generally small, sparsely populated, or in the Northeast.

The Oklahoma associate of Focus on the Family, the Oklahoma Family Policy Council (OFPC), is one of the more active state associates.

Its executive director and research director are both registered lobbyists at the state level. They lobbied against some of the provisions in the state's Living Will legislation, against the federally funded Goals 2000 educational program, against a comprehensive health plan proposed by a Democratic governor, and in favor of a law banning partial-birth abortion.

The issues the OFPC emphasized ran the gamut of the Christian conservative agenda—promoting sexual morality, strong families, and the Christian America thesis, and attacking public education—along with the traditional Republican issues of small government and reduced taxes. It administers one of the sexual abstinence grants authorized by Congress in 1996, OFPC's Kids Eagerly Endorsing Purity (KEEP) project, which conducted training programs for volunteer teachers in 1999. Another of its projects was its annual Christian Heritage Week, featuring Catherine Millard, president of Christian Heritage Ministries in Springfield, Virginia. Millard argues that "the Christian history of the nation has been deliberately rewritten and stolen from Americans over two generations since the 1930s by revisionist historians, Marxist activists, and others who hate this nation."[24]

Almost three-fourths of the Christian conservatives I interviewed in 1997 listened to the programs or read the literature of Focus on the Family and the Family Research Council. Only the Christian Coalition had a larger readership and viewership, probably because all the respondents were members of the coalition. The extent of the influence of Focus on the Family is not generally recognized because Focus on the Family, the Family Research Council, and the various associated state organizations operate under different names. On the other hand, an estimate of its political influence based only on the number of subscribers, supporters, and listeners it has would probably be too great because many of them subscribe for the family advice and may not know about or pay attention to the overtly political messages.

NOTES

1. Connie Paige, "Watch on the Right," *Ms.* 15, no. 8 (February 1987): 25.

2. Tim LaHaye, *Battle for the Mind* (Old Tappan, N.J.: Fleming H. Revell, 1980), p. 191.

3. Ibid., pp. 199–200.

4. Beverly LaHaye, *Who but a Woman?* (Nashville, Tenn.: Thomas Nelson, 1984).

5. The turnover is indicated by the listing of new area representatives in each issue of the CWA publication, *Family Voice.*

6. http://www.cwfa.org

7. Reported on CWA Web site, accessed 2 July 1999.

8. *Family Voice* (July 1999): 14.

9. William C. Martin, *With God on Our Side* (New York: Broadway Books, 1996), p. 341.

10. "Family News from Dr. Dobson," Focus on the Family newsletter, Colorado Springs, Colo., July 1987; "Family News from Dr. Dobson," March 1998.

11. Michael Gerson, "A Righteous Indignation." *U.S. News and World Report* (4 May 1998): 23; Martin, *God on Our Side,* p. 342.

12. Report of People for the American Way, April 1993.

13. Family News from Dr. Dobson, March 1998.

14. Laurie Goodstein, "Conservative Leader Takes on the GOP," *New York Times,* 12 February 1998.

15. Family News from Dr. Dobson, November 1988.

16. http://www.fotf.org

17. Those having none were Alaska, Arizona, Connecticut, Delaware, Kansas, Missouri, Montana, Nevada, New Hampshire, New Mexico, New York, North Dakota, Rhode Island, Utah, Vermont, West Virginia, and Wyoming.

18. Gary Bauer, *New York Times,* Op-Ed, 23 January 1997.

19. *Right-Wing Watch,* People for the American Way, 11 May 1998.

20. David Callahan, *$1 Billion for Ideas: Conservative Think Tanks in the 1990s* (Washington, D.C.: National Committee for Responsive Philanthropy, 1999), p. 21.

21. *Washington Watch,* newsletter of Family Research Council, 3 December 1996.

22. Bob Jones IV, "Focus on a Family Feud," *World* 13, no. 8 (28 February 1998): 14.

23. "Ring Those Bells!" *Washington Watch,* 25 September 1996.

24. Oklahoma Family Policy Council e-mail notices, 15 April 1999.

10

THE CHRISTIAN COALITION AND THE CHARISMATICS

A s Jerry Falwell faded from public notice at the end of the 1980s, Pat Robertson took over as the top newsmaker of the Christian Right. Like Jerry Falwell, Robertson had a talent for attracting publicity, but in his case, it seemed to be inadvertent. His authorship of the 1991 book *The New World Order*,[1] which appeared to many to support conspiracy theory and to be anti-Semitic, seemed reminiscent of the old days of the John Birch Society.[2] Some of those I interviewed in 1997 scoffed at Robertson's claim that he had turned Hurricane Gloria away from his home base in Virginia Beach several years before, especially since the hurricane then wreaked havoc on Long Island.

Robertson had both supporters and detractors among Christian conservatives. Those who had supported Robertson ever since his run for the presidency in 1988 trusted him implicitly. They reported that they listened regularly to his *700 Club* program and depended on his news segment to tell the truth, in contrast to network news, which they believed was too liberal.

> We try to get the news as much as we can away from the national media, because it is so slanted and so biased. We get our news from the *700 Club*. It doesn't just tell you the liberal slant. (rural wife and mother, 1997)

Pat Robertson, founder of the 700 Club and of the Christian Coalition, also ran for president in 1988. From about 1993 to 1996, the Christian Coalition was the most prominent and successful of the Christian Right organizations. (*Church and State*)

Robertson was already well known among viewers of his *700 Club* before he attained wider recognition as a candidate for the Republican nomination for president in 1988. His broadcasting career, like Jerry Falwell's, began on a shoestring. In 1960, as Robertson tells it, God told him to buy an old, poorly equipped television station in Portsmouth, Virginia. He did so, and began broadcasting with only $3 in the bank. In 1963 Robertson asked seven hundred of his listeners to pledge $10 a month to keep the broadcasts on the air. That appeal was the origin of his *700 Club*, the name given later to his best-known television program.

Instead of televising regular church services as Jerry Falwell and other televangelists were doing, Robertson used an innovative talk show format. The popular format was originally conceived by Jim Bakker in 1965, but he broke with Pat Robertson in 1972 and went on to found the PTL (Praise the Lord) network, before sinking into oblivion and disgrace.[3] By 1977, when Robertson's Christian Broadcasting Network (CBN) was well established in Virginia Beach, he founded CBN University, later renamed Regents University. With the network and the university both prospering, and having amassed a large personal fortune, Robertson began to think of involving himself in public policy. He had already concluded that "separation of church and state" was actually an abridgement of the religious freedom of Christians. As he explained in his book *The Plan*:

> For the first time, I truly realized the enormity of the plan of the ACLU, the NEA [National Endowments for the Arts], and Planned Parenthood to destroy Christian values in America. Freedom after freedom was being taken away: prayer in the schools, Bible reading, Bible clubs, Christmas activities and displays. Christians needed an organization to counter this unbelievable loss of our liberty. That year I formed the

Freedom Council to educate evangelical Christians on the vital issues
and then to get them into the public process.[4]

Robertson's later political activities, culminating in the founding of
the Christian Coalition, continued to reflect this early preoccupation with
the "Christian America" theme. In the summer of 1984, conservative
friends had begun talking to him about running for the presidency. He
heard the "still small voice of the Lord, saying over and over, 'You won't
want to do this, but . . .'" As he continued to ponder and to pray,
Robertson asked God to give him a BAC-11 airplane as a sign that he was
doing the right thing. When in February 1985 he was able to buy such a
plane for a ridiculously low price, he took it as a sign that it was indeed
God's will that he become a candidate.[5] He raised more money than any
other Republican candidate and did well in the early Iowa caucuses, but
not so well in states holding primaries.

Robertson had counted on the southern states to put him back in the
game in the Super Tuesday primaries of March 8, 1988, in which many
states held primaries simultaneously and many Republican delegates
were at stake. In Oklahoma his campaign was managed by an experienced woman who had been active in state Republican politics even
before the ERA was an issue and had worked with Ann Patterson on the
ERA campaign. Using the list of *700 Club* donors, she recruited volunteers, most of whom had no experience in politics, taught them the basics
of convention strategy, and organized them well.

Bill Morgan was one of those volunteers and *700 Club* donors. He
was a small businessman, a native of Arkansas who knew Bill Clinton,
and a life-long Democrat until sometime in the 1980s. Like the Grogan
women, he had changed his registration after reading the platforms of
both parties. Morgan attended a large Assembly of God church. Like
other members of that pentecostal denomination, he spoke in tongues. He
firmly rejected the traditional view of conservative churches that they
ought to eschew politics. He believed that "the church is called to be the
salt of the earth, and the purpose of salt on meat in the old days was to
retard corruption."

Every motivating force that drives me is based on my relationship with
God. Nothing more, nothing less. He has told me to be a good citizen,

a good father, a good husband, and He's told me to be honest, work hard, and to serve. (Bill Morgan, 1997)

After Robertson's Oklahoma County campaign coordinator asked Morgan to be responsible for canvassing a precinct, he worked so enthusiastically and so well that she assigned him almost half of the county.

With the good work of Morgan and the other campaigners, most of them women, Robertson took 21 percent of the Oklahoma Republican vote in the Super Tuesday primaries. For a moment, it seemed that the grassroots mobilization of the anti-ERA movement was being repeated. Robertson's showing in Oklahoma was better than in any other state, but the average in all the states was much worse—only 13 percent.[6] His faithful supporters had been motivated to attend caucuses, but his base of support was too narrow to win primaries. Robertson withdrew from the presidential race on April 6, 1988.[7]

In the following year, using the lists of donors to his presidential campaign, Robertson founded the Christian Coalition. His goal was to "change politics in America." To do so, he enlisted the help of Ralph Reed, who was just completing a doctorate in history at Emory University. Reed proved to be unusually talented as a political organizer. He laid out an ambitious plan to build a membership of 3 million, with chapters operating in at least 350 of the nation's 435 congressional districts, all by 1992. He hoped to succeed where all the others had failed, by building a broad grassroots organization to "unite, mobilize, educate, and activate" evangelical Protestants and conservative Catholics.[8] By the end of the first year, the Christian Coalition claimed to have 125 local chapters and 57,000 members.[9]

From its beginning in 1989, the Christian Coalition's membership and budget grew steadily, as did the attention of the media. The ambitious plan to organize core activists in every precinct was never achieved, however, despite the hiring of full-time field directors, and the development of elaborate training materials to be used in local field organizing.

After the 1995 and 1996 national conventions, which drew more than 4,000 people to Washington, D.C., the coalition had a series of setbacks. Ralph Reed's decision to back Bob Dole in the 1996 presidential election had alienated many of the hard-core members, and Dole's defeat only added to their displeasure. In 1997 Reed resigned from the coalition to

Participants at a Christian Coalition Citizen Action seminar in 1995. (*Steve Liss/TIMEpix*)

start his own consulting firm. By the end of the following year, his replacements had resigned as well.

More serious was the action of the Internal Revenue Service in revoking the Christian Coalition's provisional 501(c)4 tax-exempt status. Such organizations are not taxed on their donations. They are allowed to do some lobbying for issues and to distribute information on candidates, but the organization must be careful not to favor one party over another, or to coordinate its activities with a political party. Contributions to a 501(c)4 organization are not tax-deductible for the giver because of the limited political activity permitted to the organization.

The coalition's response to the IRS decision was to disband and reincorporate under the existing 501(c)4 tax exemption of the Texas Christian Coalition, renaming itself the Christian Coalition of America. At the same time, it set up Christian Coalition International as a separate for-profit entity. Christian Coalition fund-raising letters charged that the IRS decision was "politically motivated" because liberal groups like the National Organization for Women, Common Cause, the AFL-CIO, and the National Gay and Lesbian Task Force were never accused of violating IRS rules.[10] The letters failed to mention that both the AFL-CIO and the National Organization for Women have political action committees separate from the parent organization and not exempt from taxes. Other Christian conservative groups such as Eagle Forum, Weyrich's Free Congress Committee, and Gary Bauer's Campaign for Working Families have similar arrangements.

Political action committees (PACs,) are set up for the purpose of helping candidates, although they are subject to some restrictions. Concerned Women for America, Focus on the Family, and the Family Research Council, which do not have PACs, all distribute warnings to their members in each election year that they must avoid partisan activity. The Christian Coalition could engage in partisan political activity if it would do so through a PAC, but if it continues the same activities under the auspices of the Christian Coalition of America, it can expect to face the same IRS objections.

After the series of setbacks in 1997, the membership fell off dramatically, and the Christian Coalition magazine stopped publication. *Fortune* magazine's annual poll of Washington insiders asking which lobbying organizations were the most powerful provided further evidence of the coalition's decline. The coalition had been rated seventh in both 1997 and 1998, but it dropped to thirty-fifth in 1999.[11]

In November 1997, just as the Christian Coalition magazine was being discontinued, the policy magazine of James Dobson's Focus on the Family, *Citizen*, was upgraded from sixteen pages with three colors to twenty-four pages with full color. Maybe it was only a coincidence; it was announced as a tenth anniversary change. This was also the year that the Family Research Council's fortunes improved markedly because of contributions from the Prince and DeVos Foundations, so perhaps it was also a coincidence that the newsletter of the Family Research Council, *Washington Watch*, was also upgraded. In September 1997, it went from four pages in black and white to eight pages in full color. As evidence mounted that the Christian Coalition was not as formidable as it had been in the past, it was not surprising that other Christian conservative organizations would sense an opportunity to expand their own influence.

As late as April 1999, however, Robertson announced an ambitious program to raise $21 million, distribute 50 million voter guides in the 2000 election cycle, and elect a Congress friendly to the coalition's policy goals in the 2000 elections.[12]

1998
Voter Guide
Oklahoma
State
Legislature

CD 4,5,6, Oklahoma County, State Senate

This voter guide complies with all IRS, FEC and ethics Commission standards. Distribution in churches, synagogues and other 501(c)(3) organizations is permissible

These recorded positios of condidates were verified using .voting records, public statements, and survey responses. This voter guide is for educational purposes only and is not to be construed as an endorsement of any candidate or political party

Authorized by the Oklahoma Christian Coalition; United Founders Tower, Suite 11512, 5900 Mosteller Drive, Oklahoma City, OK 73112; Phone: 405-840-2156; Fax: 405-840-2157   E-mail: okcc@telepath.com. Web Site: www.cc.org/state/ok.us./

The Oklahoma Christian Coalition is a nonprofit 401(c)(4), pro-family, citizen action organization.

Dave Herbert (D)	State Senate, Dist. 42	John Doe (R)
Supports	Abortion on Demand	Opposes
Supports	Minors' Access to Pornography in Libraries	Opposes
Supports	Taxpayer Funding of Abortion Clinics	Opposes
Supports	Increased Federal Control of Education	Opposes
Supports	Socialized Health Care	Opposes
Supports	Decriminalized Sodomy and Beastiality	Opposes

This reproduction is enlarged to show details

The voter guide for the Oklahoma legislature which prompted a suit against the Christian Coalition. The suit was unsuccessful because of the precedent in *New York Times* v. *Sullivan*, holding that a public figure cannot claim damages even for false or misleading statements.

THE VOTER GUIDES

A staffer in the Christian Coalition's Washington office told me that voter guides are the coalition's most important project. Ken Wood, the Oklahoma director of the coalition, attributed the success of conservative candidates to the fact that the voter guides "give accurate reliable information" on the votes of "politicians who campaign conservative but vote liberal."[13] I know of no hard evidence that the voter guides did or did not affect Oklahoma elections, but the perception among Christian Coalition members is that they did. Other observers also credit the voter guides and other activities of the Christian Right movement with helping to sweep all the Democrats out of Oklahoma's congressional delegation in 1994 and 1996, although an unexpected number of open seats made it easier.[14]

The coalition depends on volunteers to distribute its voter guides on the Sunday before an election. Bill Morgan took on this task with his customary enthusiasm.

We try to identify the churches that want us and then we get the voter guides out to them. I took off work for a week, my wife took off work,

I had my son working, my daughter working, volunteers from all over, and we got over 95 percent penetration in the county.

Ninety-eight percent of those I interviewed in 1997 used the voter guides in making their own decisions and thought they were useful and unbiased. But some were aware of the possibility of bias.

They definitely are helpful to me, and I feel like they are to most people, if they really want to have the straight scoop on things. I don't think they're slanted. I feel that they are straight to the core of some of the problems we have. (retired school superintendent, 1997)

Yes, I look those over. I think that they're truthful. I've heard a lot of people try to slam them, but I think they're honest and true. . . . I would be very surprised if I found that the 700 Club Voter Guides [the respondent is confusing two of Robertson's projects, the 700 Club and the Christian Coalition] were off, I have faith in them. (housewife, rural area, 1997)

Over half of those I interviewed had actually helped to distribute the voter guides.

Yes, I pass them out. This table is left over from the last election. I had it stacked high with voter guides and other information. People would call me and ask me. They'd be busy clear up until the day before election day, and then at the last minute, they say, "I don't know who's on the ballot, tell me who the Christian men are and I'll vote for them," and that's all I've got time to say. I'll tell 'em and they'll take my word for it sometimes. (wife of a businessman, small town, 1997)

They mail them to me, and I take them to churches and distribute them and take them to the places where I hang out, there's a local beauty shop, where we go down and have kind of a roundtable there, and we sit there and discuss issues. (wife of a professional, small town, 1997)

The voter guides are small, only $8\frac{1}{2}$ x $5\frac{1}{2}$ inches. The candidates are rated on only a few issues, and categorized as supports, opposes, no response, or undecided. The voter guides' relatively simple format makes them easy to read and understand, but it also makes the guides vulnerable to charges of partisanship. The rating is supposedly based on candidate responses to questionnaires, on their voting record, or on other public statements, but candidates complain that the rating does not accurately represent their position, or in some cases, not even the response they gave on the Christian Coalition questionnaire.[15] Critics charge further that the issues included are carefully chosen to show the Republican candidates in the most favorable light, and that they are distributed by the Republican Party. Indeed, I picked some up at a Republican campaign office before the 1998 election.

Sen. Dave Herbert of the Oklahoma state senate sued the coalition for misrepresenting his positions in the 1998 election season. The Oklahoma Christian Coalition claimed in court that the statements in its voter guide were merely opinion and therefore protected by the First Amendment, although the voter guides themselves stated that the recorded positions of candidates were verified using voting records. The coalition admitted that Senator Herbert had not filled out one of their surveys, that they had not talked with him about his positions, and that some of the committee votes on which the voter guide was based were not recorded. The coalition had depended on reports of other senators on the committee and on the material put out by Oklahomans for Life for some of their information. In one case, Senator Herbert had voted against a bill in committee, but had voted for it on the floor. The coalition representative who prepared the voter guide said it was his opinion that the first vote represented the senator's true views, and the second one did not.[16]

Senator Herbert lost the case because the U.S. Supreme Court had ruled in *New York Times* v. *Sullivan* that a public official may not recover damages for a defamatory falsehood "unless he proves that the statement was made with actual malice—that is, with knowledge that it was false or with reckless disregard of whether it was false or not."[17] At the conclusion of its opinion, the Court said that even if the voter guides were defamatory, even if the coalition was negligent in preparing them, even if they were untrue, that is not enough to constitute "actual malice" as required by the *New York Times* v. *Sullivan* decision.

Because of the *Sullivan* precedent, such suits nearly always fail. However, after the suit was dismissed, Christian Coalition spokesmen were quick to claim that the "trustworthiness of our guides withstood the scrutiny of the court."[18] IRS regulations about nonpartisan politicking are more stringent, as the Christian Coalition's loss of its tax-exempt status showed. The organization Americans United for Separation of Church and State actively monitors Christian Coalition activities and files complaints with the IRS. They believe that churches may still risk losing their own tax-exemption if they distribute the voter guides.[19]

In addition to the voter guides distributed before election week, the Christian Coalition also puts out legislative scorecards, longer documents reporting every legislator's vote on certain key issues in the legislative session. Similar criticisms can be leveled at them: that the votes are selected to favor Republicans, that they do not show exactly what the provisions of a bill were or what other options were possible, or whether the vote was a substantive or procedural one.

Voter guides and scorecards have been distributed by other interest groups—the AFL-CIO, the Sierra Club, and the American Conservative Union, to name just a few—for many years. Most of them are longer and more complicated, so that a careful voter could determine exactly how the candidate voted on each particular issue and exactly what the vote meant in the legislative process. But it is unlikely that many voters actually take the trouble to decipher this more precise information. No deciphering is required for the Christian Coalition guides. Further, because they are distributed in churches the Sunday before the election, there is no opportunity for explanation or rebuttal.

CHARISMATICS IN THE CHRISTIAN RIGHT

Marion G. (Pat) Robertson is the son of a United States senator, a seminary graduate, and an ordained Southern Baptist minister. His embrace of charismatic worship began when he was introduced to the charismatic movement by a Korean woman he met while in seminary.[20] "Charismatic" is a term derived from the Greek word *charisma*, meaning grace or favor, but here it is used to mean encouraging the "spiritual gifts" of speaking in tongues, healing, and prophecy. Those practices, which formerly were almost exclusively the province of pentecostals, were adopted by some mainline churches in the "charismatic renewal" movement of the 1950s and 1960s.

Baptists and other fundamentalists have a strong theological disagreement with the pentecostal denominations, which have existed since the beginning of the twentieth century, as well as with the newer charismatics. Although recognizing that "spiritual gifts" were available to Christ's followers in biblical times, fundamentalists believe the Bible precludes their use in modern times. About 60 percent of the anti-ERA activists I interviewed in 1980 were members of fundamentalist churches and none was pentecostal.

There were many more pentecostals or charismatics among those I interviewed in 1997. About one-third were pentecostal or charismatic; most of the rest were fundamentalist. None of the charismatics reported having been recruited through their churches, but about half of the charismatics had been regular viewers of the *700 Club* on television, and a little more than a third had contributed to the Robertson presidential campaign. Almost three-fourths of the charismatics who were regular *700 Club* viewers also supported Robertson in 1988.

A national study of donors to various Republican campaign committees found that two-thirds of Robertson's campaign donors in 1988 were pentecostal or charismatic.[21] The Christian Coalition had a similar base, because the coalition's first mail solicitation went to Robertson's list of campaign contributors. Over half of all the Christian Coalition members I interviewed had been active in Robertson's presidential campaign.

A 1979 national poll by the Gallup organization found that 19 percent of the adult population called themselves charismatic or pentecostal.[22] Pentecostals are easily counted because the names of their churches identify them as such, but charismatics, or neo-pentecostals, are harder to count. They may be members of churches in one of the traditional non-pentecostal denominations—churches which have adopted a charismatic style of worship under the influence of the charismatic renewal movement. Still others belong to a charismatic nondenominational church. Therefore, each of the religious categories usually employed—evangelical, mainline, Catholic, and nondenominational—contains some charismatics, but no one knows just how many.

One charismatic among my respondents was an active member of a Methodist church, and one had grown up in the Assembly of God and remained there, but most of the charismatics were affiliated with one of the new nondenominational churches. They had grown up in Methodist, Catholic, Lutheran, Baptist, or Presbyterian churches. These respondents simply did not think denominational affiliation was important. Each respondent's pastor might have been ordained in one denomination, the

church might have been founded by another, and it might have later affiliated with still another, or with none at all. Or the church might have been
"planted" and "grown" by an energetic pastor with no denominational
connection who felt God had called him to do so. The members themselves might have grown up in one denomination and tried several others
before finding the church where they were "being fed" or "being prepared" or "learning more about the Bible."

Victory Christian Center in Tulsa, Oklahoma, is one of the nondenominational churches that had attracted several of my respondents. Its
pastor is Billy Joe Daugherty, a former Methodist and a graduate of Oral
Roberts University who served as an Assembly of God pastor before
starting his church. Oral Roberts himself, who toured the United States in
tents with preaching and faith healing crusades in the 1950s, joined the
Victory Christian Center (VCC) in 1984.

At the time of my visit to VCC in 1997, it had ten thousand members.
Seven thousand attended on the typical Sunday, in five different church
services. The church included a K–12 school, a Bible institute for laymen,
and a ministry training center. It conducts missions all over the world and
ministers to prison inmates. There were 400 staff members, including
associate pastors for each zip code in Tulsa. The church had 177 telephone extensions on three telephone lines.

Each Saturday afternoon, the custodial staff of Victory Christian
Center put down a carpet and set up chairs, a stage, and a sound system
for the Sunday services in a space that served as a gymnasium during the
week. Like other nondenominational churches, it met in a windowless
space in a building that looked more like a warehouse than a traditional
church. There were no traditional Christian symbols—often not even a
cross—and no hymnbooks. The words for congregational singing were
projected on a screen, thus freeing parishioners to raise hands to God in
the charismatic gesture of praise and worship.

Tulsa is also the headquarters of Rhema Bible churches, another
group of charismatic churches. Like Oklahoma-based Victory and
Rhema, Vineyard, Calvary Chapel, and Hope Chapel, based in southern
California, are also large independent churches that have attracted
growing numbers of worshippers. Each has its own ministry training centers and from five hundred to one thousand associated churches, created
as promising young men have been led to leave existing churches and

plant other similar ones in other cities and even in other countries. Members of these churches emphatically reject the idea that they might someday evolve into a new denomination.

In addition to churches affiliated with these five associations, the telephone directory of almost any city lists many other independent or nondenominational churches. Not all of them are charismatic, but many are. At least half of the popular preachers on radio and television are charismatic as well. The list of those mentioned by respondents included the charismatics Benny Hinn, Kenneth Copeland, and Kenneth Hagin. Other charismatic preachers are Ernest Angley, Richard Hogue, the now-retired Oral Roberts, and the now-disgraced Jim Bakker and Jimmy Swaggart. Popular televangelists who are not charismatic are James Kennedy, James Robison, Robert Schuller, and of course, Jerry Falwell.

THE FUTURE OF CONSERVATIVE CHURCHES

At least three new trends in American religion meet in the nondenominational churches to which almost two-fifths of my 1997 respondents belonged. The churches are not affiliated with any of the old denominations, either modernist or fundamentalist, their rates of growth are astonishing, and many of them, but not all, are charismatic. Donald Miller, a sociologist who has studied them in California, calls them "postmodern."[23] They are unconcerned with the old fundamentalist-modernist controversy and they reject much of church culture: the medieval architecture and symbolism, the modern formally trained clergy, traditional hymns, and the bureaucratic church hierarchy.

The statements of belief of the nondenominational groups would be acceptable to old-line fundamentalists, however. They uphold the inerrancy of the Bible, the divinity of Jesus, salvation by his Grace, and the necessity of a personal relation with Jesus as a result of a born-again experience. They require baptism by immersion, often choosing to do so in an outdoor setting, as was the baptism of Jesus by John the Baptist. But they are not so insistent on fine doctrinal points as are fundamentalists.

Another distinction between postmodernist churches and the older fundamentalist ones is perhaps less significant, but strikes the first-time visitor immediately. In accordance with their generally more casual approach to religion, jeans or shorts and T-shirts are acceptable at postmodern Sunday morning church services, as are traditional suits and dresses and everything in between.

Among my 1997 respondents, only the older ones fit the strict fundamentalist criteria. The young people were attracted to the nondenominational churches. That was confirmed when I visited nondenominational churches in my own area and noted the youthful nature of the congregations.

Public opinion surveys have consistently shown a relationship between conservative religion and conservative attitudes on such hot-button questions for the Christian Right as abortion, homosexuality, sex education in schools, and pornography.[24] The only systematic analysis of postmodern church members indicates that they hold similar views. Miller found that 87 percent of his respondents oppose abortion for any reason, 97 percent believe homosexuality is always wrong, 98 percent believe sexual relations with someone other than a marriage partner is always wrong, 64 percent oppose sex education in schools, and 62 percent identify as Republican.[25]

The extraordinary agreement of members of fundamentalist and postmodern churches with the issues espoused by the Christian Right in its meetings, its literature, and its radio and television programs does not mean that every conservative Christian is politically active on those issues. The consensus of research on the Christian Right is that almost all of its political activists are conservative Christians, but only a small proportion of conservative Christians are political activists, with a somewhat larger proportion supporting the Christian Right movement, but not active in it. That seems to be the case with the postmodern conservatives as well.

NOTES

1. Pat Robertson, *The New World Order* (Dallas: Word Publishing, 1991).

2. Michael Lind, "On Pat Robertson," *New York Review*, 20 April 1995.

3. Joe Barnhart, *Jim and Tammy* (Amherst, N.Y.: Prometheus Books, 1988), p. 45.

4. Pat Robertson, *The Plan* (Nashville: Thomas Nelson, 1989), p. 22.

5. Ibid., p. 23.

6. "Super Tuesday Primaries: The Results," *New York Times*, 10 March 1988, p. 27.

7. David E. Rosenbaum, "Robertson Ends Active Campaigning," *New York Times*, 7 April 1988, D23.

8. Ralph Reed, *After the Revolution* (Dallas: Word Publishing, 1994), p. 2.

9. Ibid., p. 197.

10. Mail from Christian Coalition, 29 November 1999.

11. Tyler Maroney and Dustin Smith, "The Influence Merchants," *Fortune* (7 December 1998): 134; Jeffrey H. Birnbaum, "Follow the Money," *Fortune* (6 December 1999): 207–208.

12. Christian Coalition: Letter from Robertson dated 24 April 1999.

13. Interview with Ken Wood, 21 November 1996.

14. "The 1994 Elections: Oklahoma and the Nation," Roundtable at Oklahoma Political Science Association Annual Meeting at University of Tulsa, 11 November 1994.

15. Mark J. Rozell and Clyde Wilcox, *Second Coming* (Baltimore: Johns Hopkins Press, 1996), p. 178; Larry J. Sabato and Glenn R. Simpson, *Dirty Little Secrets* (New York: Times Books, 1996), pp. 128–41.

16. *Honorable David Herbert* v. *Oklahoma Christian Coalition*, 992 P.2d 324. 1999 OK 90. Oklahoma Supreme Court, 9 November 1999.

17. *New York Times* v. *Sullivan*, 376 U.S. 254, 84 S. Ct. 710, 11 L. Ed 2d 686 (1964).

18. Ed Godfrey, "District Judge Dismisses Legislator's Libel Suit," *Daily Oklahoman*, 17 April 1999, p. 13.

19. Steve Benen, "Truth Squad" *Church and State* 53, no. 11 (December 2000): 252–53.

20. Rob Boston, *The Most Dangerous Man in America? Pat Robertson and the Rise of the Christian Coalition* (Amherst, N.Y.: Prometheus Books, 1996), p. 25.

21. John C. Green, "A Look at the Invisible Army: Pat Robertson's 1988 Activist Corps," chap. 4 in *Religion and the Culture Wars: Dispatches from the Front*, John C. Green, et al. (Lanham, Md.: Rowman and Littlefield, 1996).

22. "The Christianity Today-Gallup Poll: An Overview," *Christianity Today* 23, no. 28 (21 December 1979): 14.

23. Donald E. Miller, *Reinventing American Protestantism: Christianity in the New Millenium* (Berkeley: University of California Press, 1997).

24. James L. Guth and John C. Green, *The Bible and the Ballot Box: Religion and Politics in the 1988 Election* (Boulder, Colo.: Westview, 1991), p. 220; Philip E. Hammond, *Religion and Personal Autonomy: The Third Disestablishment in America* (Columbia: University of South Carolina Press, 1992), p. 33; Dean R. Hoge Benton Johnson, and Donald A. Luidens, *Vanishing Boundaries:*

The Religion of Mainline Protestant Baby Boomers (Louisville, Ky.: Westminster, Knox Press, 1994), pp. 90–91.

25. Miller, *Reinventing Protestantism,* pp. 208–11.

PART III

THE ISSUES AND HOW THEY EVOLVED

11

FOLLOWING GOD'S PLAN

ERA is against God's plan. He states in the Bible that [women and men] are to have different roles, and if this can't be in the law, then it is a violation of God's laws. (Beverly Findley, 1979)

It was important for people to understand God's plan and purpose and be in agreement so they could experience heaven right here and not wait till they got to heaven you know, and to me, all of this is part of pro-family. (urban woman, 1997)

The term "God's plan" as it was used in the anti-ERA campaign, during the first phase of the Christian conservative movement, meant "God's plan for the family." Although it was used later in a more general sense, the conflict over women's roles was the one that first motivated Christian conservatives to undertake political action. Conservative women saw the ERA not as a vehicle for gaining equality for women, but as permission for the government to interfere in their personal and family lives. What is more, their understanding of the Bible was that while women are of equal worth in God's eyes, he meant for them to have different roles and functions in the family.

Implicit in the opposition to the ERA was a fierce defense of the right of citizens to live in accordance with their religious beliefs. The fear of government intrusion into the way of life and religious practices of citizens was turned on its head in later years as Christian Right lawyers tried to gain legitimacy for religious practices or the posting of religious documents in governmental institutions—courtrooms, legislative chambers, and tax-supported schools.

During the anti-ERA campaign, 56 percent of my respondents who opposed the ERA chose as their first reason that it was "against God's plan"; of those reporting that they gave the ERA campaign the highest priority in the last few months before the deadline, all chose "against God's plan." Closely tied for second were that "it would encourage an unbiblical relationship between men and women," and that it would "weaken families." The Bible references most frequently cited in support of this view of "God's plan" were in St. Paul's letters to the early churches, for example: "Wives submit yourselves unto your own husbands as unto the Lord. For the husband is head of the wife, even as Christ is head of the church" (Eph. 5:22).[1]

The Antis also believed that if the ERA were adopted, the government would force churches to ordain women, which would violate another of St. Paul's injunctions: "Let your women keep silence in the churches, for it is not permitted unto them to speak, but they are commanded to be under obedience" (1 Cor. 14:34). ERA supporters scoffed at these fears, saying that the ERA would apply to governmental action only, and would not affect relationships within the family or within church bodies.

The question that started the whole thing: "What is the proper role for a woman?" was less contentious in 1997 than in 1980. The nation had left this issue behind and moved on to other things. Christian conservatives in 1980 held out for the "traditional family," meaning a wife who was not employed outside the home. By 1997 many had accepted families with two employed parents, and some had reluctantly accepted divorce under certain circumstances, but they were *not* ready for two parents of the same sex. In 1980 "family problems" or "family decline" meant divorces or mothers working outside the home. In 1997 it meant government usurping parents' responsibility for sex education and schools teaching creation or teaching homosexuality as an alternate lifestyle, although some older respondents still thought it best if mothers did not work outside the home.

The 1980 interviews with Christian conservatives included fifty-three women and men who were in ongoing marriages (others were single or widowed). Ten interviews were conducted with both spouses present so that I could draw some conclusions about their relationship from observing their interaction. Although I did not plan an in-depth study of their marriage relationships, I was interested in the kind of roles they had worked out between husband and wife. I questioned them about that and also asked whether they were satisfied with their marriages. Two volunteered that they were not happy in their marriages, and there was evidence of tension in one other case. Fifteen of the remaining fifty gave their marriage relationship an enthusiastic endorsement, and the other thirty-five had no complaints. Some admitted that there had been problems but that they had "worked it out." Even those who were not happy had no intention of dissolving the marriage because "it's God's plan for a woman to stay home and doing otherwise wouldn't solve the problem, so I see no reason to divorce."

Most of the women I interviewed in 1980 had been employed at some time, just after college or in the early years of their marriages before having children. But they were unanimous in believing that it was best for a woman to stay home while she had young children. A few had worked outside the home even after they had a child, but only because of financial necessity, and they all regretted having done so. Men, too, thought women should remain at home if possible.

> If a mother had to work, it would have to be an absolute emergency. If she has no husband, she would have to sacrifice a lot to communicate with that child. I would never turn my child over to someone that I did not know personally. (farmer's wife, 1980)

> I did it all backward. I wish I had stayed home, not paid all those babysitters, waited until they were in school, and then gone to work. I've paid baby-sitters over the years thousands of dollars. It wasn't very smart. (Sandra Jeter, 1980)

> Mothers shouldn't work if they can help it. It isn't good, especially if there are little children. God made it so women have the babies. Throwing men and women together in the workplace brings temptation to fornication, and the Bible is against that too. (male real estate broker, part-time minister, 1980)

In 1997 most respondents still believed that it was better for mothers to be at home while their children were small, but for various reasons some had made other choices. About half of the female respondents and the spouses of male respondents in 1997 were employed as professionals, managers, or in skilled occupations. Not all had children at home, however. The most negative comments about the consequences of mothers working outside the home came from the older women whose children were grown:

> When our girls were growing up, God spoke to me one day and told me
> . . . "I want you to stay home and teach them and take care of them."
> (urban woman, homemaker, 1997)

> That wife needs to stay home and teach those children, and they don't need
> her getting a job supposedly to buy a second car, and all that. Because when
> she gets a job, they *need* a second car. (suburban man, self-employed, 1997)

Among the thirteen families in 1997 with children still living at home, five mothers were employed and eight were full-time homemakers. One of the employed women had already resigned her teaching position for the next year because her children had reached the teenage years. Another had cut back on her working hours as her children approached their teens. A contrary example was a woman who had just begun teaching because her children were getting older and she wanted to earn money for their college expenses. Two women were employed because of immediate financial necessity. One of these women was finding it particularly difficult.

> By the time you get up early enough to get them taken care of and try
> to get a little bit of housework done and all the errands that I have to
> run, it just wears me out. I hardly ever see my husband. . . . I would like
> to be home with the children, but we just can't afford it. (suburban
> woman, computer operator, 1997)

But those who chose to stay home with their children said that it was a financial sacrifice for them too.

> It is a sacrificial decision. It doesn't make sense to have children and then
> put them in day care. A lot of people think they need the money, but they
> are too narcissistic and they buy things they can't afford. But I love to work,
> and I will do it again when the children are older. (urban woman, 1997)

> This is the second year that I've been home and it was before I even got

pregnant that I took leave of absence and my husband and I both made the decision that I would stay home. . . . We're blessed to have the financial help to let our kids go somewhere other than a public school, and to be getting a Christian education. (former teacher living in the suburbs, 1997)

In the latter case, grandparents were providing funds for the private school tuition. Two of the stay-at-home mothers were self-employed at least part-time with their own Christian ministries, one was home-schooling her children, and one had adopted several "special-needs" foster children who required a great deal of care. Two others were active in community organizations and in partisan politics.

ABORTION

The word "abortion" is not mentioned in the Bible, nor is the procedure described anywhere in it, but Christian conservatives derive their opposition to abortion from several Bible verses. "Thou shalt not kill" from the Ten Commandments (Exod. 20:13) is one. They believe the commandment is applicable to an unborn fetus because of other verses in which God recognizes the fetus: "Before I formed thee in the belly I knew thee; and before thou camest forth out of the womb, I sanctified thee . . ." (Jer.1:5).

The Supreme Court decision on abortion, *Roe* v. *Wade*, was handed down less than a year after the introduction of the ERA. Even in those early years, almost all of those I interviewed were opposed to abortion, but the ERA was engaging all of their efforts. They left the abortion issue to the Roman Catholics.

During the ERA campaign, Francis Schaeffer and Tim LaHaye began to frame the Christian Right's understanding of contemporary issues with their identification of humanism as the substitution of man's needs for God's will. They explained that abortion was the most horrifying consequence of humanism. It was the placing of the mother's convenience above obedience to God's will. In 1979 Schaeffer and Dr. C. Everett Koop traveled to eighteen cities to discuss their new book, *Whatever Happened to the Human Race?*[2] and to show a film based on the book. The book includes a brief summary of Schaeffer's analysis of humanism, as well as Koop's detailed explanation of fetal development, abortion procedures, and euthanasia.

Although the seminars and film showings were not as well attended as Koop and Schaeffer had hoped, they nevertheless brought many evangelicals into the pro-life movement, which up until then had been primarily a Roman Catholic one. Jerry Falwell picked up the theme and featured it in his *Moral Majority Report* on a regular basis, giving Schaeffer credit for his influence. During the 1980s, fundamentalist Protestants began to equal and finally to outnumber Catholics in the pro-life movement.[3] By the end of the 1990s, every Christian Right organization that polled its members on their issue priorities found that abortion was the highest priority.

Abortion was also the most important issue for 37 percent of my 1997 respondents, followed by a general concern for morals (17.8 percent) and family (16.4 percent). No other specific issue came close. Four respondents (including one who had herself had an abortion) were devoting most of their time to it. Abortion and homosexuality were the most frequently mentioned topics in Focus on the Family's *Citizen* and in Concerned Women for America's *Family Voice*. Although these two issues appeared somewhat less frequently in the Christian Coalition's *Christian American*, the increased emphasis on the abortion issue was an obvious change in the Christian Right's issue-agenda from 1980 to 1997.

About one-third of my respondents in 1997 favored a total ban on abortion, with no exceptions whatsoever. The other two-thirds wanted a ban except for cases in which the life of the mother is endangered. Other suggested exceptions (rape, incest, or a possibly deformed fetus) had no support among my respondents. The disagreement on whether it should be a total ban or an almost total one is the only abortion-related question on which 1997 respondents lacked complete unanimity.

SEX EDUCATION

When asked what could be done to reduce the number of unwanted pregnancies and therefore reduce the demand for abortion, respondents urged teaching of traditional moral values, including sexual abstinence, by home and church. Surprisingly, few of the respondents blamed increased sexual activity among the young on the sexual content of movies, television, or advertising, although William Bennett, who is generally supportive of the Christian right, does so emphatically. They attributed it instead to Planned

Parenthood's influence on the public schools and to sex education programs that actually encouraged premarital sexual experience by the young.

Many of those I interviewed blamed the Sexuality Information and Education Council of the United States (SIECUS) for the type of sex education being offered in schools. SIECUS was established in 1964, and remains the leading producer and exponent of comprehensive sex education courses for public schools.[4] It advocates the widest possible dissemination of information about all aspects of sexuality. Conservatives charge it with ignoring the moral and religious limits on sexual expression, and link it to humanism's failure to teach moral absolutes. They especially object to the SIECUS policy that masturbation and homosexuality are acceptable forms of sexual expression. In the 1997 interviews, respondents again listed sex education as one of their main objections to public schools.

Christian conservatives believe that parents are the best ones to provide sex education for young people. Some suggested that parents might profit from courses in how to teach sex education to their children. They wanted their children to learn about sex in accordance with their own moral values, and they recognized that this might not be possible in public schools.

> If [sex education] were taught, as far as I'm concerned, it should be taught from the standpoint of abstinence, like it's taught biblically, that this is a union that takes place after marriage, and it's not to be done beforehand. Contraception doesn't have to be taught. (wife of a police officer, 1997)

Christian conservatives did not want young people to be taught about contraceptives. Because they believed that public school sex education would always include such information, none wanted sex education to be taught in schools. They recognized that not all parents do an adequate job of teaching their children about sex, and they worried about it, but that was not a sufficient reason to have sex education in public schools. They believed it actually makes the situation worse. As proof, they point out that teenage pregnancy has been increasing right along with the increased availability of sex education in schools.

> That's not the answer. That's been done, over and over and over, and the birth rate keeps going up. No, contraception is not the answer. (urban businessman, 1997)

I don't believe in providing contraceptives. I think that just encourages them. And don't support but one baby. One strike and you're out. The second baby, you're on your own. (retired physician, small city, 1997)

Most of the 1980 respondents also thought sex education should be taught at home and in the church rather than in schools, but in contrast to the later respondents, some of them (almost 10 percent) were willing to have it taught in schools. Both in 1980 and in 1997 the opinions of these Christian conservatives were far different than those of the general population. A random sample survey of Oklahomans in 1980 showed that even in such a conservative state, 80 percent favored sex education in the schools.[5] The University of Virginia poll in 1996 found that 68 percent of the American public favored sex education in schools, but only 55 percent of evangelicals.[6]

The general public was also more tolerant of abortion than these Christian Right activists, but it was not entirely clear whether public opinion was moving toward or away from the conservative position. National polls by the Gallup organization found that those believing abortion should be legal under any circumstances actually increased from 21 percent to 32 percent from 1975 to 1993, while those believing it should never be legal had decreased from 22 percent to 13 percent in the same eighteen years.[7] In May 1996, 42 percent of the respondents to a Gallup Poll favored a ban except when necessary to save the mother's life,[8] the position favored by two-thirds of my interviewees.

On the other hand, the *New York Times*/CBS News poll, taken on the twenty-fifth anniversary of *Roe* v. *Wade* in January 1998, found some shift toward the pro-life position since it first asked the question in 1989: "supporters of generally available legal abortion have slipped from 40 percent to 32 percent and the ranks of those who say it should be available but stricter have increased to 45 percent from 40 percent."[9] In this 1998 poll, only 22 percent favored a total ban, in contrast to one-half of my respondents. The differing results between the Gallup and *New York Times*/CBS polls can be attributed to the different wording in the two polls, and to the ever-present volatility of public opinion on controversial subjects.

While their efforts have not been rewarded with big changes in public opinion, pro-life and pro-family activists might have taken comfort in the declining number of abortions actually performed in the United States.

Despite an inadequate system for collecting statistics on pregnancies and births, partly because the procedure is subject to so much controversy, it seems clear that the number of abortions decreased after 1990. My respondents did not rejoice in the drop, however, because it was so small, and they were not even sure they believed the figures.

The Alan Guttmacher Institute (AGI) in New York, a nongovernmental agency that tracks the official Centers for Disease Control figures and supplements them with reports from individual doctors and clinics, showed a 4.5 percent drop in abortions from 1990 to 1995.[10] The AGI suggests that the decline may be due to the reduced availability of abortion as a result of the antiabortion movement's efforts against it, particularly outside of metropolitan areas, and to reduced sexual activity and increased use of contraceptives.

Christian conservatives were suspicious of the Guttmacher Institute because of its association with Planned Parenthood. They would like to attribute the decline in abortions to abstinence-only sex education programs, the kind of sex education taught in their own churches and schools. They succeeded in getting a provision for federal government support of abstinence-only programs into the federal welfare reform bill in 1996. States first had to apply for the matching funds, however, and the actual implementation of the program did not get underway until 1998. It could not have affected the reported drop in abortion as early as 1995. The Oklahoma Family Policy Council began implementing its first grant under this legislation in spring 2000.

In the mid-1990s, the pro-life organizations found an innovative issue in what they called "partial-birth" abortion. That term was invented by the pro-life organizations; the medical profession calls it some variation of "dilation and extraction." But pro-life groups, by describing it in gruesome detail as killing the baby after it is partially delivered, and by circulating drawings showing how it is done, have succeeded in getting even some who support abortion rights to agree that this particular procedure should not be allowed. News accounts generally describe it as a "form of late-term abortion that is seldom employed."

Pro-life groups disagree with both parts of that characterization. They insist that it is sometimes used in the fifth month of pregnancy, and that it is done often. No reliable statistics are available to settle this question, although pro-lifers declare that "partial-birth" abortion is a legal term now that it has been incorporated into legislation. Although only about 1 percent of abortions occur after the twentieth week of pregnancy,[11] no one knows what proportion of those can be described as "partial-birth" abortions. In any case, appalling descriptions of the procedure may have helped to reduce support for abortions in general.[12]

Groups favoring abortion rights brought out their own appalling cases in response to the "partial-birth" abortion issue—women who had serious health problems that required this procedure. But the pro-lifers seemed to be winning the case in the court of public opinion. The Gallup Poll found in 1996 that 57 percent of Americans believed the procedure should be banned.[13] By June 2000, when the Supreme Court invalidated Nebraska's state law banning "partial-birth" abortion because it was too vague, thirty states had similar laws, and abortion opponents vowed to try again with a revised law.

HOMOSEXUALITY

While the word "homosexuality" does not appear in the Bible, there are several references to it, including "Thou shalt not lie with mankind, as with womankind: it is abomination" (Lev. 18:22). And there is the all-purpose verse forbidding all kinds of sexual sin: "Be not deceived: neither fornicators, nor idolaters, nor adulterers, nor effeminate, nor abusers of themselves with mankind" (I Cor. 6:9). The homosexual issue has been important for recruitment and fund-raising from the time of the ERA campaign to the present because its appall factor is especially high. As one pro-family leader noted in 1979, emotional issues like homosexuality are what attract attention.

Although Beverly LaHaye's *Family Voice* magazine gives roughly equal time to the abortion and homosexuality issues, her fund-raising letters for Concerned Women for America appeal for money to fight homosexuality twice as often as for abortion. Lou Sheldon's *Traditional Values Report* and his fund-raising letters devote most of their space to homosexuality. Focus on the Family mentions it less often, in only about one-third of its magazines, while the magazines and fund-raising letters of the Christian Coalition mentioned it only occasionally.

In 1980 there was little media coverage of homosexuality. By 1997 it was a regular topic in newspapers and on television news. In the meanwhile, the literature of the Christian Right and its television and radio programs had channeled listeners' opinions into a uniform way of expressing them. On this issue, perhaps more than any other, certain words and phrases appeared in many of the interviews with the second set of respondents in 1997. One oft-repeated expression is "the homosexual lifestyle," meaning promiscuous sexual activity. Another is "the homosexual agenda," meaning political pressure for same-sex marriage, allowing homosexuals to adopt children, and acceptance of homosexuality as "an acceptable alternate lifestyle." In most cases respondents had not considered the possibility that not all homosexuals push the agenda or follow the lifestyle. After all, homosexuals who live quiet lives and are not politically active in homosexual causes do not get, nor do they want, much media attention.

Both groups of respondents were nearly unanimous in believing that homosexual behavior is a sin and in opposing same-sex marriages. There were differences, however, when they were asked about some of the other practical applications of those beliefs. For instance, when I asked if a homosexual person would still be homosexual even if he did not engage in promiscuous sex, it was clear that many respondents had not thought of that before.

> Well, I don't know. I guess if you really haven't renounced it . . . well, really he's not a homosexual if he's not practicing homosexuality, I believe. (elderly housewife, knows a homosexual well, 1997)

Several suggested after some reflection that homosexuality might be likened to alcoholism, that it was an inborn tendency but that it could be controlled just as alcoholism could:

> There are some people that have a propensity for alcoholism, but that doesn't excuse their behavior. It doesn't excuse them from killing somebody on the road because they're drunk. It doesn't excuse them from anything, nor does the propensity toward lesbianism or homosexuality excuse those people from having to behave appropriately in our society. (young man, former candidate for state legislature, 1997)

When I asked if the sin of homosexuality is worse than the other things that the Bible calls an "abomination," most said no.

Well, I haven't counted [the abominations]. Homosexuality is really marked as kind of sin in a society, because in the Scripture God ordered the destruction of Sodom and Gomorrah because of that sin. . . . What we read in the Scripture is the judgment of God. It appears to me that AIDS is really a judgment because we have accepted homosexuality. (head of private Christian ministry, 1997)

Sin is sin, whether it's homosexuality or stealing, or whatever. I wrestle with this. Some sins are worse in God's eyes than other sins are, but sin is sin. All sin leads to death, it leads to a spiritual death. I am called to love the sinner, not the sin, and I try to love the sinner. (self-employed urban man, 1997)

In many cases, the interviews reflected an inward struggle about homosexuality. They were committed to the biblical stance against it, but they also recognized their responsibility to "love the sinner, while hating the sin," although it was difficult to do.

Contrary to what some research has shown, personal acquaintance with homosexuals did not affect these respondents' view of homosexuality as sin or of homosexuals as needing help to be freed from it. Even those who had close family members who were homosexual could not accept the possibility that homosexuality is inborn rather than chosen and prayed that their loved one would be released from the sin. Research suggesting that homosexuality might be inborn was categorically rejected. Their belief in the truth of God's word as it appears in the Bible made it logically impossible. For these Christian conservatives, the Bible is the ultimate authority.

Why would he say a homosexual cannot enter the kingdom of heaven if they were born that way? God would not do that. He is a loving God, and he would not call it a sin if it were something they were born with. You can't be born a sinner. (Bunny Chambers, 1979)

In 1980, a strong majority of respondents (57.2 percent) did not want homosexuals teaching in schools.

I would not want my child taught by a homosexual, or a rapist, or a drunkard. . . . A homosexual would actually be advocating by the fact they were out of the closet, even if it didn't come into his teaching, so I would not want to have a teacher like that. (urban woman, former teacher, 1980)

Twenty years later, that issue was mentioned less often, although respondents had not softened their stance. The new issue in 1997 was civil rights for homosexuals, opposed by 91 percent of respondents. Another of those oft-repeated expressions, "special rights" appears in discussion of this issue. The literature of the Christian Right has been remarkably successful in framing and redefining laws originally proposed to secure the same rights for minorities that other citizens have, as laws allowing "special rights."

> I don't oppose equal rights for homosexuals, I oppose special rights for them. I don't think they should be given. . . . I don't think they should be allowed to adopt children. That's a special right. (young man, coach at a Christian university, 1997)

But on the other hand,

> I don't think I would say that I wouldn't rent to a homosexual, if they were [chaste in their behavior]. I don't know, that's never come up. [A person like that] I trust is not gonna push that on anyone or anything like that. (elderly woman, knows a homosexual well, 1997)

Slightly more than half of the respondents thought landlords should have a right to refuse to rent to homosexuals and that employers should have a right to refuse to hire homosexuals. Many saw this issue as a conflict of rights. Most believed that businesspeople should have a right to choose the employees with whom they have to work on a day-to-day basis and that property owners should have a right to choose the renters who live in their own homes. And yet they recognized that homosexuals need to be able to find a job and a place to live. The consensus, if there is one, is that small business owners and owner-landlords should be given more leeway than large corporate employers and large apartment complex landlords.

> They're here and they've got to live and I say they're just going to have to get by with that. That's what I've done all my life. They can have a place to live, if they leave off what they're asking for. (retired farmer, 1997)

> There are going to be all kinds of people in that one hundred-unit apartment complex that are going to be doing things that you don't believe

are right, but I believe it falls under different things than an individual piece of property. (wife of a businessman, 1997)

I think that probably depends on the job. I wouldn't want my daughter being taught by a homosexual or my son. I really wouldn't. The same reason I wouldn't want them taught by an agnostic. (young man, former legislative candidate, 1997)

These active church members are especially sensitive to the issue of churches being forced to do something that violates their religious principles, such as hiring homosexuals to work for the church. The same argument surfaced in the ERA campaign about equal rights for women.

. . . that churches might at some point in time have to hire them. You know, churches being forced to hire and employ people to be around their kids, that's not religious freedom, those are special rights. A homosexual has every right I have right now. He's got it made, he doesn't need special rights. They have the rights of other workers, but I don't want it crammed down my throat. (urban businessman, 1997)

While opposing rights laws for homosexuals, almost all the respondents agreed to the need for civil rights laws for people of color who cannot help the color of their skin. Only about half approved of equal rights laws for women, although women cannot help their sex either. But the strong belief that homosexuality is a choice colored their opinion on equal rights laws for homosexuals.

I think it is a special right to not allow not hiring homosexuals. Black people can't help what color they are, but homosexuals can help being homosexual. (young man, head of private ministry opposing abortion, 1997)

The unyielding stand of the Christian conservatives on most aspects of homosexuality has hardly changed since 1972. They would say that this is simply because the Bible has not changed. But in the meanwhile, the American public has gradually become more accepting of homosexuality. Gallup Polls show that the percentage of Americans believing that homosexuality should be considered an acceptable alternative lifestyle increased from 34 percent in 1982 to 50 percent in 1999.[14]

Trend, Opinions on Homosexuality
Gallup Polls, 1977-1999

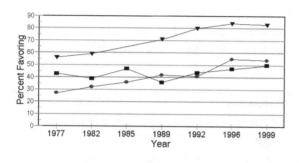

Year

—■— Legalized   —▼— Equal Jobs   —●— Elem. Tchrs.

Question 1:
Do you think homosexual relations between consenting adults should or should not be legal?

Question 2:
In general, do you think homosexuals should or should not have equal rights in term of job opportunities?

Question 3:
Do you think homosexuals should or should not be hired as elementary teachers?

Source: Lydia Saad, "Americans Growing More Tolerant of Gays," *Gallup Poll Monthly* 375 (December 1996): 12–14; Mark Gillespie, "Americans Support Hate Crimes Legislation That Includes Protection for Gays," *Gallup Poll Monthly* 403 (April 1999): 25–26.

Gallup Polls also showed a steady increase in those saying homosexuals should have equal rights in job opportunities, from 56 percent in 1977 to 83 percent in 1999. Those willing to accept homosexuals even as elementary school teachers, something my respondents strongly opposed, increased from 27 percent in 1977 to 54 percent in 1999.[15] But the American public in 1996 was still strongly opposed (68 percent) to making same-sex marriages legal.

Those who oppose the Christian Right note that its emphasis on sexual sin does not accurately represent the teachings of Jesus, who spoke about responsibility for the poor more frequently than about sexual misconduct. And Francis Schaeffer, whose writings were the foundation for much of the Christian Right's political agenda, lamented in an interview late in his life that evangelical reviewers never mentioned the things he considered most important: "the Christian responsibility for the compassionate use of accumulated wealth and the racial situation."[16]

While this criticism is valid in terms of the Christian Right's appeals for political action, it is only fair to note that a great many of those I interviewed do participate in church activities to help the poor. They work at homeless shelters and crisis pregnancy centers. They also gather food and clothing to distribute in their local communities and in their missions around the world. It is *government* help for the poor that they object to. About the bombing of the Oklahoma City federal building, one respondent said:

> The outpouring of volunteer help in Oklahoma City [after the bombing] proved that people can take care of their own. We don't need government to take care of us. (urban woman, 1996)

In summary, Christian conservatives have come to accept the diversity of women's roles and that many women need and want to work outside the home. But their views in comparison to those reflected in national opinion polls are less tolerant of abortion, much less tolerant of homosexuality, and less willing to accept sex education in the public schools. The public may be moving ever-so-slightly toward the Christian conservatives' opinions on abortion, although the evidence is mixed and depends on the wording of the questions. Public opinion is moving away from their views on homosexuality, but agrees with them in disapproving same-sex marriages.

NOTES

1. These and all subsequent Bible references are to the Authorized (King James) Version.

2. Francis Schaeffer, *Whatever Happened to the Human Race?* (Tappan, N.J.: Fleming H. Revell, 1979).

3. Dallas Blanchard, *The Anti-Abortion Movement: References and Resources* (New York: Prentice-Hall, 1996), p. 5.

4. See the March 1969 article in *American Opinion* by Gary Allen, "Sex Education Problems" and the book published in 1977 by the John Birch Society's press, Western Islands, *The SIECUS Circle: A Humanist Revolution*, by Claire Chambers.

5. Norma Haston Turner, *Analysis of Attitudes of Oklahomans of Voting Age toward Sex Education, Teen Contraception, and Abortion*, D.P.H. dissertation, University of Oklahoma, 1981, pp. 51–52.

6. James D. Hunter and Carl Bowman, *The State of Disunion*, vol. II, Fieldwork conducted by the Gallup Organization (Ivy, Va.: In Medias Res Educational Foundation, 1996), question 96-f.

7. Leslie McAneny and Lydia Saad, "Strong Ties between Religious Commitment and Abortion Views," *Gallup Poll Monthly* 330 (April 1993): 35–30.

8. Lydia Saad, "Issue Referendum Reveals Populist Leanings," *Gallup Monthly Report* 367 (May 1996): 2–4.

9. Carey Goldberg and Janet Elder, "Public Still Backs Abortion, but Wants Limits, Poll Says," *New York Times*, 16 January 1998, A1.

10. Tamar Lewin, "Abortion Rate Declined Again in '95," *New York Times*, 5 December 1997, A14.

11. "Facts in Brief: Induced Abortion," The Alan Guttmacher Institute Web site, http://www.agi-usa.org/pubs/fb_abortion2/fb_abort2.html, accessed 17 July 1998.

12. Richard L. Berke, "For Republicans, a Narrower Focus on Abortion Pays," *New York Times,* 21 October 1997, A1.

13. Saad, "Populist Leanings," p. 3.

14. David W. Moore, "Public Opposes Gay Marriages," *Gallup Poll Monthly* 366 (April 1996): 19–21.

15. Lydia Saad, "Americans Growing More Tolerant of Gays," *Gallup Poll Monthly* 375 (December 1996): 12–14; Mark Gillespie, "Americans Support Hate Crimes Legislation That Includes Protection for Gays," *Gallup Poll Monthly* 403 (April 1999): 25–26.

16. Philip Yancey, "Schaeffer on Schaeffer, Part II" *Christianity Today*, 6 April 1979, p. 22.

12

GUARDING
AGAINST HUMANISM

We've become a hedonistic society. . . . Personally, I believe our nation
is very much comparable to the Roman empire. . . . Rome became a
hedonistic society, where there was self-gratification and self-pleasure,
no thought of tomorrow, no thought of the consequences, no commitment to others or to marriage. . . . They became dependent on government, became a welfare state. Everything that makes a decaying civilization was there. (urban woman, 1980)

Historians question the details of this version of Roman history,
but in the 1970s, the "immorality of Rome" theme was a
common one from the pulpits of fundamentalist churches, along with its
corollary, that America will go the way of Rome if she does not mend her
ways. Because I heard this theme so often during the conflict over the
ERA, I began asking those who favored the ERA as well as those who
opposed it if they felt that things were getting worse. I found clear differences in the responses of the two groups to the following question:

A lot of people say that our society has lots of problems, like crime,
divorce, teenage pregnancy, and so on. Do you really think things are
worse now than they used to be, or better, or are they about the same?

The typical answer of the conservative Christians opposing the ERA to this question was:

> Yes, they are getting worse. There is a breakdown of the home. Women are working and not caring for children. There is immorality, dishonesty, and people are more interested in themselves than in others. And the worst thing of all is that now immorality is accepted, whereas it used to be frowned upon. (urban woman, 1980)

In contrast, the typical answer of someone supporting the ERA was:

> No, I think people who say that just don't know their history. There have always been problems, but now we've started becoming more aware of them and are trying to do something about them, so I think things are actually better now than before.

Another typical feminist response was:

> Well, there are a lot of problems, of course, but they are caused by changes in technology and industrialization. I certainly wouldn't want to go back to washing on the washboard, so I think we will just have to go to work to solve the new problems that come with social change.

These statements give credence to the claim that the Christian Right movement is a protest against modernism, not only in biblical interpretation, but also in the characteristics of postindustrial society. But the Antis were quite willing to accept the advantages of modern technology. It is not modern society in general that they deplore, but the erosion of traditional moral standards. Their perception may have been colored by their different environment. They lived, worked, attended church, and established friendships in a different cultural milieu than did the Pros. Each group's viewpoint was understandable in the context of their lives and experiences. Individuals in each group also reflected the viewpoint of the churches they attended.

When asked what concerned them most, the first response of the Antis was nearly always some variation of the "moral decline" theme. When pressed for an explanation, they cited the failure of societal institutions—families, schools, and communities—to teach morality as they had in the past.

I believe in the Bible very strongly. The home and family life are more to blame. Working mothers do not teach their children, and it just declines with each generation. (small-town woman, 1980)

I think there really are more and worse problems than before. We accept bad behavior where we didn't used to. It used to be that if you went down the street and saw a child misbehaving, you could speak to it and say "Your mother wouldn't want you to do that," but now everyone just accepts it as normal. (farm wife, 1980)

I think our morals are getting worse. We do not allow moralizing in schools, but just as in the old saying, "not to decide is to decide." Not to moralize is to moralize. I don't think it's a conspiracy, but it is a gradual creeping thing. We have been asleep at the switch and have let the humanists take over the content of our schools in a very subtle way. (part-time secretary, 1980)

In the 1997 interviews, the most common first response was still "moral decline" although it no longer came in the context of the ERA's violation of God's plan. This view that "things are getting worse," so widespread among my respondents, was spelled out in detail in unconfirmed Supreme Court nominee Robert Bork's *Slouching Toward Gomorrah*, published in 1996, and eagerly mentioned to me by some of those I interviewed.

HUMANISM

Not only were Christian conservatives troubled that social institutions were no longer teaching morality, but they saw the very basis for morality that had always guided their own lives being questioned. During the ERA campaign, and to a lesser extent in the later decades of the Christian Right, those most involved in it identified "humanism" as the root cause of all the trends they deplored. Students of history and philosophy know humanism as a sixteenth-century movement to revive ancient classical works. Later the word came to stand for the belief that art, science, philosophy, and sometimes even theology should be judged primarily in terms of their effect on the welfare of humanity. But for fundamentalists/evangelicals, humanism, especially when preceded by the modifier "secular"—as it usually was in their writings—is an antireligious and corrupting dogma. Betty Grogan, who in 1977 had fought off a particular "humanist program" scheduled for her local library, put it this way: "If we are not on guard, humanism will be brought into our community, in a dramatic, enticing, subtle way."

Lottie Beth Hobbs, the Fort Worth woman who started Women Who Want to be Women, later renamed Pro-Family Forum, discovered the other meaning of humanism in 1974. She does not remember exactly how she first heard about it, but however it came to her attention, she immediately began to study the subject and became convinced that the ERA was only one manifestation of the larger threat of secular humanism. She presented the results of her research at meetings of conservative groups and in the publications of her Pro-Family Forum. So that her members might be better informed, she also purchased the little booklet *Humanist Manifestos I and II* in bulk for resale.[1] The *Humanist Manifestos* were drafted by the American Humanist Association and signed by several dozen prominent humanists. Christian conservatives used the list of signers to identify those who were spreading what they saw as a dangerous philosophy.

Francis Schaeffer, a conservative Presbyterian minister who had moved to Switzerland and devoted himself to studying philosophy and theology, set up the frames within which evangelicals understood humanism. Schaeffer wrote several books, each more insistent than the one before, that Christians must resist humanism and its disastrous consequences. His first book on the subject, *How Should We Then Live?,* published in 1976, took readers quickly through Western history from ancient Rome to the modern United States, tracing the course of "biblically based" Christian ways of thinking and the opposing humanistic viewpoint.[2]

Schaeffer contended that the Reformation briefly "removed the humanistic distortions which had entered the Catholic church" and placed Reformation churches in their proper place *under* the authority of the Bible— "not above it and not equal to it."[3] His favorite expression was "the biblical base"; it meant that the Bible was the *only* proper basis for science, art, philosophy, or ethics, as well as religion. Humanism, as he saw it, substituted man's reason or ecclesiastical authority for this biblical base.

Schaeffer's analysis of humanism is essential to understanding the

Christian conservatives of today, for their positions on issues from abortion through the ERA and evolution to prayer in schools were informed by Schaeffer's discussion of humanism. This is not to say that all of them had read Schaeffer's work themselves. In many cases, they had learned of it indirectly from their pastors or from Christian Right literature.

The core of the problem for Schaeffer was that humanism offered no fixed standard for behavior. "If there is no absolute moral standard, then one cannot say in a final sense that anything is right or wrong."[4] Humanists claim that their standard is the welfare of humanity, but this can change, or be different for different people. Only the Bible offers a final, ultimate, and unchanging standard. To the fundamentalists of the early decades of the twentieth century, and also to those in later years who were more likely to call themselves evangelicals, the Bible cannot be wrong, and its truths are eternal. Everything in it is true, all the events actually happened as described, and its moral lessons are still applicable in today's world.

Tim LaHaye published his own book on humanism four years later, using the "secular" modifier throughout. Titled *Battle for the Mind* and published in 1980, it was dedicated to Schaeffer.[5] The early chapters summarized Schaeffer's book, but LaHaye condensed and simplified the ideas. While Schaeffer's book was difficult reading for the nonexpert in philosophy, history, and art, LaHaye made it accessible to the average layman. Both books were criticized for errors of historical fact, but they nevertheless shaped and framed the political agenda of the Christian conservatives.

According to the last three chapters in Schaeffer's book, humanism had influenced modern society, from Communism in Europe to the loss of the work ethic and misguided Supreme Court decisions in America. LaHaye spelled it out. He accused humanists of infiltrating American education, encouraging the sexual revolution, controlling the media, and infecting politics with their acceptance of shifting standards of behavior. In short, every evil trend could be traced to humanism. To LaHaye, as it had been to Lottie Beth Hobbs, the influence of secular humanism was the key that unlocked all the puzzles and explained all the disturbing trends in modern America. LaHaye's contribution was to disseminate the ideas widely among Christian conservatives.

To make this key available to fundamentalist evangelicals, LaHaye's San Diego church distributed his book to 85,000 pastors all across the country. They responded by spreading its message to their congregations in special "seminars," a brief version of which I heard at a Pro-Family Forum meeting. The analysis of humanism was presented by a Church of Christ minister, who read excerpts from the *Humanist Manifestos*, and claimed that Gloria Steinem and Betty Friedan were among the signers, although Steinem's name was not in the book I purchased. Then he explained what humanism meant, illustrating it by the size of the lectern. "If there is a dispute about it, we can get a ruler and measure it, but without a ruler, there is no way of knowing how big it is. It's the same with morality. If we don't have God as a measure of morality, there is no way of telling what is right and what is wrong."

Humanism was mentioned by almost everyone in the interviews I conducted and the conferences and meetings I attended from 1976 to 1983. Those who were most active in political campaigns or in the anti-ERA movement were the best informed about it. Others knew about it, but were less certain about its meaning. Humanism was mentioned less frequently in the 1997 interviews, and again, it was the most involved and most thoughtful respondents who knew the most about it. Frank Compton, a self-employed businessman who had read Francis Schaeffer and had a well-developed personal philosophy, said:

> We're into what's commonly called secular humanism. [It means that] I
> become my own person, my own law unto myself. I do my own thing,
> I do what's good for me. If it's good do it. (1997)

But Compton was exceptional. Despite all the efforts to educate Christian conservatives about it, secular humanism may have been too abstract an enemy to rally the rank and file. Respondents in 1997 were more likely to identify the problem as relativism—the loss of moral absolutes—a meaning similar to that used by Schaeffer. One young woman in 1997 explained it this way: "Well I think that today there are no morals being taught, there are no absolutes. Family values are in a decline." Another young woman laid the blame on sociology, a favorite target of Christian conservatives:

> I've got concerns with sociology. [An approach] apart from God can
> really wreak havoc with one's world view. Sociology can teach
> humanism, can teach an absence of absolutes and I want my child

growing up and knowing that there are moral absolutes as well as physical absolutes. Not only when you drop the rock will it fall, but also if
you sow, you shall also reap. (suburban woman, 1997)

Christian conservatives were especially upset that what they saw as
humanism was being taught in public schools. Myrtle Kelly was an articulate, intelligent woman who became a pro-family activist and a regional
star because her children encountered values clarification in their school
classes. After reading about the program in a 1978 issue of *Better Homes
and Gardens,*[6] she was horrified to learn that her own children had been
exposed to it in their school. She believed that some of the teaching exercises, such as choosing who would be allowed to remain in an over-
crowded lifeboat, had upset her son.

> When he came in with [talking about] games about a lifeboat turning
> over—he never went into detail—but I think the impact was such that
> he didn't want to talk about it. Because I can remember one day he came
> in from school and went to his room, and he cried, and he cried, and he
> cried. We never could get him to tell us what it was. He'd always told
> us what was bothering him before.
>   And I would almost guarantee that that was the day that they went
> through the little thing of the lifeboat, and you choose whether your
> mother or your father or you die. And I don't care who it is, in the little
> boy's mind, he's going to be the one that lives. And I think he came
> home and I think subconsciously that child realized that he'd let his
> father drown! I think it's . . . think it's just that simple. I hate to think
> about it again—I get so upset every time I talk about it. That's what
> started me on the pro-family group. (Myrtle Kelly, 1997)

That the questioning of moral values in the 1960s left many people
adrift was recognized by both liberals and conservatives. Sociologists, who
are indeed likely to be liberal, describe it as "anomie" or lack of moral consensus. But liberals and conservatives proposed different solutions. To the
conservatives in the pro-family movement of the 1970s and 1980s, the moral
absolutes of the Bible were the answer. They opposed school curricula based
on the theories of the Swiss developmental psychologist Jean Piaget and of
Lawrence Kohlberg. Kohlberg was a psychology professor at Harvard who
theorized that moral development follows certain stages from the simple "I

can't reach it," to "The rules say I shouldn't take it," to the more advanced "It doesn't belong to me, so it would be wrong for me to take it." Kohlberg and Sidney Simon of the University of Massachusetts proposed that schools should be involved in helping children reach more consistent and more firmly grounded moral values.

Working with Louis Raths at Ohio State University, and others, Simon developed specific strategies and curricula for teachers to use. Raths argued that children who grow up without the support of consistent family and community values tend to be apathetic, flighty, overconforming or overdissenting.[7] His curriculum was an attempt to help individuals sort out their own values and priorities, by a series of questions, pencil-and-paper exercises, hypothetical situations, and sometimes by role-playing. The lifeboat scenario, as described above, was frequently used with adult groups, as well as in school classrooms.

Christian conservatives believed that Raths's ideas were in fact a part of the problem, especially when he advised teachers to treat alternative solutions as if they were of equal value. When discussing value questions, he recommended that teachers make nonjudgmental comments, give additional information, or ask for an opinion, but not tell the children what is right or express their own opinions. Values were to be worked out by and for each individual through the process of considering all possible alternatives in many different situations. To Christian conservatives, this was a perfect example of humanism's failure to espouse moral absolutes.

In response to the conflict over values clarification in schools, Sen. Orrin Hatch (R-Utah) proposed a Pupil Rights Amendment to the General Education Provisions Act, which became law in 1978. It provided that parents should have an opportunity to examine any materials used in the classrooms, and that children should not be asked personal questions about sex, religion, or their family lives. But Christian conservatives objected that there was no effort to enforce the new amendment, and no regulations were proposed to implement it. As a result of their protests, the Department of Education held hearings in seven cities in spring 1984. Some of the women I had interviewed, including Myrtle Kelly and Anna Mayer, testified at the hearings. Phyllis Schlafly excerpted the testimony at the hearings and published it in a book called *Child Abuse in the Classroom*.[8] New regulations embodying these changes were finally promulgated in November 1984.

At just about the same time, a new conflict over humanism erupted in

Hawkins County, Tennessee, when Vicky Frost objected to textbooks her daughter was using in school because they included witches, magic, and evolution; were favorable to feminism and pacifism; and promoted humanist values. The complaints were similar to those raised by the parents in Kanawha County, West Virginia, in 1978. In the Tennessee case, the series, published by Holt, Rinehart, and Winston, was a popular one, used in classrooms all across the United States. Frost was unfairly accused of "censorship"; she did not ask the school to stop using the textbooks, but only to provide alternative materials for those whose parents objected to them.

The parents objected to "A Visit to Mars," which seemed to embody thought transfer or telepathy,[9] to a story in which it was suggested that lies might be appropriate in certain situations, and to a sixth-grade book that said "eons ago the world was ice and mud and fish climbed out of the sea to become reptiles on land and then dinosaurs and mammals."[10]

Frost was arrested for trespassing in November 1983 when she removed her daughter from a reading class and began teaching the child herself in the school library. Represented by an attorney from Beverly LaHaye's Concerned Women for America (CWA), the Frosts and four other families filed suit against the school board. The case, *Mozert* v. *Hawkins*, was named for Bob Mozert, another of the protesting parents. The media dubbed it Scopes II. Like the Scopes trial in 1925, it was tried in Tennessee, and received nationwide publicity. But in this case the state of Tennessee opposed the fundamentalists and defended the textbooks, along with People for the American Way and the publishers. LaHaye accused the media of being anti-Christian by printing exaggerated reports of the issues in the case.

Concerned Women for America had four attorneys on the case and spent over $100,000. It was one of a whole series of "religious freedom" cases that the CWA's lead attorney, Michael Farris, undertook during the mid-1980s. Pat Robertson's National Legal Foundation also provided attorneys for the case. The parents won the textbook case in federal district court, securing Frost's release and gaining permission for her to teach her children at home. The American Civil Liberties Union, after some doubts about it, decided to join the case for the appeal. The appeals court voided the district court ruling on a technicality, and the U.S. Supreme Court refused to hear it in 1988.[11] In the meanwhile, the children had been enrolled in private Christian schools.

CREATION

The final outcome of *Mozert* v. *Hawkins* was thus similar to that of the original Scopes trial. In 1925 the fundamentalists seemed to have won when John Scopes was convicted of illegally teaching evolution and fined $100. H. L. Mencken's newspaper paid his fine. But the Tennessee Supreme Court reversed the lower court a year later on a technicality. After the reversal and the negative publicity engendered by Mencken, fundamentalists withdrew from public defense of their beliefs. The contemporary Christian conservative movement, no longer politically quiescent, revived the controversy. In the intervening years, the fundamentalist/evangelical belief in "biblical inerrancy" has not changed. It is the foundation of the believers' still-implacable opposition to the teaching of evolution. If the Bible cannot be wrong—and they believe it cannot—then the creation story in Genesis is true as written.

Fundamentalists do not want their children to be told in school that Earth and the life on it are a product of an evolutionary process. They believe that creation was a result of God's action, as described in the Bible, or, "intelligent design," and that evolution is another example of the humanist view of the world. What is more, they believe that teaching creation actually opens the door to moral decline. Evolution is just another tool by which the government schools interfere with the right of Christians to teach their children in a moral context. "Humanism is the philosophy and evolution makes man an animal. They go hand in hand," said a Baptist minister in 1980. Myrtle Kelly put it this way:

> Once you accept the idea that maybe it did happen that way, maybe we did evolve, then you have lost the foundation of the belief. If man is nothing special at all, then it really doesn't matter what people do, if we just came into existence by accident. But if we were created by a divine being, we are something special and need to hold fast to these principles. (1980)

Kevin Hunter, a young man whose children were home-schooled, argued that the consequences of teaching evolution were partly responsible for the prevalence of abortion.

> If you tell somebody for a generation that we are nothing but apes, we

shouldn't be surprised if we start acting like that, and if you convince somebody that the only difference between them and an ape is that they have been born to this race and not to that race . . . then you can actually be convinced that to have an abortion would be the moral and right thing to do. (1997)

In 1972, the same year that the ERA was sent to the states for ratification, Tim LaHaye, Henry Morris, and two professors at American Heritage College associated with LaHaye's church founded the Institute for Creation Research as a branch of the college. Henry Morris is president of the institute, which became separate and independent of the college in 1981. By the 1990s, the materials produced by the institute had developed specific arguments to show that the biblical story of creation is actually true. Beverly LaHaye endorsed the work of the institute in one of her fund-raising letters:

If William Jennings Bryan had had the massive creation evidence at his disposal that has been gathered by God-respecting scientists in recent years, evolution would not now be being taught as fact in our public schools.[12]

The Scopes trial of 1925 was a test of a law forbidding the teaching of evolution in schools. In addition to Tennessee, Oklahoma, Florida, Mississippi, North Carolina, and Kentucky had similar laws. Although the laws forbidding evolution were struck down, creation was not forbidden. It continued to be taught in many schools in the South. With the revival of fundamentalist activism, and with the help of the Creation Research Institute, conservative Christian groups began urging states to pass new laws making creationism an acceptable part of the curricula.

The Institute for Creation Research is but one example of the development of a parallel culture in the closing years of the twentieth century. Christian children and young adults are not only attending different schools; they are being taught a growing body of different scholarship on scientific issues like these. A whole complex of associations, publishing houses, and research institutes supports the alternative scholarship. In the case of creation, however, the alternative scholarship runs up against the First Amendment. Despite their conviction that evolution is false and creation is true, creationists have learned that courts will not accept laws banning evolution. Courts have also refused to allow public schools to teach Bible-based creationism. In an attempt to meet that objection, the Creation Research Institute calls its materials "creation science." Its materials dispute the validity of carbon-dating techniques, point to gaps in the fossil record supporting evolution, and accuse secular scientists of bias against creationism. Those materials have been distributed to Christian schools and to home-schooling associations. Their faculty members are invited to present their ideas in many settings all over the country.

Kevin Hunter described the way his home-schooled children are taught:

> We do not teach evolution, in fact my children are extremely adept at rolling their eyes, and shaking their heads anytime they say, "and we found this bone and it is 150 million years old," and we go: "Oh really, were you there, how do you know that?" My kids know that when you carbon date something, the mathematical equation that you plug all the information into has fourteen assumptions built into it. Now those assumptions are based on the evolutionary model. Now if you have fourteen assumptions, biased toward evolution, you can plug in whatever you want and it's going to come out 16 billion years old. How could it not?
>
> We believe in a six-day literal creation. We believe there is a voluminous amount of scientific evidence to support that, and we believe that Earth and the universe is probably five or six thousand years old, roughly. We're not really apologetic about it, and if anybody brings up certain points, we've pretty much got answers. (1997)

The creationists have lost every court case in which they have tried to show that "creation science" is actually a science, but they have been more successful in getting schools, particularly in the South, to give it "equal time." They argue that evolution is only a theory that is no more proven than creationism is, and that it is unfair to teach evolution if creationism is excluded. A Louisiana law based on this idea was declared unconstitutional by the U.S. Supreme Court in 1987 in *Edwards* v. *Aguillard*.[13] Since then, they have had better luck with other less obvious approaches. For instance, Alabama authorities require that science textbooks carry a disclaimer stating that evolution is

a controversial theory some scientists present as a scientific explanation for the origin of living things. . . . No one was present when life first appeared on Earth. Therefore, any statement about life's origins should be considered as theory, not fact.[14]

The "theory versus fact" argument is a common one among contemporary conservative Christians, including this young suburban woman I interviewed in 1997:

I don't believe that evolution is any more than a theory, I don't think it's been proved, so I think they should both be taught. I was just amazed when about 1989 the son of the man that I worked for—his son came home from school one summer and I said "Did you know that evolution is just a theory?" and he said "No, I've been taught all my life it was a fact." He'd never heard of it at all. The theory of evolution—so much of it has been disproved and is more so all the time.

This argument implies that a theory is no more than a "hunch" and that if theories are true they will at some point be proven and turn into facts. Creationists argue that there are frequent revisions in the theory of evolution, and that if it were a fact, it would not need to be revised. But scientists say that teachers should have no objection to teaching evolution as a theory, for both evolution and creation are indeed theories, while facts are in a different category altogether. Facts are not former theories, but are bits of evidence that either support or cast doubt on a theory. Scientists stand ready to revise any theory if new facts require a revision, or to discard a theory altogether if a preponderance of facts disproves it. They accuse creationists of beginning with a conviction that their theory is true and of seeking facts to support it.

Creationists turn this argument on its head. They believe that it is the scientists who are so blinded by their preconceived notions that they cannot recognize the validity of the facts that support creationism. But scientists believe the facts being discovered support and strengthen the theory of evolution rather than weaken it. The argument has been going on for a long time and will probably continue to do so, but in the meantime creationists have won a near victory in public opinion. A Gallup Poll taken in June 1999 showed that 47 percent of the public believes that God created human beings, 49 percent accept the theory of evolution, and 68 percent favor teaching both in schools.[15] Among my 1997 respondents, 93 percent believed creation should be taught.

> They should teach creation, absolutely. They taught creation and evolution said, "it's not right, you have to give them a choice," and now evolution is the only thing they teach and creation says, "give them a choice," and they say, "oh no, you can't do that," but there is scientific data to support creation. (urban businesswoman, former legislative candidate, 1997)

Favorable public opinion has made it possible for creationists to affect the way science is taught by affecting individual teachers and districts, and not only in the South. They have, for example, criticized teachers who teach evolution in Friendly, Nevada; dominated school boards in charter schools in Paradise, California, and Berlin, Michigan; and influenced the actions of an individual administrator in Moon, Pennsylvania.[16] Perhaps their best-publicized success was to persuade the elected Kansas Board of Education in 1999 to remove any references to evolution from the standardized tests used in the schools. That decision was overturned when an election the following year removed a majority of the board members who favored it. The most significant result of the controversy is that it has discouraged teachers from dealing with the subject forthrightly, thus ensuring that evolution in many districts is taught poorly if at all.

That the Bible is a true account of the creation of Earth has been a tenet of fundamentalism ever since the word "fundamentalism" came into the American lexicon back at the beginning of the twentieth century. That there are certain absolute standards of right and wrong has also been an integral part of fundamentalist belief. Both follow logically from their belief that the words of the Bible are true as written: God created heaven and Earth, and the behavioral rules that were handed down by God are applicable throughout his creation. The ideas are not new.

What *is* new in the creation arena since the early 1970s is the institutions, research projects, articulate spokespersons, and detailed books supporting these points of view with other kinds of evidence than that of biblical texts. According to the Creation Research Institute and the work of their graduates in other institutions across the country, it is not only the Bible, but physical evidence that supports creation. According to Francis

Schaeffer, it is not only the Bible, but the historical record of societies espousing humanism that supports the view of humanism as an evil.

These more sophisticated arguments are the backdrop for the beliefs of the ordinary people whom I interviewed. Not all of them are familiar with the sophisticated sources, but they have heard simplified versions of them in their churches and on Christian radio, seen them on Christian television, and read them in magazines of the Christian conservative organizations. That half of Americans believe in creation is testimony to their success.

NOTES

1. *Humanist Manifestos I and II* (Amherst, N.Y.: Prometheus Books, 1973).

2. Francis A. Schaeffer, *How Should We Then Live?* (Tappan, N.J.: Fleming H. Revell, 1976), p. 82.

3. Ibid., p. 82.

4. Ibid., p. 145.

5. Tim LaHaye, *The Battle for the Mind* (Old Tappan, N.J.: Fleming H. Revell, 1980).

6. "What Are Your Children Being Taught about Morality?" *Better Homes and Gardens* 56 (September 1978): 16ff.

7. Louis Raths, Merrill B. Harmin, and Sidney B. Simon, *Values and Teaching* (Columbus, Ohio: Charles E. Merrill, 1966); Sidney B. Simon, Leland W. Howe, and Howard Kirschenbaum, *Values Clarification: A Handbook of Practical Strategies for Teachers and Students* (New York: Hart, 1972).

8. Phyllis Schlafly, ed., *Child Abuse in the Classroom* (Alton, Ill.: Pere Marquette, 1984).

9. Dudley Clendinen, "Fundamentalist Parents Put Textbooks on Trial," *New York Times*, 14 July 1986, p. 8.

10. *Riders on the Earth* (New York: Holt, Rinehart & Winston), 6th grade students' edition, p. 350.

11. Kathy Hacker, "A Woman of Action," *Philadelphia Inquirer*, 6 March 1988, p. I6.

12. CWA fund-raising letter, no date.

13. 482 U.S. 578, 107 S.Ct. 2573 (1987).

14. Peter Applebome, "Seventy Years after Scopes Trial, Creation Debate Lives," *New York Times*, 10 May 1996, p. A1.

15. David W. Moore, "Americans Support Teaching Creationism as Well as Evolution in Public Schools," *Gallup Poll Monthly* 407 (August 1999): 35–37.

16. Eugenie C. Scott, "Monkey Business," *Sciences* 36, no. 1 (January–February 1996): 20 (6 pages), published by the New York Academy of Sciences.

13

AMERICA'S CHRISTIAN HERITAGE

Even the Founding Fathers, when they were trying to write our Constitution, they were having prayer before every session, that God would guide them in what they did. People came here for the sole purpose originally . . . for religious freedom from England. (suburban woman, 1997)

The Pilgrims started it. They came for religious purposes, and what we've done, our schools have quit teaching it. . . . America is supposedly a Christian country. It was founded on a Christian base. (small-town pastor, 1980)

The conviction that God looks with favor on America because of the "faith of the forefathers" has been a recurring theme throughout the thirty years of the Christian Right. Respondents in both periods were appalled at what they saw as America's moral decline, not only because they personally disapproved of societal trends and attitudes, but because they believed that God's favor is conditional.

We have gotten away from traditional Judeo-Christian values on which the country was founded and became great. I'm really pessimistic about it. I believe that there is a chance [to return to the traditional values], and as a Christian, I have to work hard and do all I can to bring it about, but I can't be optimistic about it. Christians are our only hope. (urban woman, 1980)

> I really believe because of the faith of our forefathers, that God has blessed this country. I don't think it's because we were smarter. . . . I went on a mission trip to [a former Communist country] where things have been so hard, and I can foresee where if things don't change here, we could really go into a dark period, too. (urban woman, 1997)

Cleon Skousen is a former FBI agent, Salt Lake City police chief, and professor at Brigham Young University who has written books on Communism and "constitutional studies." He founded the Freemen Institute in 1971, with Ezra Taft Benson as a principal speaker. In 1980 Carol Ellison, one of the regional stars in the anti-ERA campaign, showed me the thick loose-leaf book of seminar materials that she had received when she attended one of Skousen's Freemen Institute seminars. Ellison was one of the most enthusiastic workers in the anti-ERA campaign. She had been active in the Republican Party even during the years when the state was overwhelmingly Democratic. She went to the institute course to see if the Farm Bureau should consider sponsoring it locally.

> I went to the Freemen Institute. . . . It just built me back up again, because they say we have four years to make a change in the country again, or this could be a dictatorship. It was two weekends, it was an eighteen-hour course, and you could get college credit for it. It really brushed me up on the Constitution of the United States. They read through it together during the sessions, and everyone had to fill in the blanks, and they went through the whole book of it. Also, they've got monthly publications that you can subscribe to, and you can buy the publications. Skousen is marvelous, I could listen to him all day. (Carol Ellison, October 24, 1980)

The study book began with the historical background of the Constitution, then went through the Constitution phrase by phrase, giving interpretations and U.S. Supreme Court decisions. The basic facts were there, but the interpretations, the emphasis, and the choice of Court decisions were different from those in standard American government textbooks. For instance, the section on the "right to bear arms" quoted not the Court case most often cited in standard textbooks, which declared that the Second Amendment does *not* preclude regulation of firearms, but other less well known ones. There was also more emphasis on the Tenth Amendment, which is used by conservatives to argue for greater states' rights.

As I know from my own experience teaching American government to adults, and as news sources regularly report, most Americans know very little about their government. American schools and colleges have largely failed to educate our citizens about government and about the Constitution. Skousen and other Christian conservatives are filling that "knowledge gap" with their own version. They charge that historians and textbook writers willfully ignore our Christian heritage, and that what students do learn about American history and government is wrong.

> I think they twisted that around, I think that they are trying to say that religious faiths don't belong here whereas it was supposed to be in the beginning. When I was in school, you could hear about Christians in your history textbook, now they've taken all that stuff out, they say it doesn't belong there. (urban young woman, 1997)

> The public schools are not teaching history. It's so distorted, particularly Christian history, the Christianity in this country, and the fact that this whole country was founded for the propagation of the gospel, and for missionary work among the Indians. (self-employed urban man, 1997)

A second and related belief of all of my respondents, whether in 1980 or 1997, was that U.S. Supreme Court decisions about the separation of church and state are wrong because they misinterpret the First Amendment's Establishment Clause.[1] In 1980 the Christian conservative view was relatively simple, that prayer should be allowed in schools, and that atheist Madalyn Murray O'Hair had caused a misguided Supreme Court to ban it. "Throwing God out of the schools" is how some of my respondents described it. Many argued further that "when they took prayer out of the schools, dropouts and drugs increased."

In fact, the Supreme Court's *Engel* v. *Vitale* (1962) decision, and a companion decision in 1963, *Abington Township School District* v. *Schempp* on Bible reading and the recitation of the Lord's Prayer,[2] each settled a whole group of cases. O'Hair was only one of many plaintiffs in the second group of cases. (In multicase decisions, the legal citations list the case beginning with the letter nearest the front of the alphabet. O'Hair's case was *Murray* v. *Curlett*.) Those decisions were more limited, banning only prayers that were written or prescribed by the school authorities and/or conducted by teachers. Basing their decisions on the clause in the Constitution forbidding "establishment of religion," the Supreme Court has consistently ruled that for school officials to mandate any kind of religious exercise for students who are required by law to attend, is a form of "establishment."

Many schools, especially in the South, continued prayers in schools despite the 1962 and 1963 decisions. Voluntary prayer has never been banned by law or by the Supreme Court, however. Some schools, fearing lawsuits, interpreted the rules more strictly than necessary, forbidding even voluntary, student-initiated prayer. This overreaction by school officials created examples that added to the pressure for "religious freedom." The very decentralization of schools, which conservatives favor, makes ensuring uniform application of Supreme Court decisions difficult. Because of the tradition of local control of schools in the United States, it is virtually impossible to make any widespread changes in school policies at the national level despite attempts by those of both the left and the right.

Concerned Women for America's (CWA) attorney, Michael Farris, had defended a variety of "religious freedom" cases in the 1980s, most notably *Mozert* v. *Hawkins*, about school textbooks.[3] The CWA dropped its school litigation project after Farris moved on to become head of the Homeschool Legal Defense Association. Those who believe their religious rights have been violated now can seek help from Pat Robertson's American Center for Law and Justice, John Whitehead's Rutherford Institute, or the Alliance Defense Fund, a sort of superfund set up in 1994 by ten Christian conservative organizations.[4] The Rutherford Institute, named for Samuel Rutherford, an obscure Scottish clergyman, was founded for just that purpose. Whitehead explained his legal theory on the separation of church and state in his book, *The Second American Revolution*,[5] drawing heavily on another book by Francis Schaeffer, *The Christian Manifesto*.[6] Both appeared at about the same time.

CHRISTIAN CONSERVATIVES AND CHURCH-STATE SEPARATION

Both Schaeffer and Whitehead credited Samuel Rutherford with influencing the Founding Fathers as they wrote the Declaration of Independence and the United States Constitution. They believed the writers of the Constitution had the "Christian base," even if they were not all Christians, for they lived "within the circle of that which a Christian consensus brings forth."[7] Because of this background, the original Constitution was legitimate, but after secular humanism replaced the Christian base, judges began making sociological law, substituting human judgment for that of the Bible and for the plain words of the Constitution.

Whitehead pointed out, correctly, that the phrase "separation of church and state" does not appear in the original Constitution or in the First Amendment, which was intended to forbid an established church: "Congress shall make no law respecting an establishment of religion." Even this provision, referring only to congressional action, did not at first apply to the states. As Justice Hugo Black had acknowledged in the *Engel v. Vitale* school prayer decision, at least eight of the thirteen original colonies actually had established state churches at the time of the Revolution. But Supreme Court decisions in the twentieth century interpreted the First Amendment as limiting state action as well.

The Christian conservative insistence on biblical inerrancy, making no allowance for different circumstances or revised interpretations in different historical periods, is reflected in their view of constitutional interpretation. Their interpretation of the Constitution can be described as "constitutional inerrancy," although I am not aware that the conservative legal scholars themselves have used the phrase. "Constitutional inerrancy" leads conservative Christians to reject the series of Court decisions applying the provisions of the Bill of Rights to the states. While the Bill of Rights originally applied only to the national government, its later application to the states was derived from an interpretation of the Fourteenth Amendment.

Fifty-seven years after the Fourteenth Amendment was added to the Constitution, the Supreme Court handed down the first of a series of decisions using what is now known as the "doctrine of incorporation."[8] The doctrine of incorporation means that the provisions of the Bill of Rights have become part of, or "incorporated in" the Fourteenth Amendment's simple statement limiting the states' authority to deprive persons of life, liberty, or property. Applying the doctrine of incorporation—a "modernist" interpretation of the Constitution comparable to the modernist interpretation of the Bible—subsequent Supreme Courts have applied the provisions of different parts of the Bill of Rights, one by one, to the states as well as to the federal government.

In the 1947 case *Everson* v. *Board of Education*, the Supreme Court incorporated the establishment clause, requiring that states also must avoid entangling the state with religion. Further, the Court has taken "establishment" to mean not only actual tax support of a church—the common usage at the time of the Revolution—but any kind of religious activity by or in a tax-supported entity. To constitutional inerrantists these interpretations have stretched the plain words of the Constitution unacceptably far.[9]

Whitehead argues further that the Constitution was originally intended to protect the Christian religion but that in a series of decisions beginning with the 1879 case involving the Mormon practice of polygamy[10] (fundamentalists generally do not regard Mormons as Christians) and continuing into the twentieth century, the Court has gradually broadened the definition of religion. In *Torcaso* v. *Watkins*,[11] Whitehead argues that the Court actually classified secular humanism as a religion.[12] The *Torcaso* decision was used by those who oppose humanism to bring cases arguing that schools unconstitutionally discriminate against the Christian religion when they allow "humanistic religion" while keeping out Christian teaching.

The "religious freedom" cases initiated by the Christian Right are also based on the second part of the First Amendment, which says that "[Congress shall make no law] prohibiting the free exercise [of religion]." Prohibiting interference with free exercise of religion can seem contradictory to prohibiting the establishment of religion as "establishment" is now interpreted by the courts. Clearly, the people are protected in their free exercise of religion from government interference in homes, churches, and businesses, but are they also free to exercise their religion on tax-supported property, in tax-supported institutions, or using funds provided by taxpayers? This is the point at which Christian conservatives disagree with supporters of church-state separation.

The arguments of the Christian Right in these cases are more plausible if one accepts the premises that constitutional interpretation should be limited to the actual words of the original Constitution, and that practices common in the early nineteenth century should therefore be allowed in the late twentieth century as well. Chief Justice William Rehnquist argued for these premises in his dissent in *Wallace* v. *Jaffree* (1985),[13] but dissenting opinions do not become part of the legal framework. The decision in that case struck down an Alabama law providing for a minute of silence at the beginning of the school day during which teachers could, if they wished, read a prayer. In his dissent, Rehnquist described the deliberations during the formulation of the First Amendment clauses and subsequent Supreme Court interpretations of those clauses, but without Whitehead's emphasis on a biblical foundation.

Just as Tim LaHaye popularized and publicized Schaeffer's analysis of humanism, David Barton, the Christian Rights advocate, is chiefly responsible for the wide dissemination and popularization of Whitehead's somewhat technical legal arguments.[14] By the 1990s, Barton had taken the place of the eighty-year-old Skousen as the authority for Christian conservatives on the basic documents of American history. At a Christian Coalition meeting, I saw Barton's video on George Washington, *America's Christian Heritage,* emphasizing Washington's miraculous escapes in battle and his religious faith. Another of Barton's videos is *America's Godly Heritage,*[15] with excerpts from court cases showing "that for 160 years, Christian principles were inseparable from public affairs."

The use of that film in a class in American history in a public school was one of several complaints raised in 1993 by the Herdahl family of Ecru, Mississippi. While the case was working its way through the courts, Mrs. Herdahl testified before Sen. Orrin Hatch's (R-Utah) Judiciary Committee in 1995 that her family members, who were also Christians, were harassed by other residents of the town after they filed the case.[16] In the case, *Herdahl* v. *Pontotoc County School District* (1996),[17] Judge Neal B. Biggers of the U.S. District Court of Northern Mississippi decided in favor of the Herdahls on all the complaints they raised. The judge agreed with the Herdahls that the Barton tape was not objective history, but sectarian religious material.[18] The school district did not appeal, so the case never reached the Supreme Court.

According to his Web site, Barton graduated from Oral Roberts University in Tulsa, Oklahoma, with a B.A. degree in Education and taught math and science for eight years before founding Wallbuilders, his publishing and marketing company, in 1971.[19] He has appeared at state and national conventions of the Christian Coalition and has spoken on Focus on the Family radio programs. Jerry Falwell's Liberty University recommends Barton's work to readers and to the students at his university. Barton declares that moral decline, and even the decline of SAT scores, had actually been set in motion by the Supreme Court decisions declaring school-initiated prayers to be unconstitutional.

David Barton is head of Wallbuilders, an organization promoting the idea that the separation of church and state is a misinterpretation of what the Constitution says and the Founding Fathers intended. (*Church and State photo*)

Barton's energetic marketing of his materials has made them ubiquitous among Christian conservatives. His books and videos were in the homes of many of my respondents. Others had heard him speak or had heard about him on other Christian programs. Even those who had not were familiar with the arguments he makes. But none of the respondents knew that Barton had been forced to admit that many of the quotations from the Founding Fathers or from historical documents on which he bases his arguments are, in fact, inaccurate— or, as he puts it, "unconfirmed." His work, including the questionable quotations, is quoted in congressional debates, in letters to the editor, and on Pat Robertson's *700 Club*.

Professor Robert S. Alley of the University of Richmond, who had attended some of the hearings in the *Herdahl* v. *Pontotoc School District* case, had searched databases and consulted experts on James Madison, Thomas Jefferson, Patrick Henry, and others whom Barton had quoted. When he could not find a record of a particular quotation, he tried to determine if it was consistent with that person's other writings before he accused Barton of having used a false quotation. He discussed his findings when he appeared, along with Pat Robertson, at a 1995 symposium at William and Mary College.[20]

After Alley's disclosure, Barton posted on his Web site a list of the "unconfirmed" quotations, arguing that in all except one case it was a minor point, and that the person quoted had actually said something similar. However, he later reissued his book, *The Myth of Separation*, with a new title, and without the questionable quotations. The Web site then advertised the book with its new title, *Original Intent: The Courts, The Constitution, and Religion*. In spite of the new edition having been published, the book I bought at a Christian Coalition convention in 1996 was the original version.

The National Center for Constitutional Studies, the successor to Cleon Skousen's Freemen Institute, also offers seminars and a home-study course with conservative interpretations of the Constitution. Updated versions of the Skousen materials are also available on a Web site, http://www.xmission.com/~nccs/, and on a CD-ROM.[21]

The ideas in these books are not taught in secular universities, although law students usually study dissenting opinions, and these include the arguments favored by the Christian conservatives. The books themselves, published by private or little-known presses, are not generally available in public or university libraries, but they are in the libraries of conservative religious colleges and universities. The small conservative colleges have now been joined by large accredited universities like Oral Roberts University, Pat Robertson's Regents University, and Jerry Falwell's Liberty University. Christian conservatives hope that as more and more students graduate from these universities and their law schools, their alternative legal scholarship will become better known and accepted, and that justices sympathetic to it will be appointed to the Supreme Court in the future.

The Christian conservative emphasis on the "Christian base" of the Founding Fathers, however, is questioned even by fellow evangelicals who are also historians. In *The Search for Christian America*, George Marsden, a well-regarded historian of religion, argues that Reformation Christianity was only one of many sources of the political beliefs of the founders. He believes that the historical emphasis on Reformation Christianity "attributes to the Bible things that were not drawn from the Bible." The founders desired to establish the United States as a secular nation precisely because of their experience with Protestant Bible common-wealths in Europe. Finally, he believes that today's Christians should work for "social, political, and moral renewal" but should not dream of making America a "Christian" nation.[22]

THE NEW VICTIMS

My 1997 respondents, having been exposed to Whitehead's and Barton's ideas by way of the Christian Coalition and other Christian conservative organizations, believe they are victims of discrimination because of their beliefs. Fueling their resentment at the time of the interviews was an incident that had occurred the previous winter when a Tulsa fire station was forced to take down a nativity scene on its premises. At about the same time, a suburb of Oklahoma City was required to remove a cross from its city seal. In both cases, suits had been filed by the American Civil Liberties Union; there have been similar cases in other states. Also fueling resentment were the sometimes exaggerated accounts in Christian Coalition mailings of what court decisions required.

> I believe that separation of church and state means that the government does not have a right to set up a government church and does not have a right to tell the churches how to conduct their business. I don't think it ever meant that churches were not to affect the public in any such way. (Kathy Williams, 1997)

Respondents blamed the American Civil Liberties Union, People for the American Way, and in some cases, Communists for having fostered the constitutional interpretations with which they disagreed. In the 1997 interviews, there was another villain—immigration and the push for diversity. A small minority argued that Christians founded our country, and those who came later should not be allowed to change the rules.

> I think that's one of our problems. This country was founded on a belief in God, and if we let these other people live here, OK, but I don't think we ought to let them tell us what we can do. I'm sorry we've taken God out of government, out of public displays. Letting these other groups in that don't believe in God is part of the problem. (rural farm wife, 1997)

> I believe we have moved over to let all the Arabs tell us what to do. I mean if they want to come to our schools, why can't they accept the teaching that is given, or the prayers or whatever is done in the school? These other people didn't have to accept it. They came here, they have to obey the rules of the land, why not the school? I can't understand that. (small-town woman, 1997)

In 1997 Rep. Ernest Istook (R-Okla.) introduced the Religious Freedom Amendment specifying that prayer and religious observances in schools were not prohibited by the Constitution. There were at least two other similar amendments proposed by other representatives, but none was submitted to the states. By that time, there had been still more "misguided" court decisions. An Alabama judge had forbidden the posting of the Ten Commandments in a courtroom, courts in Oklahoma and Illinois had required cities to remove Christian symbols from their city seals, and students had been criticized for writing term papers about Jesus or for referring to their faith in a graduation speech. The Ten Commandments cases are just one example of how these issues develop and take on a life of their own.

Rep. Ernest Istook (R-Okla.) crafted a constitutional amendment to permit prayer in schools, hoping to pick up enough support in Congress so that it would be submitted to the states for ratification. Despite efforts to consult with many different interest groups, he was unable to get that support. (*Church and State photo*)

THE TEN COMMAND-MENTS ISSUE

In 1980 the Supreme Court ruled in *Stone* v. *Graham*,[23] that a Kentucky law requiring the Ten Commandments to be posted in schools was unconstitutional.[23] The Ten Commandments became contentious again in 1997, two years after County Circuit Judge Roy Moore of Etowah County, Alabama, had posted a plaque of the Protestant version of the Ten Commandments in his courtroom and begun opening court sessions with prayer. The American Civil Liberties Union had sued him in 1995 and a local judge had ordered him to take down the plaque and stop the prayers, but the order was stayed while the case was appealed to the state supreme court.

After James Dobson discussed the case on his Focus on the Family radio program on February 12, 1997, he reported that 17,000 letters of support came into the offices of Alabama governor Fob James, including some from other state governors. The Christian Coalition's *Christian American* and *Religious Rights Watch* and the magazines of Focus on the

Family and the American Family Association all reported the progress of the case and used it in fund-raising letters. At a rally in Montgomery two months later, Governor James spoke, declaring to a crowd waving Confederate battle flags that he would use National Guard troops to protect the Ten Commandments. The rally was attended by leaders of the Christian Right from all over the country, including Ralph Reed.

Rep. Robert Aderholt (R-Ala.), the congressman from Judge Moore's district, introduced a nonbinding resolution of support for Judge Moore in the House of Representatives that passed it on March 5, 1997. Professor Alley noted the use of other inaccurate quotations from the Founding Fathers in support of the Ten Commandments in that debate.[24] Rep. Joe Scarborough (R-Fla.) quoted Madison as saying that the entire future of American civilization depended upon the power of "the individual to govern himself . . . according to the Ten Commandments of God." This was one of the "unconfirmed" quotations that David Barton had removed from his books conceding that it could not be found in any of Madison's writings. Scarborough also claimed that George Washington had said in his Farewell Address that "it is impossible to govern rightly without God and the Ten Commandments." This is a further misquotation of one of Barton's misquotations, and neither version could be found in a computer check of all of Washington's writings.

On January 23, 1998, the Alabama Supreme Court refused to rule on the Ten Commandments case for technical reasons. Both sides could claim victory; the last ruling by a court had been that the judge's practices were unconstitutional, but the practices could continue. In the meantime, Christian Right organizations had a wonderful fund-raising issue as they blamed separationist organizations for attacking religion by forbidding display of the Ten Commandments. Those organizations, the American Civil Liberties Union and Americans United for Separation of Church and State, however, pointed out that any individual, any privately owned business, or any church can display the Ten Commandments or any other religious material inside or on the grounds of its own property. The display violates the First Amendment only when it appears on government property, indicating government support for a particular religion. Since there are actually three different versions of the Ten Commandments— Protestant, Catholic, and Jewish—choosing any one of them would give a preference to that religion.

Judge Moore's case inspired a series of other attempts to display the Ten Commandments on government property. The city council in Charleston, South Carolina, voted to display the Decalogue in council chambers, and in California, a businessman paid for advertising space at the city schools' baseball field, then used the space to list the Ten Commandments, with the title "Rules to Live By." When the school district removed the sign, he sued them. In 1998 the crusade came to Indiana, when the Focus on the Family associate for that state urged officials to post the Ten Commandments in courthouses and on the state capitol grounds.

Still another episode in the Ten Commandments controversy, but probably not the last, came in June 1999, when Rep. Robert Aderholt, Judge Roy Moore's congressman, put another version of his Ten Commandments Defense Act into regular legislation. He had tried to do the same thing two years earlier, but had succeeded in getting only a nonbinding resolution. This time, he added it to a juvenile justice bill passed after the shootings at Columbine High School in Colorado. The rider directed federal courts not to rule about government-sponsored Ten Commandments displays. Although of questionable constitutionality, the measure passed the House of Representatives. In the 2000 elections, Judge Moore had a victory of sorts, when he was elected chief justice of the Alabama Supreme Court.

GRASSROOTS RESPONSE TO CHURCH-STATE ISSUES

The Christian Coalition devoted more space in its written material to the Christian heritage/religious freedom issue than any of the other Christian conservative organizations. Its use of this theme is consistent with Pat Robertson's speeches and writing throughout his public career. In 1999 the Christian Coalition sent a "Survey on Religion in American Public Life" to its mailing list. The survey, received in May 1999, is an example of the kind of communication that adds to the sense of victimhood among Christian conservatives. It included the following questions:

1. Do you believe efforts to strip all traces of religion from society and public life are hurting our country and destroying America's moral fiber?
2. The Bill of Rights guarantees freedom of religious expression, yet

a series of Supreme Court rulings has banned and censored religious speech in America. Do you believe Congress should pass a
constitutional amendment designed to protect religious freedom?
3. As a result of lawsuits filed by the American Civil Liberties Union
and People for the American Way, Christian symbols have been
removed from public places all over America. Do you believe our
elected officials should protect the right to religious expression in
public and respect religion and the traditional morality and family
values America was built on?

The premises of these questions reflect the rhetoric on church-state
issues that is common in Christian conservative mailings and literature:
that courts have banned all religious speech and removed all religious
symbols from public places. In fact, the decisions apply only to tax-supported property or institutions. Privately owned businesses, individuals,
and of course, churches, are free to do and say anything of a religious
nature on their own property, even if it is visible and public.

The Christian Coalition distributes a one-page monthly publication
called *Religious Rights Watch*, along with a form to be returned with a
"monthly contribution" to the work of the Christian Coalition. *Religious
Rights Watch* included a note urging readers to send in letters and dated
newspaper clippings about threats to religious freedom. Their reports of
incidents all around the country were then summarized in the publication
itself. Although I met no Christian Coalition member who made the
requested monthly contribution, all were well aware of the religious
freedom stories. They had come to see themselves as victims of an anti-
Christian campaign.

There's not any such thing [as separation of church and state]. It's not in
the Constitution, that's just ignorance. (doctor's wife, small city, 1997)

I think that [separation of church and state] was a concept that was
introduced more recently to our country by some people that were really
trying to rid our country of the influence of the Bible. The First Amendment doesn't say anything about separation of church and state. (young
man, head of private Christian ministry, 1997)

If I had my way, I'd put the American Civil Liberties Union out of business. . . . They try to make it wrong, anything the Christians do. (small-town widow, 1997)

Horror stories abound, and were reported in *Religious Rights Watch* about seemingly unreasonable attempts to stop religious practices. Because so many people from so many different places make such decisions for local government and local schools, it is inevitable that some incorrect decisions are made. But there have been horror stories of the opposite kind as well, which are not so well publicized—for instance, the teacher in a small Oklahoma school who accused one of her pupils of collaborating with the devil and predicted that she would suffer eternal damnation because she had worn a witch costume on Halloween.

The belief that God has given us "this beautiful land" and that it will be taken from us if we "are not faithful," soon evolved into a demand that government policy should favor Christianity. For many conservative Christians, the courts became the enemy of Christianity when they began interpreting the First Amendment as forbidding religious symbols on government property or verbal expressions of religion by government officials or tax-supported teachers. From the perspective of more than thirty years after the *Engel* v. *Vitale* decision, it seems that those who favored separation of church and state failed to recognize how deeply offensive the decisions would be to devout Christians.

If they had, they might have explained the basis for these decisions in the desire of the Founding Fathers to avoid the kind of religious entanglement that they had known in Europe. They might also have made more of an effort to educate school and other government officials about what kinds of religious expression, in what kinds of settings, would be constitutional, as President Clinton did in 1997. By then it was too late. The Christian Right had already taken control of the issue; the American Center for Law and Justice had issued detailed guidelines on workers' rights in the workplace, students' rights in public schools, and individual rights in public places. Americans United for Separation of Church and State might have disagreed with some of the details, but in general, the guidelines were carefully worded and footnoted.

NOTES

1. "Congress shall make no law respecting an establishment of religion, or prohibiting the free exercise thereof."

2. *Engel v. Vitale*, 370 U.S. 421 (1962); *Abington Township School District v. Schempp*, 374 U.S. 203 (1963).

3. *Mozert v. Hawkins County Public Schools*, 827 F. 2d, 1058 U.S. 102 (1987).

4. Joseph L. Conn, "The Airwaves Ayatollahs," *Church and State* 47, no. 3 (March 1994): 588.

5. John Whitehead, *The Second American Revolution* (Wheaton, Ill.: Crossway Books, 1982).

6. Francis A. Schaeffer, *The Christian Manifesto* (Wheaton, Ill.: Crossway Books, 1981).

7. Francis A. Schaeffer, *How Shall We Then Live?* (Old Tappan, N.J.: Fleming H. Revell, 1976), p. 110.

8. *Gitlow v. New York*, 268 U.S. 652 (1925).

9. Whitehead, *Second Revolution,* pp. 97–99. Whitehead's complete argument against the incorporation doctrine is contained in his Essay III on page 201.

10. *Reynolds v. U.S.*, 98 U.S. 145 (1879).

11. *Torcaso v. Watkins*, 367 U.S. 488 (1961).

12. Whitehead, *Second Revolution,* pp.104–109.

13. *Wallace v. Jaffree,* 472 U.S. 38 (1985). *Amicus curiae* briefs supporting the Alabama law were filed by Michael Turpen, then Oklahoma's attorney general; John W. Whitehead, then of the Legal Foundation of America; and the Moral Majority, among others.

14. David Barton, *The Myth of Separation* (Aledo, Tex.: Wallbuilder, 1992); John W. Whitehead, *The Separation Illusion* (Milford, Mich.: Mott Media, 1982).

15. Available from Wallbuilders, P.O. Box 397, Aledo, Texas 76008.

16. Robert S. Alley, *Without a Prayer: Religious Expression in the Public Schools* (Amherst, N.Y.: Prometheus Books, 1996), pp. 187–90.

17. 3:94 CV 188-B-A, 3 June 1996.

18. Alley, *Without a Prayer,* pp. 251–52.

19. http://www.christiananswers.net/resume.html, accessed 1999.

20. Robert S. Alley, "Public Education and the Public Good," *William and Mary Bill of Rights Journal* 4, no. 1 (summer 1995): 277–350.

21. David Barton (Wallbuilders, P.O. Box 397, Aledo, Texas 76008); The Freemen Institute, now the National Center for Constitutional Studies (Box 1056, Malta, Idaho 83342).

22. George M. Marsden, "Return to Christian America: a Political Agenda,"

chap. 6 in *The Search for Christian America,* Mark A. Noll, Nathan O. Hatch, and George M. Marsden, exp. ed. (Colorado Springs: Helmers and Howard, 1989).

23. *Stone et al.* v. *Graham,* 449 U.S. 39 (1980).

24. Robert S. Alley, "Memo to the U.S. Congress: Thou Shalt Not Bear False History," *Church & State* 50, no. 6 (June 1997): 21.

14

CHURCH, STATE, AND SCHOOLS

T he White House Conference on Families brought school issues to the attention of many in the pro-family movement who had not been involved in the earlier, localized protests of school curricula. Public schools soon became one of the leading reasons for a Christian conservative to be appalled. The conference transcripts showed a depth of anger and resentment against the public schools that had not been widely recognized before. If the moderator did not exercise his or her prerogative to keep the discussion on the assigned topic, any session on any topic was likely to turn into an airing of pro-family grievances against public education.

Conservatives came to the Oklahoma conference expecting to find opposition because they had been told that the conference would be dominated by anti-family forces. Yet a majority of the conferees, even of those not associated with the pro-family movement, agreed with them on many issues. One woman who was in this category, from rural western Oklahoma, found herself in an uncomfortable position. She was a member of a Church of Christ who agreed with the pro-family movement on almost every issue, but she had also been a schoolteacher for most of her adult life. At the White House conference, she found herself defending the public schools.

> I tell you, they ripped education up one side and down the other. They had a mindset. I told 'em I didn't think they were on the right track, and a lot of them, I felt like, were kinda misinformed about some of the poli-

cies that some of the schools and education were taking, and they didn't like me very well for that. (schoolteacher, rural area, 1980)

Whether the complaints were justified or not, and whether or not the complainers were misinformed, there is no mistaking the depth of their resentment about the direction of public education. Parents believed that teachers did not want them to know what was going on in school.[1]

Some of these teachers have already made up their minds what they are going to do, and they just won't listen to the parents.

Parents sometimes volunteer to help in the school because otherwise the teachers won't let them come in.

Teachers create bad self-images in the students, then when the parents inquire, they won't respond.

Some of the teachers won't allow volunteers to help in the classroom. They say they aren't trained well enough, but I think they just don't want parents to know what is going on.

Some remembered the schools of their youth and compared present-day schools unfavorably with them:

When I was in school, we got a grade card every month, and when my daughter was in school they were getting it every two months. Two months is too long for the parents to know what the child is doing.

When I was in school, teachers felt that they could teach you courtesy, teach you to love your country, correct you. Every morning they said "Did you brush your teeth? Did you clean your fingernails?" this sort of thing, and they felt a responsibility for the children they taught.

Another complaint was that schools do not do a good job with their basic task of teaching children to read, write, and figure:

We had a second cousin come over here from England, and we took him to Sunday school, and when we passed around the class reading the lesson, he read so beautifully that they asked him to read the whole thing. Why can't our kids here learn to read like that? I'm disgusted with the educational system—we spend billions of dollars, and we get nothin'! (farmer, 1980)

I have a daughter who is excellent in almost every subject, but you know, she can't do fractions, and she is in the twelfth grade, and that's where federal education gets you!

Finally, and this is the issue about which parents were the most bitter, they believed that the schools were undermining the values that parents have tried to teach their children. Myrtle Kelly put it most directly and most emphatically: "The schools, with federal funding, are making a frontal attack on the Judeo-Christian value system!" Other parents, also speaking from their own experience, were just as upset:

Parents should be involved in writing textbooks so they do not undermine their values.

There should be a mechanism for removing textbooks from the classroom if parents find them offensive.

The federal government is trying to control minds and morals. They don't recognize that there are thousands concerned with looking for an absolute. The Bible should have a place, and be taught to children, as opposed to the humanistic approach.

We are allowing homosexuality to be brought before our children, and they are told that this is normal. It's been crammed down our throats, like it or not. We don't have the right to choose. When we educate children, we don't want them taught [that] this is normal. We can't allow them to make a choice. The farmer when he plants his corn—he doesn't leave it alone, but he takes care of it. Children are just as important.

The White House conferences of 1979 and 1980 could have been an early warning to the education establishment of the grassroots alienation from the public school system, which only intensified during later decades. The complaints of these respondents were echoed through the years in other parts of the country. There were three kinds of complaints: parents' concerns are not respected, educational basics are neglected, and religious values are undermined by teaching humanism and by teaching about sex without including moral values.

Both Eagle Forum and Pro-Family Forum took note of the grassroots concern about schools, and shifted their attention to schools after the defeat of the ERA. Lottie Beth Hobbs changed the name of her Pro-Family Forum newsletter to *The Family Educator*, before discontinuing it in 1994. Phyllis Schlafly encouraged her members to speak at the 1984 Department of Education hearings on a pupil rights act, which was supposed to allow parents to examine and object to books used in their children's schools. She objected that the department had not properly implemented the bill. After the hearings, Schlafly published a book of excerpts from the hearings, *Child Abuse in the Classroom*.[2] In February 1986, she began producing a new publication, *Education Reporter*, to deal exclusively with education issues.

Schlafly also offered copies of the *McGuffey Readers* for sale. Christian conservatives recommend the *McGuffey Readers* because they have serious content, and best of all, biblical and moral content. Schlafly even produced her own reading curriculum using the phonics method, which the Christian conservatives believe is the only way to teach reading. She had always touted her own success in teaching her children to read, and urged her followers to do the same, even before their children started attending school.

DEVELOPMENT OF THE ISSUE

Even during the heat of the ERA campaign, school issues continued to energize the grassroots in scattered local protests and briefly in nationally coordinated ones. It is not hard to understand why school issues resonate so strongly with the public. What is more important to a parent than the feeling that his or her children are learning what they need to assure their earning power as adults, that the values of the school are in sync with those of the parents, and that the children are physically safe at school? Or, to approach it from the point of view of an organization trying to mobilize volunteers and raise money, what better way to appall parents than to raise doubts about the efficacy, safety, and moral standards of the schools their children attend?

Although several organizations tried, no single organization focusing on schools gained national recognition in the way that Phyllis Schlafly's Eagle Forum, Jerry Falwell's Moral Majority, or Pat Robertson's Christian Coalition did. That may be because the education issue has so many different subissues and because so many different organizations aspire to lead the charge. Or, it may be, as the Christian conservatives themselves believe, because the public schools are simply too tightly controlled by unions and bureaucracies to implement meaningful change. This argument continued to be made ever more forcefully by think tanks funded by wealthy foundations, which had some success in persuading the American public of their views. To cover the whole range of education issues thoroughly would easily fill another book. This chapter can do no more than provide a quick overview of some of the specific issues.

HUMANISM IN THE CURRICULUM

Humanism was a catchall category, including a variety of complaints about curricula. As mentioned earlier, to the Christian conservatives, humanism meant relativism, which in turn meant a loosening of traditional moral standards. Sex education, previously discussed in chapter 11, was one of the sore points. It was a hot issue in 1980 when I conducted my first series of interviews. Those who favored sex education—and a statewide survey showed that a strong majority of the state's population did—saw it as a necessary corrective to an increasingly sex-saturated popular culture. But most of the Christian conservatives thought it was actually a cause of increased sexual activity.

Christian conservatives thought that the failure of textbooks to teach what they understood to be the Christian values of the Founding Fathers and the Christian basis of the Constitution was another example of humanism. The textbook controversy in the 1970s in Kanawha County, West Virginia, was the first broad attack on school textbooks to gain national attention. Although the local protesters did not at first define their objections as related to humanism, they were soon informed about it by outsiders offering to help them.

Mel and Norma Gabler of Longview, Texas, offered their own research to textbook protesters anywhere in the country. The easy availability of their files probably increased the likelihood of protracted textbook controversies. The Gablers came to be feared by publishers all over the United States because the Texas system was large enough that a lost textbook purchase there meant a serious drop in sales. It was even more serious when ad hoc committees in other states began to do similar analyses and make similar complaints to state textbook commissions. The Gablers saw themselves as guardians against liberal permissiveness, lack of a patriotic emphasis, and sex education.

Some of the excerpts provided by the Gablers for Kanawha County activists were not even in the textbooks under consideration in Kanawha County, but they were accepted unquestioningly by the local protesters. School boards in other local communities did not learn from the Kanawha County controversy. Some of the more thoughtful commentators in that case had noted that school policies, not just in Kanawha County, but all over the country, typically do not allow for input from parents.[3] Just as some parents complain, and as Alice Moore from Kanawha County had found, the official responses to parental input often seemed to be dismissive and arrogant. The spread of textbook protests in other communities across the nation, earlier in Anaheim, California; and later in Hawkins County and Church Hill, Tennessee; and in Mobile, Alabama, indicated that conservatives in other communities also found the schools unresponsive.

The protesters were influenced and eventually shoved aside by other individuals and groups eager to take advantage of the controversy. The violence in Kanawha County did not come from Moore or from the other parents who originally supported her, but from others who were attracted by the national publicity. Representatives from the Heritage Foundation in Washington, D.C., came to West Virginia, not to foment violence, but to mobilize conservative Christians for their own national conservative agenda.

The American Library Association reported in 1981 that "about one public school in five was pressured each year to remove books that someone finds offensive." In a survey of 1,891 librarians, principals, and superintendents, they found that more than two hundred books had been subjected to censorship pressures in 1980.[4] Nearly half the challenges asserted that the books were obscene, used objectionable language, or dealt with sexuality, but others concerned the portrayal of U.S. history, evolution, and contempt for traditional family values. In the 1980s, the attorney for Concerned Women for America took on several cases in which plaintiffs made similar charges about school textbooks and school policies.

During all of this agitation and protest against the public schools, Ronald Reagan was elected president in 1980. Christian conservatives had opposed Jimmy Carter's creation of the Department of Education, but they were pleased when President Reagan appointed several of their own to positions in that department. Onalee McGraw, who had been the education director of the Heritage Foundation and had written Heritage's original 1976 report on secular humanism in the schools, was named a member of the National Council on Education Research. Gary Bauer, little known at the time but better known later, was appointed deputy undersecretary of education and then became undersecretary. Robert Simonds, who had recently formed the National Association of Christian Educators as an alternative to the National Education Association, was appointed to serve on Reagan's task force to implement the famous *Nation at Risk* report, which decried the deficiencies of public education.

As a result of that experience, Simonds created a new organization for parents in 1983 called Citizens for Excellence in Education (CEE). It has since merged with his National Association of Christian Educators. Simonds, who had taught math in a California community college, had been asked to resign after students complained of his aggressive religious proselytizing in class. His organization was not well known nationally, and not always well known even in communities where his followers succeeded in gaining election to local school boards. His approach at that time might be described as "If you can't beat 'em, join 'em," or "If the school board won't do what you want, get on the school board yourself!" He pioneered the "stealth" approach, suggesting that candidates not identify themselves as part of his organization, or even as supporting its goals. Once elected, they pushed their agenda of "academic excellence, godly morals, and traditional values"[5] in schools. This wasn't always successful either, for the new board members often created so much conflict on the boards that they were defeated at the next election.

The CEE office in Costa Mesa, California, distributed a School Awareness Kit that included a pamphlet entitled "How to Elect Christians to Public Office." In 1993 Simonds claimed to have 1,250 chapters in the United States and that the organization had helped to elect a total of 5,561 school board members in the previous four years.[6] But during the 1990s, the Christian conservative movement was beginning to shift its educational emphasis again, from improving the public schools to establishing private schools and trying to get government funding for them.

In 1998 Simonds began urging Christians to withdraw their children from the public school system. Many of his supporters were not ready for that change in strategy; his contributions dropped off after the announcement, and in 1999 he was sending out an emergency request to his supporters for more funds. Citizens for Excellence in Education was the nearest thing to a single national organization focusing specifically on education. Although it never caught the attention of the national media, it was still in existence in 1999.

DESEGREGATION

Discontent with public schools first reached significant levels in the 1960s as a result of court decisions. When the Supreme Court ruled in *Brown* v. *Board of Education* in 1954 that separate schooling for black and white children should end "with all deliberate speed," southern communities responded by establishing private "segregation academies," often in churches. Northern parents expressed their anger by organizing massive protests against the busing ordered to implement the *Brown* decision. The protesters' concern about their children's school experience was accompanied by a resentment of the "feds'" interference in what had always been a local responsibility for public education.

Robert Billings, as head of the National Christian Action Coalition, organized a massive letter-writing campaign in 1978 against the IRS proposal to revoke the tax exemption of private schools if they were racially segregated. Billings had been principal of a Christian high school and claimed to have inspired the founding of over four hundred other Christian schools.[7] This incident, described in chapter 6, was successful from the point of view of the protesters, for the IRS abandoned its plans. Like the anti-ERA movement, it was an example of mobilization in the face of a specific threat, but unlike the ERA, the issue was quickly resolved.

PRAYER AND BIBLE READING IN SCHOOLS

If the 1954 *Brown* v. *Board of Education* decision envisioned a public school system in which blacks and whites study amicably together on equal terms in equally well equipped facilities, the ideal has not been achieved, but since about 1980, the desegregation issue has simmered rather than boiled. The fears of parents, Christian conservatives, and others that the schools undermine their values while failing to provide a good solid education have been a far more volatile mix. The 1962 and 1963 Supreme Court decisions that teacher-led school prayer and Bible reading were unconstitutional contributed to the belief that government was an accomplice in undermining traditional values in the public schools.

The conflict over prayer at graduation exercises is just one of many possible examples of the struggle between supporters of church-state separation and the desire of the majority of parents for religious exercises in the schools. In 1992 the Supreme Court declared in *Lee* v. *Weisman* that school-sponsored prayer at graduation exercises was unconstitutional.[8] Following that decision, there was a series of attempts to slip graduation prayer past the courts. The most obvious solution was for the prayer to be initiated by students, or to be included in the valedictorian's speech. Several states tried to pass laws permitting such expressions. Some of the cases and some of the laws were approved by local and state courts, but others were not. The problem was that other students who might be of a different religion than the speaker would be a captive audience in such a situation.

By 1996 three different U.S. circuit courts had ruled in such cases, one permitting graduation prayer if a majority of students had voted for it, and two ruling it unconstitutional. In July 1999, still another U.S. circuit court, in Atlanta, ruled that student-initiated voluntary prayer would be permissible over the school's intercom system and at graduation exercises. The Supreme Court rendered a decision at the end of the 2000 term definitively declaring it unconstitutional even with the so-called circuit breakers, which the defendants had claimed removed the school administration from responsibility for the prayer.

Ever since the first decisions in 1963, a solid majority of the American public has agreed with the Christian conservative opposition to the Supreme Court decisions on school prayer and/or Bible reading. The public also favors a constitutional amendment to overturn the decisions, although the majority declined from 65.9 percent in 1974 to 52.8 percent in 1998.[9] The General Social Survey poll in figure 14.1 shows the results on this question. A Gallup Poll in 1999 showed again that strong majorities of 70 percent favor prayer in classrooms and 83 percent favor it at graduation exercises.[10]

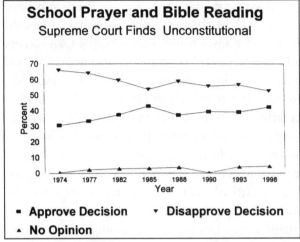

School Prayer and Bible Reading
Supreme Court Finds Unconstitutional

- **Approve Decision** ▾ **Disapprove Decision**
- ▲ **No Opinion**

FIGURE 14.1
Question 314:

The United States Supreme Court has ruled that no state or local government may require the reading of the Lord's Prayer or Bible verses in public schools. What are your views on this—do you approve or disapprove of the Court ruling?

Source: *General Social Surveys, 1974–1998,* James Allan Davis and Tom W. Smith, principal investigators (Chicago: National Opinion Research Center). Analysis performed on MicroCase Explorit Software, Microcase Corporation Bellevue, Washington.

BUT HOW TO DO IT?

Given that the Supreme Court decisions in question are based on the justices' reading of the First Amendment clause forbidding an "establishment of religion," the only way to overturn the decisions is to amend the First Amendment. Just as constitutional amendments outlawing abortion have fallen victim to disagreements among conservatives about just how to do it, the Christian conservative desire to amend the constitution to permit religious practices on government property has also been delayed by differing viewpoints. First, many, but not all, Baptists, whose forebears were the most vigorous supporters of church-state separation when the First Amendment was adopted, objected to it. Some of my Baptist respondents had been cautioned by their pastors that allowing religious practices in schools or on government property would open the door to similar practices by other religions and actually make the situation worse.

Others, including David Barton, have helped to draft an amendment; James Dobson and Lou Sheldon of the Traditional Values Coalition have also taken an interest in the project. In 1995 and 1996 various versions were introduced in the House of Representatives by Reps. Henry Hyde (R-Ill.), Dick Armey (R-Tex.), and Ernest Istook (R-Okla.), and in the

Senate by Orrin Hatch (R-Utah). Some wanted to limit it to prayer in schools, others wanted to include government aid and funding for religiously based charitable organizations. Rep. Ernest Istook, whose amendment dealt only with school prayer, was the most persistent in talking to all the various religious groups—Protestant, Catholic, and Jewish—and trying to achieve a compromise. Despite his efforts, he did not succeed.

Why are devout Christians, who conduct prayer and Bible study in their homes and attend it in their churches, thus making sure that their children are exposed to their faith, so determined to have it in the schools as well? Some think it is necessary because of their belief that America is a Christian nation, and that God has favored us because we recognize him in our public lives. Others say that the school shootings have shown that "kicking God out of the schools" has led to horrible tragedies. And in some cases, respondents claimed to favor it because some children are not exposed to religion at home. For whatever reason, a strong majority of the American public favors some kind of religious exercises in schools.

> I think that once we took prayer out of schools, that was the biggest mistake, because I've seen a rise in gang activity in our neighborhoods, I've seen my little brother get kicked out of school. He's in there with no prayer in the school. There's no Christian activity and I think he just gets involved with kids that were not raised in a godly family, that don't believe that God's watching, so why not do anything we can? (young woman, student, and part-time sales clerk, 1997)

> It probably would not make a whole lot of difference if there is no religious training at home but the issue is really a lot more than prayer, it really has to do with the Bible and the influence of the Bible in our school system, because our country was founded not only on freedom of religion, but on Bible principles, and a lot of people don't understand that. (older woman, small town, 1997)

Almost all of my respondents think that student-led religious activities should be allowed in public schools. But having learned the realities of what the courts will allow (even if they do not agree with it) and being aware of the diversity of the student population today, slightly less than half think teachers should lead prayer in schools.

> I'm torn. On the one hand, if they're all good Baptist teachers, fine, but I
> don't think I'd want an Islamic person leading a prayer in school, so I think
> they should allow them a moment of silence. But as far as actually leading
> them in prayer, I don't think so. (young woman, former sales clerk, 1997)

Those responding to a national poll conducted by the Gallup organization for the Phi Delta Kappa educational fraternity in 1995 also gave
strong support for a constitutional amendment permitting spoken prayers,
but 81 percent recognized that it might be necessary to include the prayers
of other religious groups as well. Seventy percent would actually choose
a moment of silent prayer or contemplation over spoken prayers, as did
about 15 percent of my respondents.[11]

> I think they should have a moment of silence just to settle them down,
> and if they do know how to pray and if they have met the Lord, I think
> it is certainly an orderly thing to do. Wherever I am and that's
> announced, everybody bows their head for a moment of silence and
> children can do the same thing. I remember as a child praying silently.
> (urban businesswoman, 1997)

ALTERNATIVES TO PUBLIC SCHOOLS

Michael Farris, the Concerned Women for America attorney who had represented parents objecting to textbooks in several court cases, left CWA
in 1987 to run for office, then became the head of the Homeschool Legal
Defense Association. Christian conservatives of the 1990s had come to
realize that the kind of religious and moral training they would like to
have their children exposed to in the schools would not be allowed
because of the First Amendment. This realization, in combination with
their doubts about the quality of public education itself, was an impetus
to the search for alternatives. The Christian schools that Robert Billings
had encouraged were one alternative. The home-schooling that Farris
defended was another.

In 1980 none of those I interviewed was utilizing Christian schools or
home-schooling, but in 1997, 90 percent of those with children or grandchildren of school age had at least one child or grandchild attending Christian

schools. Some were paying tuition for their grandchildren. About half as many had children or grandchildren being home-schooled. Both parents and grandparents thought it important for children to have that religious training.

> Well, it's kinda like sex education. If you say I'm all for prayer in schools, I am for that, but I would worry about how it's done with the type of teachers that are coming out of the teachers' colleges, and this is why I am very strong for either home-schooling or Christian schools. (housewife, long-time Eagle Forum leader, 1997)

The majority of those who had chosen Christian schools or home-schooling did so because they wanted schools to reinforce their own Christian values, or because they wanted to avoid humanistic values, the teaching of evolution, and/or exposure to sex education of the kind they disapproved. But there were many other objections: the low academic standards of the public schools, the lack of discipline, the "whole-language" method of teaching (instead of phonics), the history books that criticized America instead of instilling patriotism, and the government programs that they objected to, such as School-to-Work, Goals 2000, and Outcome-Based Education. All of these were government programs offering government grants if local schools would use certain procedures or programs in their classrooms.

The older respondents did not have firsthand knowledge of these problems in schools; they had been told by their children, or had read examples in the literature from the Christian Coalition or Concerned Women for America. Some of the younger parents had horror stories of their own to tell: the children who were allowed to watch frivolous videotapes or who went on field trips of doubtful value so often that there seemed to be no time left for learning, the teacher who smoked marijuana during recess, and the child who still had not learned to read by the third grade, but who learned quickly when she was put in a private school.

Only three of these respondents had a good word to say about the public schools. The 1998 Phi Delta Kappa poll also found a negative view of public schools, but somewhat higher ratings among those whose children attended public schools than among those whose children did not. Sixty-two percent of all those polled gave As or Bs to the public schools their own children attended, and 52 percent gave similarly high grades to the schools in their community, but only 39 percent of those whose children attended private schools rated the community schools as highly.[12]

The opinions of public schools in general have become more negative in the ten years that the Phi Delta Kappa has commissioned these polls, while the opinions of local community schools have stayed about the same. This suggests that the lower ratings for public schools nationally may have been influenced by negative publicity about public schools, much of it generated by conservative organizations. Only 18 percent of all those polled in 1998 gave As or Bs to the public schools of the nation, and of those whose children attend private schools, only 12 percent gave high grades to public schools.[13] Figures 14.2 and 14.3 show comparisons from Phi Delta Kappa polls in the 1990s.[14]

CREATING A CLIMATE FOR PUBLIC SCHOOL ALTERNATIVES

As more and more parents opted to take their children out of the public schools, the pressure for help for those families to pay private tuition grew. If their children did not attend public schools, they objected to paying taxes for them. They would be delighted if they could receive a portion of the money their district would otherwise use to support public schools as a voucher they could use to pay for private school or for home-schooling materials. It is not surprising that the Phi Delta Kappa surveys also showed support for vouchers rising as approval of public schools falls.

The Phi Delta Kappa polls, however, show that approval of vouchers was higher when the question was asked in terms of helping parents pay for private schools, but lower when the question asked if they favored government funds going to private schools. There is still some reluctance to take money away from the public schools. Well-funded institutes and centers are working to change that reluctance. The Bradley Foundation of Wisconsin was instrumental in changing the climate of opinion about vouchers.

In earlier decades, such a policy had few supporters because it was seen as potentially undermining the public school system on which poor and immigrant children had always depended for a foothold in the nation's economy. Voucher proponents never spoke of it in those terms, however. They framed it differently: as a means of helping poor children escape failing

Figure 14.2

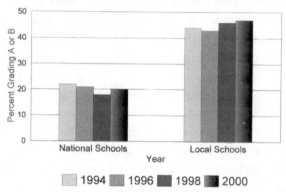

Grading the Public Schools
All Parents, Phi Delta Kappa Polls

Question: Students are often given the grades, A, B, C, D and Fail to denote the quality of their work. Suppose the public schools themselves, in this community, or in the nation as a whole, were graded in the same way. What grade would you give the public schools?

Source: "The Thirty-second Annual Phi Delta Kappa/Gallup Pole of the Public's Attitudes toward the Public Schools," http://www.pdkintl.org/kappan/kpo10 009.htm, accessed 22 August 2000.

Figure 14.3

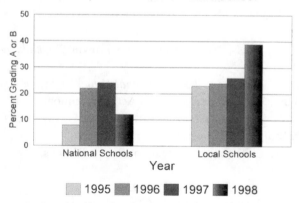

Grading the Public Schools
Parents, Children not in Public School

Question: Same as figure 14.2.

Source: Lowell C. Rose and Alec M. Gallup. "The Public's Attitudes toward the Public Schools," *Phi Delta Kappan* 80 (September 1998): 45–46.

public schools. Liberals who opposed vouchers failed to make the case that voucher programs seldom provide enough money to pay private school tuition, or that removing money from public schools would only make it harder for them to provide a good education for the students remaining.

After the Wisconsin legislature in 1989 provided for a voucher program limited to secular or private schools, and it was challenged in court, the Bradley Foundation provided funds to pay for students to enroll in private schools including religious ones.[15] Having thus created a constituency for the voucher program, the foundation continued to support it when the state adopted a new voucher plan including religious schools. That program was subject to a more serious court challenge on the basis of the First Amendment, but Bradley recruited a legal team including Kenneth Starr (later to become a nationally known special prosecutor), and arranged the financing to fight it.

NOTES

1. This and subsequent unidentified quotations are from the transcripts of the sessions of the Oklahoma White House Conference on Families, in which speakers are not named.

2. Phyllis Schlafly, ed., *Child Abuse in the Classroom: Official Transcript of Proceedings before the Department of Education* (Alton, Ill.: Pere Marquette, 1984).

3. David Brudnoy, "For a Limited Jubilee," *New York Times*, op-ed, 24 October 1974.

4. Associated Press, "School Censorship Growing," *Oklahoma City Times*, 31 July 1981.

5. Robert W. Klous, ed., *The Traditional Values in Action Resource Directory* (Lynchburg, Va.: Christian Values in Action Coalition, 1995), p. 188.

6. Robert L. Simonds, "Christian Parents Should Serve on School Boards," *California School Boards Journal* (winter 1993).

7. Robert McG. Thomas, "Obituary of Robert Billings," *New York Times*, 1 June 1995.

8. *Lee* v. *Weisman*, 505 U.S. 577 (1992).

9. James Allan Davis and Tom W. Smith, principal investigators, *General Social Surveys, 1974–1998* (Chicago: National Opinion Research Center). Analysis performed on MicroCase ExplorIt software created by Microcase Corporation, Bellevue, Washington. Question 314.

10. Mark Gillespie, "Most Americans Support Prayer in Public Schools," *Gallup Poll Monthly* 406 (July 1999).

11. Stanley M. Elam and Lowell C. Rose, "The Phi Delta Kappa/Gallup Poll of the Public's Attitudes toward the Public Schools," *Phi Delta Kappan* 77 (September 1995): 50–51.

12. Lowell C. Rose and Alec M. Gallup, "The Public's Attitudes toward the Public Schools," *Phi Delta Kappan* 80 (September 1998): 45–46.

13. Ibid., pp. 42–43.

14. "The Thirty-second Annual Phi Delta Kappa/Gallup Poll of the Public's Attitudes toward the Public Schools," http://www.pdkintl.org/kappan/kpol 0009.htm, accessed 22 August 2000.

15. James A. Barnes, "Banker with a Cause," *National Journal*, 6 March 1993, p. 566.

CHAPTER 15

CONCLUSION: LOOKING BACK, LOOKING FORWARD

B y the end of the twentieth century, the Christian conservative defense of religious freedom was presented from a different perspective than it had been twenty-five years earlier. The women in the 1970s who opposed the Equal Rights Amendment saw it as a government threat to God's plan for the family. By opposing it, they understood that they were defending their religious freedom as wives and mothers. What started as simple opposition to the ERA evolved into the pro-family movement and then the Christian Right.

Twenty-five years later, the Christian Right's agenda was clearly in opposition to the separation of church and state. The movement's Christian conservative adherents objected to contemporary interpretations of the First Amendment's religion clauses. Both in the movement's legislative proposals and in the cases brought to trial by their lawyers, they argued for "religious freedom" by seeking to have the Ten Commandments posted in government buildings and Christian prayers said in school classrooms and at assemblies and football games. In other cases, the lawyers sought to prevent schools from teaching tolerance of homosexuality and to allow landlords to refuse to rent to homosexual couples, claiming that any accommodation to homosexuality violated the religious belief of Christians.

The three sources of Christian Right activism in the anti-ERA crusade—women, fundamentalists, and southerners—were still important at the end of those twenty-five years, but each had undergone some changes.

WOMEN IN THE CHRISTIAN RIGHT

The women of the 1970s who mobilized to defeat the Equal Rights Amendment were living a paradox: they were taking an active public role while promoting the ideal of the stay-at-home wife and mother. Feminists thought Phyllis Schlafly was the premier example of that paradox, for she had been politically active for most of her adult life. Actually, she was able to resolve the conflict and to "have it all," for she had unusual stamina, a talent for organization, and hired help. Those of her followers who were not so fortunate had to resolve the conflict in their own way. They continued to believe that it was better for mothers to stay at home while their children were small, but not all were able to realize that ideal in their own lives.

Although the ERA was not ratified, the visibility of the issue did produce some changes in women's legal status. Women in later years had easier access to education, credit, and a wider variety of jobs, but little was done to help them accommodate their family roles to their new opportunities outside the home. If the antifeminists wanted to return to the old ideal of "separate spheres" for women, they did not succeed. But neither did the feminists succeed in restructuring society and its workplaces to fit the needs of families with children. It was still the responsibility of each individual woman to work out the conflict between work and family for herself.

Women were in high-level positions in the movement itself at the end of the century, but few could be said to be "in charge." Phyllis Schlafly was still active as a member of the Christian Right's Council for National Policy, a regular speaker at Christian Coalition meetings, and a strong advocate at each Republican convention for the strict antiabortion plank in the party's platform. Although Lottie Beth Hobbs, the other national anti-ERA leader, went back to her own private career in 1984, another woman, Beverly LaHaye, along with her husband, Tim, still had a prominent role.

Most of the Christian Right organizations were still headed by men, but some women were near the top level. That was in keeping with the policy of conservative churches, where the senior pastor was usually a man. Roberta Combs, former head of the Christian Coalition of South

Carolina, became the national coalition's executive vice president after Ralph Reed and his successors, Don Hodel and Randy Tate, all resigned or were dismissed in the space of a few months. Pat Robertson was still the president. As old age crept up on the original male entrepreneurs of the Christian conservative organizations, many of them took a reduced role while turning the day-to-day management over to their sons, and in one case a daughter. Andrea Sheldon, the daughter of Lou Sheldon, became legislative affairs director and later executive director of her father's Traditional Values Coalition. Beverly LaHaye moved back to California in 1998, but kept the title of chairman of Concerned Women for America; the new president was another woman, Carmen Pate.

CONSERVATIVE CHURCHES IN THE CHRISTIAN RIGHT

Conservative churches in America, whether fundamentalist or charismatic, grew faster than the population from 1970 to 1997, while the modernist/liberal churches actually lost membership even as the population increased. The Nazarenes grew by 65 percent, the Mormons by 116 percent, and the Assemblies of God by an astonishing 281 percent in that period. In those same three decades, four liberal churches were all losing membership: the United Methodists by 22.3 percent, the Episcopalians by 24.9 percent, the United Church of Christ by 27.6 percent, and the Christian Church (Disciples of Christ) by 41.6 percent. The growth curve of the Southern Baptist Convention was an intriguing contrast. Although it grew rapidly from 1960 to about 1980, its growth slowed dramatically in the 1980s and actually failed to keep pace with population growth in the 1990s, after hard-line conservatives took control of the convention offices.[1]

At century's end, conservative churches still provided most of the activists for Christian Right organizations, just as they had in the early pro-family movement. But the face of conservative Christianity had changed. Women from fundamentalist churches were the grassroots activists of the anti-ERA campaign, along with some members of the modernist or liberal churches who were dissidents in their churches. In the 1990s, a new and growing constituency for the Christian Right came from the postmodern nondenominational and charismatic, but still conservative, churches. Their numerical growth and the increasing levels of education and affluence of their members gave conservative Christians more potential leverage in politics.

THE SOUTH AND THE CHRISTIAN RIGHT

The South is still the home base of conservative religion, but southern religion and its accompanying cultural beliefs have spread beyond the borders of the Old South. This is the "Southernization of America" described by John Egerton in 1974.[2] The other half of Egerton's thesis is the "Americanization of Dixie." Not only are southern people, southern ideas, and southern problems to be found in the North as well as the South, but northerners with different racial attitudes have come into the South as the South's economy has modernized. The two regions are still different, but the differences are not as great as they once were. Religion is one of the important indicators of that change.

The distribution of conservative Christians is becoming somewhat more equal in different regions of the country. In 1972, 60.4 percent of self-identified fundamentalists responding to the General Social Survey were southern, almost twice as high as the proportion (30.9 percent of all respondents who were southern). In 1998, a slightly smaller percentage (54.8 percent) of fundamentalists were southern, but 36.1 percent of all respondents were. Fundamentalists were twice as likely as the general population to be southern in 1972, but only 1.5 times as likely to be southern in 1998.[3]

The southern view of womanhood, supported by fundamentalist theology, was upheld by nine of the eleven states of the old Confederacy in their refusal to ratify the Woman Suffrage Amendment in 1920. The Equal Rights Amendment, which also challenged women's traditional roles, was rejected by the same number of old Confederate states, but it was rejected outside of the South as well.

Southern churches bore some responsibility for southern culture's unequal treatment of both African Americans and women, for southern churches had found justification in the Bible for both. That heritage was not entirely gone at the turn of the century, but the new postmodern churches were trying to move beyond it. All of the nondenominational churches that I visited in Oklahoma had women in responsible positions, although they were not senior pastors. One of the nondenominational preachers featured on the Trinity Broadcasting (television) Network is also a woman. Meanwhile, the Southern Baptist Convention was reiterating its belief that women should not be pastors at all. The nondenominational churches I visited always included sizeable numbers of worshippers of African and Hispanic descent.

Not only neo-pentecostals, but the older pentecostal churches practiced racial tolerance, possibly because one of the earliest pentecostal pastors was William Seymour, an African American who conducted the Azusa Street Revivals in Los Angeles from 1904 to 1906. Seymour's religious style and oral liturgy were of African derivation. His revivals, along with those of his Caucasian mentor in Topeka, Kansas, were the beginning of the Assemblies of God, the largest pentecostal denomination in America at the end of the century.[4]

The rapid growth of the postmodern churches may have had some influence on the racial climate. Those churches are also advancing the revitalization and partial modernization of a fundamentalism that might otherwise die with its older rural conservative adherents. In the South, as elsewhere in the country, the new suburbs, with their younger and better-educated residents, are where the postmodern churches are prospering. The conservative social attitudes of the old fundamentalists on abortion, pornography, and sex education still affect southern politics, even as they spread to other regions.

At the end of William Hixson's historical review of research on the Christian Right, he suggests that the search for the locus of the popular support for the Christian Right was misplaced, and that the more interesting question would have been why the Republicans were willing to listen to it.[5] Surely one reason is that so many of the Republicans now *are* southerners who were willing to listen to campaign rhetoric tailored to their traditional social conservatism.

Conservative social attitudes on sexual, reproductive, and family issues are now represented in Congress by the Republicans of the New South, just as the Democrats of the Old Solid South represented their constituents when they delayed the passage of civil rights laws for so many years. The Christian Right is now as essential to the Republican coalition as the segregationists were essential to the Democratic coalition in the

1940s and 1950s. In 1998 Republicans held eight governorships in the eleven states of the old Confederacy, the same number that Democrats held in 1980. Republicans held fifteen of twenty-two U.S. Senate seats from the South in 1998; Democrats held sixteen in 1980. The Republican advantage in southern seats in the House of Representatives was 71 to 54, reversing a Democratic majority of 77 to 31 in 1980.[6]

In the Congresses of the 1940s and 1950s, the Democrats were careful to represent their constituents on segregation, but voted with northern Democrats on most other issues. Now segregation is a less significant issue and southern Republicans are listening to their constituents on sexual, reproductive, and family issues. My suggestion in the introduction to this book that the Republicanization of the South was responsible for the conservatization of the Republican Party should have been modified to specify which kind of conservatism.

WHAT HAS THE CHRISTIAN RIGHT ACCOMPLISHED?

In addition to the growth in membership, organizational offices, staffs, and communication channels, and the new cooperation between religious groups, the Christian Right can take some satisfaction in substantive progress on their political agenda. The movement seems to have brought citizens who had previously shunned it into the political process. That is even more significant because political participation in general was declining at the same time. Voter turnout has been falling ever since the 1960s. The increasing political apathy of the American electorate, especially those under fifty, is one of the Christian Right's greatest assets, one that was given to it free of charge. Figure 15.1 shows the relatively low levels of participation for younger voters compared to older ones.[7]

The movement was also at least partially responsible for the increased Republican presence in the U.S. Congress, in state governorships, and in state legislatures. Although the Christian Coalition insisted (in its effort to justify its tax-exempt status) that it was not tied to any particular party, its own survey of the national membership in 1995 showed that 68 percent were Republican, 20 percent independent, and only 5 percent Democrat.[8] All but one of my respondents were Republicans. Fur-

Political Participation
Gallup, University of Virginia, 1996

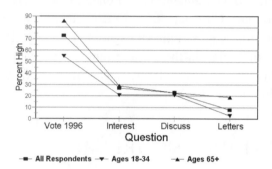

- All Respondents - Ages 18-34 - Ages 65+

FIGURE 15.1
Question 1. #25. Percent who voted in 1996.
Question 2. #99. Percent very interested in politics and national affairs.
Question 3. #30. Percent who discuss politics and politicians often with other people.
Question 4. #32. Percent who write letters often to government or to someone else of influence about needs or problems.

Source: James D. Hunter and Carl Bowman. *The State of Disunion*, Vol. II, Fieldwork conducted by the Gallup Organization (Ivy, Va.: In Medias Res Educational Foundation, 1996).

ther, it is clear that the kind of legislation they want is more likely to receive the support of Republicans than Democrats.

Since 1994, the Christian Right has been particularly successful in legislation around the edges of the abortion issue, such as mandatory parental consent, mandatory waiting periods, and the new law providing federal funds for abstinence-only sex education. Conservatives were able to get a ban on what they call partial-birth abortion through the 1997–1998 Congress, although President Clinton's veto kept the ban from becoming law. With the election of a Republican president in 2000, they may have fewer occasions to contend with a presidential veto of their legislation.

While they have been thwarted in many of their legislative attempts, at least the issues the Christian Right cares about were being talked about. For them, that was progress of a sort. Public airing of their desire to push homosexuals back into the closet, to outlaw abortion, to allow religious exercises in public schools, and to allow parents to use their share of public school money for private or Christian schools may cause more citizens to pay attention to those issues and to form opinions on them. It remains to be seen whether more people will then come around to the Christian Right's point of view.

The *Fortune* poll of Washington insiders rated the Christian Coalition as the seventh most influential lobby in both 1997 and 1998, but it slipped to thirty-fifth in 1999. The National Right-to-Life Committee, on the other hand, was moving up. It was tenth in 1997, ninth in 1998, and eighth in 1999. Some of the groups frequently mentioned in the Christian Right's direct mail as the "anti-Christian left" were rated as less successful. The National Abortion Rights Action League and Planned Parenthood were both below the radar, in the sixtieth range. The National Education Association was rated ninth in 1997, sank to twenty-first in 1998, but rose again to ninth in 1999.[9]

DO THEY REPRESENT THE MAINSTREAM?

Many of those I interviewed were the very conservative Christian Right activists, who may be no more than 5 percent of the population, according to one estimate.[10] Those who identify with the Christian Right but are less active were somewhat less conservative. One estimate places them at about 14 percent of the population.[11] Finally, we can expect the views of the larger group of evangelicals, roughly 25 to 30 percent of the population, to be even less conservative, but still more conservative than the general public.

Figure 15.2 compares the opinions of the broader category of evangelicals with the general public on five of the issues that are most salient for the Christian conservatives.[12] The patterns are similar for both groups, but evangelicals are clearly more conservative than the general public. If the poll had tabulated answers to the same questions for Christian Right activists, the line representing their more conservative views would have been above all of these lines. The opinions of evangelicals about women's roles have moved close to those of the general public since 1972, but evangelicals are still more conservative than the general public on homosexuality, sex education in public schools, abortion, and voluntary prayer in public schools.

ARE THEY EXTREMIST?

Christian conservatives are *extremely* sensitive about being called radical or extremist. They complain that the media is too quick to identify extremist views or actions, such as abortion clinic shootings, with those

**FIGURE
15.2**

Opinions on Christian Right Issues
Gallup, University of Virginia, 1996

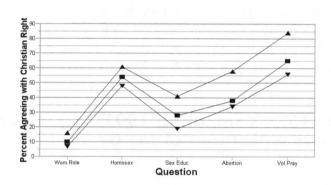

-▲- **All Evangelicals**   -■- **All Respondents**   -▼- **All, Age 18-34**

Question 1. #6-a. Do you feel that changes in the role of women in society are either mostly bad or very bad?

Question 2. #6-g. Do you feel that more acceptance of homosexuality is either very bad or mostly bad?

Question 3. #96-f. Do you disagree mostly or completely that public schools have a responsibility to provide sex education to teenagers?

Question 4. #94-i. Do you feel that abortion is just as bad as killing a person who has already been born—it is murder?

Question 5. #10-c. Do you favor allowing voluntary prayer in public schools?

Source: James D. Hunter and Carl Bowman, *The State of Disunion*. Fieldwork conducted by the Gallup Organization (Ivy, Va.: In Medias Res Educational Foundation, 1996).

of the movement as a whole. The direct mail of groups opposing the Christian Right indeed routinely labels them "extremist" and "radical." If extremism is the use of violent and/or illegal means to advance their causes, the truly extremist groups were the Weather Underground of the 1960s on the left and the Ku Klux Klan, neo-Nazis, paramilitary groups, and clinic bombers on the right, all of which were denounced by my respondents. It is true, however, that the hot rhetoric of organizational direct mail activates those with the more extreme opinions, and encourages those opinions. As in any organization, the more strongly ideological members are likely to be the most activist.

If extremism means holding opinions shared by only a small proportion of the general public, the Christian Right may or may not be extremist, depending on what proportion is chosen as the criterion. Table 15.3 shows that the views of my respondents on some issues probably are extremist when compared to public opinion polls. The percentage-point differences range from 24.3 on prayer in schools to 73.9 on homosexuality.

Table 15.3. Comparing 1997 Respondents' Views with Those of the General Public

Issue	Percents favoring Respondts	Public	Diff.
1. Homosexuals should have equal rights	8.1	82.0	73.9
2. Sex education in general	n.a.	68.0	68.0
3. Moment of silence beginning school day	15.0	70.0	55.0
4. Abortion available only strict limits	n.a.	45.0	46.4
5. Homosexuality acceptable lifestyle	0.0	44.0	44.0
6. Vouchers/tax credits/private schools	15.4	50.0	34.6
7. Abortion legal in all cases	0.0	32.0	32.0
8. Approve of public schools	11.0	43.0	32.0
9. Ban on abortion except to save mother	72.3	42.0	30.3
10. Teaching creation in public schools	93.2	58.0	25.2
11. Overturn school prayer decisions	97.3	73.0	24.3
12. Same-sex marriage	4.3	28.0	23.7
13. Abortion ban except life, rape, incest	91.4	n.a.	
14. Teacher-led prayer in public schools	46.0	n.a.	
15. Student-led prayer in public schools	97.0	n.a	
16. Sex education with abstinence emphasis	71.1	n.a.	
17. Sex education with contraceptive info.	0.0	n.a.	

Sources for the opinions of the general public are as follows:

Questions Nos. 1, 9, 10, 11, and 12, Gallup, 1996
Questions Nos. 2 and 5, University of Virginia, 1996
Question No. 3, Gallup, 1995
Question No. 4 and 7, *New York Times*, 1998
Question No. 6, Gallup, 1993
Question No. 8, Phi Delta Kappa Poll, 1997

Because my respondents are among the most activist of the Christian Right in Oklahoma, their answers may not accurately represent all of the Christian Right even in Oklahoma. It should be noted also that public opinion poll responses vary with the wording of the questions, the organization doing the polling, and the time that the surveying was done. The questions shown in the table were chosen to be as similar as possible to the ones I asked my respondents, but the correspondence is not perfect.

The concern of Christian conservatives about moral decline is shared by many who are not conservative. They have that concern in common with mainstream America, although others use different terms and propose different solutions. For instance, a group of liberal women with whom I discussed my research agreed that there is a moral crisis in America today. Some of them believed that lack of parental responsibility and family breakdown were partially responsible, just as the Christian Right respondents had. But the liberal women mentioned corporate greed and tax loopholes as well, and most disagreed with the solutions of the Christian Right, such as school vouchers, banning abortions, or opposing gay rights laws. Similar views were found in a national poll by the *Wall Street Journal* and NBC News in 1999. About two-thirds of those questioned agreed "that social and moral values were higher when they were growing up than they are today. As a corollary, two-thirds believe that standards of acceptable and unacceptable behavior are lower today than in recent years."[13]

The Christian conservatives might find the key to electoral success if they could tap into this unease among the general public, without alienating it with unpopular stances on abortion and homosexuality. Presidential candidates of both parties were trying to do exactly that as they maneuvered toward the 2000 elections. But for Christian conservatives, that is difficult to do. Their belief that they represent God's truth as well as their need to maintain "appallment" to keep the contributions coming will stand in the way of compromise in our political system.

Despite its rhetoric of distrust in government, the Christian conservative movement has sought solutions in government action: prohibiting abortion, same-sex marriages, and homosexual adoptions, or government sponsorship of prayer and Ten Commandments displays. It seems unlikely that the movement would agree to abandon these positions. But the same *Wall Street Journal/NBC News* poll finds that most of the public wants individual families and communities, not government, to solve the problems of moral decline. Meanwhile, some influential voices in evangelicalism are calling for a return to its historic role of strengthening families and communities instead of turning to political and governmental solutions.[14]

LOOKING AHEAD

By the end of the twentieth century, the organizations of the Christian Right were burdened with large fixed costs. The offices in Washington, D.C., and in the states with their paid staffers, the glossy magazines, and the TV programs were expensive. Direct mail, which had been an excellent source of funds when it was a relatively new technology, was less effective twenty years later. The fund-raising letters became ever more insistent, and the threats of imminent bankruptcy ever more dire. The monthly publications began carrying advertisements, and in summer 2000, a letter from Concerned Women for America for the first time included pitches for credit cards and printed books of checks with a portion of the proceeds to go to the organization.

By the beginning of the year 2000, there was a real possibility that age might soon force some of the Christian Right entrepreneurs to retire. James Dobson was the youngest at sixty-three, and Phyllis Schlafly the oldest at seventy-five. LaHaye, Schlafly, and Dobson had already taken a less active role and made plans for choosing a successor. It is unlikely that any successor will be able to attract enthusiastic followers and plan strategy as well as those who started the organizations.

The Christian Coalition's obituary had already been prepared by the year 2000, but that was not the first media declaration that the Christian Right was dead. It remains to be seen whether a new organization will take the coaliltion's place, or if Dobson's Focus on the Family or the Family Research Council will become the leading Christian conservative organization. But whatever happens to the organizations, the Christian conservative movement still has its base in the growing membership of the conservative churches. The Christian Right persuaded conservative Christians that they should seek a place in the American political system. Barring the unlikely possibility that they change their minds again, Christian conservatives will continue to be a significant interest group regardless of what happens to a particular organization.

Convinced that the secular media and the public schools were all defeating their attempts to teach moral values to their children, Christian conservatives have created their own media and schools. Convinced that politicians, agency heads, and judges were not doing their part to sustain a moral culture, they have seen to it that their own young people are being trained to fill those positions. Their children's schooling, often in Christian schools or in their own homes, is carefully supervised to inculcate their values. Well-financed organizations are subsidizing conservative newspapers on college campuses and offering handsome college scholarships to conservative young people. Accredited institutions like Oral Roberts University, Jerry Falwell's Liberty University, and Pat Robertson's Regents University now provide postsecondary, graduate, and legal education. Annual meetings of the American Political Science Association, long perceived as a hotbed of liberalism, now feature papers by graduate students and professors from these conservative universities. The graduates of these schools, colleges, and universities will become doctors, lawyers, journalists, and professors as well as preachers and entrepreneurs. They will be in a position to shape the culture for coming generations, for they know that the political changes they have achieved will not last unless those changes reside in the hearts and minds of the people.

NOTES

1. Calculated from statistics in the 1970 to 1997 *Yearbooks of American and Canadian Churches* (Nashville: Abingdon). Each book includes the latest available statistics from the denominations; often they were as much as two years behind the date of the book.

2. John Egerton, *The Americanization of Dixie, the Southernization of America* (New York: Harper's, 1974).

3. James A. Davis and Tom W. Smith, principal investigators, *General Social Surveys, 1972–1998* (Chicago: National Opinion Research Center). Analysis performed on MicroCase Analysis System, created and sold by MicroCase Corporation, Bellevue, Washington.

4. Margaret M. Poloma, *The Assemblies of God at the Crossroads: Charisma and Institutional Dilemmas* (Knoxville: University of Tennessee Press, 1989), p. 26.

5. William B. Hixson, *The Search for the American Right Wing* (Princeton, N.J.: Princeton University Press, 1992), p. 268.

6. Kevin Sack, "The Solid South Has Switched Sides," *New York Times,* 16 March 1998.

7. James D. Hunter and Carl Bowman, *The State of Disunion,* vol. I (Ivy, Va.: In Medias Res Educational Foundation, 1996) questions 25, 9, 30, and 32.

8. Richard Berke, "Christian Coalition Is United on Morality, but Not Politics," *New York Times*, 8 September 1995, p. D18.

9. Tyler Maroney and Dustin Smith, "The Influence Merchants," *Fortune,* 7 December 1998, p. 134; Jeffrey H. Birnbaum, "Follow the Money," *Fortune,* 6 July 2000, p. 140.

10. Hunter and Bowman, *Disunion,* p. 52.

11. Tom W. Smith, *Analysis of the Survey of the Religious Right,* conducted by the Gallup International Institute (New York: American Jewish Committee, 1996).

12. Hunter and Bowman, *Disunion*, questions 6-a, 6-g, 96-f, and 94-i

13 Bernard Wysocki Jr., "Most Turn to Family, More Than to State, for Answers," *Wall Street Journal*, 24 June 1999, p. A9.

14. Cal Thomas and Ed Dobson, *Blinded by Might: Can the Religious Right Save America?* (Grand Rapids, Mich.: Zondervan Publishing, 1999).

APPENDIX

METHODOLOGICAL NOTE

In a study of a social movement that extends from 1972 to the present, and which had members in every state of the Union, it is obviously impossible for one person—or even a group of persons—to know everything that transpired everywhere. For specific information about motivation, mobilization, recruitment, leadership styles, and movement culture, I conducted interviews with grassroots members and leaders themselves, as well as engaging in participant observation at meetings, lobbying events, and national and regional conferences. For information about organizational activities in other states and for analyses by other observers, I read the magazines, direct-mail solicitations, and position papers that the movement produced, and books and articles about the movement from the secular media and academic presses.

PARTICIPANTS AND LEADER INTERVIEWS: PARTICIPANT OBSERVATION

From 1976 to 1983 I conducted about a hundred in-depth interviews and attended organizational meetings and lobbying events. After the ERA was finally defeated, I conducted a mail survey using random samples from both the STOP-ERA and OK-ERA lists to learn about what they had done in the ERA campaign and why.

From 1995 to 1998 I interviewed another generation of activists, about seventy-two altogether, and observed another set of organizations. From these interviews I learned how they had been recruited to the movement, what they hoped to accomplish in it, and what they thought about the issues.

To find interview respondents in a more systematic way, I used random samples of lists provided by the 1979 Oklahoma White House Conference on Families and the Oklahoma Christian Coalition office. While neither list is a random sample of all Oklahoma Christian conservatives, those in the samples were diverse in age, educational level, involvement in movement activity, and type of residence—urban or rural. By the time I did the second set of interviews, most of the earlier respondents had dropped out or moved away, and some had died. But I was able to locate a few for reinterviewing, and one actually appeared in both samples.

In addition to the sample interviews, I interviewed as many as I could find of those who had been identified as leaders, either holding formal office or having informal leadership qualities. There were also interviews with national leaders in Washington, D.C., and with ordinary participants during breaks in regional or national conferences.

While there are some advantages to sampling movement participants from all across the nation, there are also advantages to staying in the same place and watching the movement grow from its first stages through its period of expansion and professionalization to its present status as a player in national politics. An additional benefit was that I could see respondents in many different situations and observe the extent to which some of them changed over time. Why did I choose Oklahoma? First, of course, because I was there, but it was serendipitous. The state is part of the bloc of southern and western states where the pro-family movement is strongest. It is also where the pro-family movement began.

PRINTED SOURCES, MOVEMENT SOURCES, BOOKS AND NEWSPAPERS ARTICLES

In the early years movement literature was typed in the homes of members, copied, and distributed in churches or on car windshields. Later there were national organizations producing slick magazines, direct-mail solicitations, and radio and television programs. Again, it was impossible to sample all of it, but I joined several organizations in order to be on their mailing lists. The library of People for the American Way in Washington, D.C., has wonderfully complete files of most of the organizations' literature, and I spent many hours there copying things I had not received myself. A final source of data was books about the pro-family movement by academic authors and stories in secular newspapers and newsmagazines.

RESOURCES

Ammerman, Nancy Tatom. *Baptist Battles.* New Brunswick, N.J.: Rutgers University Press, 1995.

Bendroth, Margaret Lamberts. "Fundamentalism and the Family: Gender, Culture, and the American Pro-family Movement." *Journal of Women's History* 10, no. 4 (winter 1999).

Blumenthal, Sidney. *Pledging Allegiance: The Last Campaign of the Cold War.* New York: HarperCollins, 1990.

Callahan, David. *$1 Billion for Ideas: Conservative Think Tanks in the 1990s.* Washington, D.C.: National Committee for Responsive Philanthropy, 1999.

Crawford, Alan. *Thunder on the Right.* New York: Pantheon Books, 1980.

Egerton, John. *The Americanization of Dixie, the Southernization of America.* New York: Harpers, 1974.

Felsenthal, Carol. *The Sweetheart of the Silent Majority.* Garden City, N.Y.: Doubleday, 1981.

Finke, Roger, and Rodney Stark. *The Churching of America, 1776–1990: Winners and Losers in Our Religious Economy.* New Brunswick, N.J.: Rutgers University Press, 1992.

Hadden, Jerry, and Charles Swann. *Prime-Time Preachers.* Reading, Mass.: Addison Wesley, 1981.

Hammond, Philip E. *Religion and Personal Autonomy: The Third Disestablishment in America.* Columbia: University of South Carolina Press, 1992.

Himmelstein, Jerome L. *To the Right: The Transformation of American Conservatism.* Berkeley: University of California Press, 1990.

Hixson, William B. *The Search for the American Right Wing*. Princeton, N.J.: Princeton University Press, 1992.

Kelley, Dean M. *Why Conservative Churches Are Growing*. New York: Harper and Row, 1972.

Liebman, Robert C., and Robert Wuthnow. *The New Christian Right*. New York: Aldine, 1983.

Marsden, George M. *Religion and American Culture*. New York: Harcourt-Brace Jovanovich, 1990.

Marshall, Susan. *Splintered Sisterhood: Gender and Class in the Campaign against Woman Suffrage*. Madison: University of Wisconsin Press, 1997.

Martin, William C. *With God on Our Side*. New York: Broadway Books, 1996.

Marty, Martin. *Righteous Empire: The Protestant Experience in America*. New York: Dial, 1970.

Mathews, Donald G., and Jane Sherron DeHart. *Sex, Gender, and the Politics of ERA*. New York: Oxford University Press, 1990.

Miller, Donald E. *Reinventing American Protestantism: Christianity in the New Millenium*. Berkeley: University of California Press, 1997.

Moen, Matthew. *The Transformation of the Christian Right*. Tuscaloosa: University of Alabama Press, 1992.

Noll, Mark A. Nathan O. Hatch, and George M. Marsden. *The Search for Christian America,* Exp. Ed. Colorado Springs: Helmers and Howard, 1989.

Paige, Connie. *The Right to Lifers, Who They Are, How They Operate, Where They Get Their Money*. New York: Summit Books, 1983.

Stefancic, Jean, and Richard Delgado. *No Mercy: How Conservative Think Tanks and Foundations Changed America's Social Agenda*. Philadelphia: Temple University Press, 1996.

Thomas, Cal, and Ed Dobson. *Blinded by Might: Can the Religious Right Save America?* Grand Rapids, Mich.: Zondervan Publishing, 1999.

CHRISTIAN RIGHT PUBLICATIONS

Barton, David. *The Myth of Separation*. Aledo, Tex.: Wallbuilder, 1992.

Falwell, Jerry. *Strength for the Journey*. New York: Simon and Schuster, 1987.

——. *Listen America!* New York: Bantam (Doubleday), 1980.

LaHaye, Beverly. *Who but a Woman?* Nashville: Thomas Nelson, 1984.

LaHaye, Tim. *Battle for the Mind*. Old Tappan, N.J.: Fleming H. Revell, 1980.

Lindell, Harold. *The Battle for the Bible*. Grand Rapids, Mich.: Zondervan, 1976.

Morgan, Marabel. *Total Woman*. New York: Pocket Books, 1973.

Reed, Ralph. *After the Revolution.* Dallas: Word Publishing, 1994.

Robertson, Pat. *The Plan.* Nashville: Thomas Nelson, 1989.

———. *The New World Order.* Dallas: Word Publishing, 1991.

Schaeffer, Francis A. *How Should We Then Live?* Old Tappan, N.J.: Fleming H. Revell, 1976.

———. *Whatever Happened to the Human Race?* Old Tappan, N.J.: Fleming H. Revell, 1979.

———. *The Christian Manifesto.* Wheaton, Ill.: Crossway Books, 1981.

Schlafly, Phyllis. *A Choice Not an Echo.* Alton, Ill.: Pere Marquette, 1964.

———. *The Power of the Christian Woman.* Cincinnati, Ohio: Standard Publishing, 1981.

Thomson, Rosemary. The *Price of LIBerty.* Carol Stream, Ill.: Mansions Press, 1978.

———. *Withstanding Humanism's Challenge to Families: Anatomy of a White House Conference.* Morton, Ill.: Traditional Publications, 1981.

Viguerie, Richard A. *The New Right: We're Ready to Lead.* Falls Church, Va.: Viguerie, 1981.

Whitehead, John W. *The Second American Revolution.* Wheaton, Ill.: Crossway Books, 1982.

———. *The Separation Illusion.* Milford, Mich.: Mott Media, 1982.

IF YOU WANT TO LEARN MORE

The Wilcox Collection of the Spencer Library at the University of Kansas in Lawrence specializes in both right-wing and left-wing organizations.

Columbia University in New York has the files of *Group Research Report,* a newsletter about the right, published by Wes McCune from 1961 to 1983.

People for the American Way in Washington, D.C., has an extensive collection of videotapes and periodicals produced by the Christian Right, at 2000 M Street, N.W. #400, Washington, D.C. 20036; 202-467-4999; www.pfaw.org.

The Diamond Collection at the Bancroft Library of the University of California in Berkeley includes material from the entire spectrum of right-wing oganizations.

There is also a Right Wing Collection at the University of Iowa in Iowa City, Iowa.

Most of the organizations mentioned in this book have sites on the Internet, and some of them offer a tremendous variety of information, but their addresses change frequently. Use your browser to find them if you are interested.

The following organizations, which oppose the Christian Right agenda, can also provide information about the movement:

Americans United for Separation of Church and State, 1816 Jefferson Place, N.W., Washington, DC 20036; 202-466-3234; www.au.org.
Institute for First Amendment Studies, P.O. Box 589, Great Barrington, MA, 01230; 800-370-3329; www.ifas.org.
National Abortion Rights League: www.naral.org.

INDEX

Page numbers in *italics* refer to illustrations.

293

"stealth" school board candidates in, 259

vouchers and, 266–68

and White House Conference on Families, 253–56

Education Department, U.S., 226, 256, 259

Education Reporter, 256

Education Research Analysis, 125

Edwards v. *Aguillard,* 230

Egerton, John, 22, 274

Eisenhower, Dwight, 50

elections of 1964, 48

elections of 1976, 142, 159

elections of 1980, 90, 157, 159, 160, 259

elections of 1984, 160

elections of 1988, 185–86, 193

elections of 1996, 186

elections of 2000, 136

Ellis, Tottie, 78

Ellison, Carol, 96, 97, 236

employment, homosexuality and, 179

Employment Non-Discrimination Act (ENDA), 179

Engel v. *Vitale,* 237, 239, 249

Episcopalians

anti-ERA efforts and, 31, 36

declining membership of, 273

fundamentalists among, 72

history of, 18

liturgy used by, 36

Equal Rights Amendment (ERA), 17, 21, 23

as "against God's plan," 70, 71, 201–202, 271

Baptists in efforts against, 35, 69, 77, 94, 97, 162, 163

Bible and opinions over, 71–72

in Christian Right's development, 123–24, 135

Church of Christ and efforts against, 31, 34, 35, 36, 38, 39, 64, 69, 70, 75–76, 77, 78, 90, 94, 97

demographics on opponents of, 69–70, 83, 162

demographics on proponents of, 83

Eagle Forum in efforts against, 50–61

fear in activism against, 88–89

feminists and, 15, 21, 30, 57–58, 100, 152, 272

finances in battle over, 43–45

Findley's efforts against, 31, 34, 37–38, 39, 45, 63, 74, 75, 86, 201

Hobbs's efforts against, 39–43, *40,* 61, 65, 66–67, 75, 78, 90

homosexuality and, 85, 115, 210, 213, 214

interdenominational distrust and, 77–79

IWY conferences and, 104, 105, 106, 109

John Birch Society opposition to, 32, 33, 35, 44, 49, 50, 51, 57, 94, 97

LaHayes and, 167

law journal articles on, 41

leadership styles in battle over, 54, 93–95

legal arguments against, 32–33

legislators' mail on, 88

local coordination against, 56–57

Methodists in efforts against, 69, 97

Mormons in efforts against, 35, 43–44, 69, 76–77, 78, 89, 92, 93, 94, 97

Oklahoma hearings on, 33–34